A PERFECTLY BEAUTIFUL PLACE

A Perfectly Beautiful Place

by

Michael Elcock

OOLICHAN BOOKS
LANTZVILLE, BRITISH COLUMBIA, CANADA
2004

National Library of Canada Cataloguing in Publication

Elcock, Michael

A perfectly beautiful place / Michael Elcock.

ISBN 0-88982-189-5

1. Elcock, Michael—Travel. 2. Voyages and travels. I. Title.

G465.E42 2004   910.4   C2004-901002-6

The Canada Council | Le Conseil des Arts
for the Arts | du Canada

We gratefully acknowledge the support of the Canada Council for the Arts for our publishing program.

BRITISH
COLUMBIA
ARTS COUNCIL
Supported by the Province of British Columbia

Grateful acknowledgement is also made to the BC Ministry of Tourism, Small Business and Culture for their financial support.

We acknowledge the financial support of the Government of Canada through the Book Publishing Industry Development Program for our publishing activities.

Published by
Oolichan Books
P.O. Box 10, Lantzville
British Columbia, Canada
V0R 2H0

Printed in Canada

For Marilyn

Contents

A Perfectly Beautiful Place

The Seville Diaries

Introduction

I was two when I was stuffed into the luggage compartment of a Tiger Moth, behind the open cockpit carrying my mother and Derek Malcolm-Brown, the head of West African Airways. We took off in the little bi-plane from the airport at Lagos, flew down the Niger delta and landed on hard wet sand at Lighthouse Beach for a picnic of sandwiches and cake and tea. The Tiger Moth, already ancient when I flew in it, vanished soon afterwards when 'Uncle' Derek acquired a new wife.

Travel has been central to my life ever since and the explorations that are an inevitable part of it remain endlessly fascinating, immeasurably instructive, infinitely rewarding. And humbling. It's the best of classrooms, the best way to find out about the people who inhabit this planet. It's also a way to look at ourselves as others see us, the best way to find out about ourselves.

This book is about the idea of change and the way that time and history alter the ways we view our world, and how we live our lives. It's about viewing these changes through a personal lens—taking my own cut at the state of things, not just relying on the interpretations of journalists and academics.

Apart from the obvious insecurities associated with journeying to faraway places and unfamiliar cultures, the best examples of our constantly altering relationship with the world are wrought daily by what we now consider to be commonplace technologies. My grandfather knew how to ride a horse, drive a carriage. It was his way of getting about. My grandfather lived through those days to the advent of the motorcar, the telephone, radio and television. He lived to see the gigantic Boeing 747—an aeroplane the size of a small passenger ship in his youth—lift into the air with four hundred people on board and spirit them in a matter of hours to the far side of the world. He lived to see men orbiting the earth.

I remember my grandfather well; I used to have long conversations with him, and the memory of these talks helps now to invest such phenomenal shifts with an element of the surreal. It is still difficult for me to get my head around the *idea* of all the changes that occurred from the start of his life to the middle of mine; what they actually mean to people. We have lost much of the memory of it.

The effects of change can be particularly emphatic in the old border zones of Europe, the cockpit of so many brutal wars for so many centuries. When the old lady, Helene Detry-Gustin, spoke to me from the doorway of her cottage in Belgium saying, "Cologne is a long way from here," I thought nothing of it. Of course Cologne is a long way from the middle of the Ardennes forests. Had it not taken us several days, meandering along old country roads, to reach her village? It was only later that I realised she was talking out of another generation; that the modern reality is that Cologne is not much more than an hour away from her little village, now that there are fast new highways and no border posts.

The world is changing quickly; its cultural and social divisions altering as political barriers come down, or go up. Every advance in electronic communication shrinks it further, and so people of different generations often view the world through different frames of reference. This can cause misunderstandings and problems. But it can also mean that people from different cultures talk to each other without reference to time and space—and often without reference to history. This is enormously important because it reduces barriers that are often intellectually artificial in the first place. History sometimes gets in the way of tolerance and understanding.

But such changes can also mean that experience can be forgotten, knowledge misplaced. If history is put aside in order to facilitate cordial relationships between peoples, it should not be discarded. History is knowledge, and it has the power to enrich our lives and our musings, offer us wisdom and spiritual richness, bring unimaginable dimensions into our wanderings. I didn't know when I went to Malta that I'd come across old bomb-blast berms and air raid shelters, and all the past events and lives—including my father's—that they can quickly conjure up. Or that an innocuous trip on a train from Venice to Vienna would direct me to an almost forgotten story of genocide, perpetrated in the heart of Europe by Russians with the assistance of British politicians, and facilitated by the British Army. I didn't know when I went back to my birthplace that I'd find derelict Nissen huts, aircraft hard stands and the brick ruins of my father's old air force Mess on a nearby farm which used to be a training airfield. I had no idea that a trip to France, following my wife's grandfather seventy years after a devastating war, would be the visceral experience it was, and bring me such profound connections to nearly forgotten people and events. I could just as easily have examined the pages of books for the factual information I gleaned from these travels, or watched television documentaries. But if I'd done that I wouldn't have smelled the hot summer sun baking the earth in Andalusia, felt the brush of salt, tropical air on my skin in Panama, or heard the soporific buzzing of bumble bees in Picardy—where the appreciation of such things was once imbued by circumstances and conflict with a terrible immediacy.

A   Perfectly Beautiful Place

". . . it was perhaps the most surprising of all the day's surprises to smell the sweet smell of summer grass, a smell of cattle and peace and sun that had warmed the earth some other time when summer was real."

—Martha Gellhorn, Normandy, June 1944

Beirut

I'm staring at a photograph in an old copy of *Time Magazine*, a picture of the destruction caused by the fighting between Hezbollah and the Israelis in West Beirut during the nineteen-eighties. The apartment where I used to live stands in the middle of the frame. It has no front wall; all the floors are visible, and all the rooms, opened up like a child's doll's house. Carpets spill over the landings; beds and chairs hang crookedly from buckled floors as if they're about to fall all the way down to the ground. I can see a tilted bathtub and a broken toilet, look into bedrooms with plaster-white blankets on neatly made beds. There are couches and tables and fallen pots with plants in them. Paintings hang drunkenly on the walls. There is dust. You can tell from the photograph that there is dust.

It's a long time since I lived in that apartment. I've grown up since then; the boy who lived there no longer exists. But I have memories of it, and I go back there sometimes in the half-sleep of early morning when I hear the soft susurration of a sweeping broom, the most Mediterranean of sounds.

✦

The apartment stands almost at the tip of Pigeon Point in West Beirut. A short stretch of scrub-covered waste ground spreads out in front of it, crossed by a zigzag road where the tyres of big-finned DeSoto taxis screech on the hot tarmac. Beyond that the Mediterranean Sea reaches all the way to the curve of the horizon, which I can measure against the exact line of the metal rail on our balcony.

On the other side of the waste ground, stairs lead down to a beach club, a kind of concrete lido under the cliffs, with tables and chairs and coloured umbrellas. Down there the sea is cool and calm and there are little flat-topped canoe-shaped boats for rent. I often take one out just to sit on the gentle up and down motion of the water in the bay. It's a peaceful bay, hidden from the city by high cliffs. Pigeon Rock rises up in its centre; a high, guano-white rock with a cavernous hole through its middle and a patch of sun-burned grass on its flat top. I sprint through the hole in my little flat-topped boat on a surging aquamarine wave, as if I'm shooting rapids in Colorado.

Each night after supper the sun sinks down big and red in front of our balcony. When it's gone it leaves a wide, wet crimson path across the sea all the way to where I'm watching. On Thursdays a cruise ship called the *Agamemnon* sails through the setting sun, cocky and streamlined with its raked funnel.

Beirut sits on a narrow littoral between the mountains and the sea. The coastal plain is dry and dusty, though it is said to have been quite fertile through the ages, a place of orange groves and olive trees. To the south lie the ancient Phoenician ports of Tyre and Sidon. Beyond them lies unstable border country, and Israel. When I lived there, Beirut was trying to shed its French colonial cloak. French was still the second language after Arabic, and few Lebanese Arabs spoke English.

One day we drove up into the mountains to see the famous cedars of Lebanon, which date from biblical times and were revered by Solomon. The cedars are the country's national symbol, but only a handful of these majestic trees are still left. When I saw them they were wreathed in mist, standing in snow.

My father and I are driving a switchback road over the mountains through little villages with European-Arabic names like Sofia and Bhamdoun. Neat, white-painted concrete markers on corners define sheer drop-offs. When we come out of the mist we can see the road dropping sharply away to the Beka'a Valley, lying flat and green far below.

The road runs straight and true through the Beka'a for miles. It is like travelling along the bottom of a dried-up lake, its sides rising steep on both sides of us.

Baalbek, the main town in the Beka'a, is notorious now as a centre of shadowy anti-western guerrilla organisations. Long ago it was inhabited by the Phoenicians, and then conquerors followed. When the Romans came, they used the name the Greeks had given it, and knew the place as Heliopolis, the 'City of the Sun". Here they built some of the most impressively engineered structures in their whole great empire—not only out of respect for their deities, but also perhaps as a kind of architectural intimidation against the burgeoning Christianity which was already beginning to destabilise their empire. Other peoples and armies and rulers followed the Romans, but the temples of Baalbek were eventually brought down, not by wars but by a series of great earthquakes.

The ruins are magnificent, cared for and striking, as if they have been left by creatures from another planet. Only six pillars are left of the Temple of Jupiter, standing rebellious against gravity, topped by massive stone lintels balanced seventy feet above the ground. My father points out the Temple of Bacchus as a place of great importance, although I don't quite understand why he does this, don't yet appreciate his lifelong affinity for good beer. It's simply part of a land full of exotic sights and smells, and ancient riches which have been absorbed into the daily lives of the people who live here.

But I remember that Bacchus's temple was well preserved, as if it had been pickled and dried by arid desert airs; remember feeling that all of it was a long, long way from Edinburgh where I lived, although not so distant from the Latin and Greek studies we suffered through at school. I remember too that my father, who I hardly knew then, squeezed this excursion in on one of his days off from work as the Middle East Airlines Station Manager at Beirut's international airport.

Inspired perhaps by these classical associations, my father decides to rent a Baby Grand piano. In due course a shiny black piano arrives at our apartment on the back of a flat-deck lorry. The driver climbs down from his cab and stands there for a long time, staring up at the building, working things out. He walks in and out of the front door several times, and climbs up to the first floor landing, examining the stairwell, calculating angles. Our flat is on the fifth floor. There are six floors in the building altogether and there is no elevator.

In the end the delivery man undoes some screws and takes off the piano legs, and then slings a complicated system of leather belts around his chest and shoulders and forehead, and straps the piano onto his back. When he's ready he takes several deep breaths and carries it all the way up to our apartment; five flights of stairs, all by himself. It's hot in Lebanon; he is leaking bountiful quantities of sweat by the time he reaches our front door.

But there is something wrong with the piano when my father sits down to play it that evening. He calls the rental company the next morning and they send a man to re-tune it, but he can't get it to sound right. The piano tuner says he'll arrange for the company to send us another one.

The same delivery man comes to take the black piano away. He has an assistant this time to help him, but the stairs are too narrow for both of them to carry it and the assistant isn't much help. The delivery man makes the trip back down the stairs with the black piano strapped on his back, the assistant murmuring directions.

Two hours later the pair of them come back, this time with an ivory-white baby grand piano in the back of the truck. The delivery man straps himself onto the white piano with the help of his assistant; then he carries it all the way up the stairs again. It is another steaming hot day.

After dinner the piano makes perfect sound. I walk out onto the balcony while my father plays, and watch the sun dropping off the rim of the earth. The *Agamemnon* carefully parts the sunset. Something catches my eye and I lean out and look down the front of the apartment building. People are standing out on all the balconies below me, listening. It is Chopin, and it sounds like the music of the setting sun.

Malta

High above the Mediterranean we come upon dozens of extraordinary, towering spiral clouds. They're purest white on the outside, dark and forbidding at their centres. Although we're flying at thirty-five thousand feet they reach far above us, like celestial pillars supporting the sky itself. Beyond them the heavens are deep, deep blue.

I've never seen clouds like these before. They stand astride our heading like sentinels, stretching out on either side of us as far as I can see—as if they could pluck at the aeroplane and tear it to pieces, like the mythic Scylla and Charybdis. Our pilot picks his way warily past them and we begin the long descent into Malta.

When I was a child I thought this sky, to the south of Naples, the most dangerous in the world. One black night when I was twelve, the aeroplane taking me to India suddenly fell two thousand feet here. In those days, BOAC gave their fleet of Canadair Argonauts names from Greek mythology, and the one I was flying in was called *Ariadne*. We dropped like a stone, so hard that the passengers who hadn't fastened their seat belts were pinned to the cabin ceiling for what seemed like minutes, until we stopped falling and they smashed down onto the floor. This is the place too, where the Comet 1, the first commercial jet airliner, fell out of the sky with all its passengers in the early nineteen-fifties, torn apart by a combination of violent turbulence and metal fatigue.

We pass on to the southeast, leaving the unpredictable cloud-pillars behind us, and lose height until we're drifting low like a shadow over aquamarine shallows, a rocky shoreline and then dusty, grey-brown land. The old wartime dispersal bays at Malta's main airport at Luqa are overgrown with weeds, still enclosed by the high earth berms which were built to protect Malta's tiny WWII fighter force from Axis bomb blasts.

My father landed here one night in 1942 with his crew, sheltered his bomber behind one of these crumbling dirt ramparts and waited anxiously for a German air raid to end so that he could refuel and continue his journey. He was lucky even to get this far; he and his crew very nearly didn't find Malta on that black Mediterranean night. It feels strange to me to gaze out of the window of this modern British Airways aeroplane, to be here, knowing that statistically, bomber pilots like my father should have been killed three times over during their tour of thirty operations. In this wartime theatre, my father flew thirty-five.

Our aircraft taxis slowly to the terminal, and we wait as the engines run down. The airport buildings are down-at-heel and spartan, furnished with scratched metal tables and chairs. Linoleum lifts from the floor, and the bare walls create echoes. A Maltese Customs Officer asks me some cursory questions and then waves me through. Carm Borg, a chunky, dark-suited man from the Malta Olympic Committee is here to meet me, with his colleague Philippe, the Treasurer, who is appropriately thin and bookish and bespectacled. I've come here for several days of meetings with them in conjunction with Victoria's bid to host the Commonwealth Games in western Canada. They take me off to the Holiday Inn in Sliema.

*In the photograph, four of them are standing in front of a Welling-
ton bomber at the RAF Operational Training Unit at Bassingbourne,
in the south of England. They're impossibly young, shy and confi-
dent, slouched under the perspex nose of the aeroplane. My father's
parachute lies at his feet, an RAF kitbag slung over his shoulder. It's
the summer of 1942 and they're just about to leave for Gibraltar
and Malta, on their way to the Middle East. Two of the boys in the
picture are New Zealanders, one is Canadian, my father the only
Englishman.*

*They lose an engine minutes after they take off from Portreath in
Cornwall, and only just make it back to the airfield. A felicitous
updraft scrapes them over the top of the cliff at the edge of the air-
field and they crash-land on the grass, shearing off the undercar-
riage and wrecking the new bomber. The Wellington is full of fuel
for the long flight to Gibraltar and the crew jumps out and hares
away across the grass before it blows up. None of them is hurt, al-
though the New Zealand Wireless Operator has lost his false teeth.
It's a close thing.*

*The accident holds them up for two weeks until a Board of En-
quiry clears them of blame. The Board finds that the engine failed
because of carburettor icing, something they didn't know much
about at the time.*

Sliema is a suburb of Valetta. It sits like the fighting claw of a
crab at the left side of the capital's head, protecting the har-
bour of Marsamxett. I had misgivings when I was told that I
was booked into the Holiday Inn, but this hotel is magnificent,
unlike any Holiday Inn I've ever seen before. The furniture is a
comfortable colonial rattan, the armchairs overflowing with
puffy, pastel-coloured cushions. A ceiling fan turns slowly,
breaking up the sullen air. A huge king-sized bed fills the cen-
tre of the room, and a big bowl of fresh fruit sits on the dress-
ing table. The sea glints through French windows, beyond a
balcony with a white table and chair. But the weather outside
is dull, the air still and heavy: brittle.

"Certified that original Log Book was destroyed in crash of Wellington aircraft HF 829 at Portreath, Cornwall, on 10th May 1942."

S/LDR. O.C. "F" Flight. Harwell

As I make my way through Valetta's busy streets, the geography of the place is at first confusing. The map makes some of it clear. There must be miles and miles of shoreline here, bent and serrated like the magnified blade of a carpenter's jigsaw. Ancient forts and barracks are etched into the capital's tentacled peninsulas, along the sides of the inlets that the Maltese call creeks. Tigne Fort guards Sliema and the western approaches; Fort St. Elmo stands square on the tip of Valetta. A stone's throw to the east sits Ricassoli Fort, guarding the entrance to Grand Harbour. Below it lies Fort St. Angelo, at the head of the township of Vittoriosa. A few yards to the south, across Dockyard Creek, Senglea's fortified walls repelled the great Ottoman siege which began in 1565.

A motor scooter with no muffler rips past with a noise like tearing calico, trailing blue exhaust smoke. Washing hangs in the listless air from high windows in the narrow streets. It's difficult to distinguish between the different towns that make up the mass of the capital. All of them are joined together. But the place carries the scars of Luftwaffe bombs and Napoleon's cannon, the architectures of Venice and Istanbul and of the stateless Knights of Saint John. Every corner of it exudes tales of history, and breathes the sweet, composted air of the ancients.

Nowhere on Malta is far from the sea; there are little harbours everywhere. I work my way up a flight of dusty steps to the top of a rise, and there, framed among the flaking plaster of old buildings, lies the blue Mediterranean. Up here, on the central spine of this old city, I can turn around amidst the scurrying traffic and look down four streets. At the foot of three of them sits sun-sparkled water and it's easy to see the enormous value this place has had for the navies of the sea powers over the centuries; no less for the Phoenicians or the Egyptians than for the British in more recent times.

Most of the boats in Valetta's harbours are painted yellow and blue, some with delicate red lines, and panels of ochre and green. Nearly all of them have an eye painted just below the prow, to reflect back the evil eye and ward off bad spirits. This eye comes from far, far back in history: from pre-Pharaonic times, when it was given to the region by the Egyptian god Horus, a provider of solace and hope. It has been adopted as a talisman by most Mediterranean cultures; these brightly painted fishing boats would not be out of place beside a wharf on Mikonos, or Kyrenia.

Pilot's Flying Log Book—May 29, 1942
Wellington DV607 – Pilot "Self" – Lyneham-Gibraltar – 10hrs 30mins
At the end of May they take off again for Gibraltar and the Middle East in a new aeroplane, this time from Lyneham in Wiltshire.

Nineteen aircraft leave England for Cairo on this day, with orders to fly south-west down the English Channel, round the tip of Brittany and then track south across the Bay of Biscay at a height of two thousand feet. They're to keep radio silence to avoid alerting German fighter stations in western France. The Germans occupy all of France, and the first half of the route lies within range of their aircraft. After dark the Wellington must show no navigation lights at all.

Somewhere over the Bay of Biscay someone takes a shot at the bomber from a fishing boat, putting a hole through one of the propeller blades and causing some engine vibration; but they make it into Gibraltar and land safely after dark. The flight has taken ten and a half hours. A ground crew replaces the propeller blade during the night.

Fifty-six years later, after a lifetime in civil aviation, this remains the longest continuous stretch of time my father has ever spent in the air.

✦

The Malta Olympic Committee functions on enthusiasm and grit. The volunteers who staff it are keen, and they seem to work extraordinarily hard. The whole operation runs on a shoestring out of a tiny two-room office up a long uneven stairway in a dilapidated part of Valetta. It strikes me that it must be a constant grind for them to raise enough money to do anything at all. They show me proudly around the little Olympic Museum in their threadbare office, and project a short Olympic solidarity film onto the whitewashed wall.

On Sunday morning my new friends take me over to Senglea for the opening ceremonies of the Commonwealth Weightlifting Championships, which they are hosting. These are held in a rundown gymnasium at La Salle School. There are no opulent Olympic trappings here; no trumpets or fanfares or balloons; no fancy sound and light show, only scratchy, taped music piping out of ancient tannoy speakers high up in the dusty rafters. But it's a touching affair, with a group of young schoolgirls giving a demonstration of traditional Maltese dances for the audience. The lifting begins.

Pilot's Flying Log Book – May 30, 1942
Wellington DV607 – Self & Crew – Gibraltar-Malta – 2hrs 30mins (Returned To Base)
My father taxis the bomber out for take-off. He sits at the controls and stares up at the massive rock of Gibraltar, and down the runway to Algeciras Bay. The runway is short, the sea frighteningly close. He squints into the late afternoon sun, and tries to make out the strange shapes he can see sticking out of the water.

"What the hell are those?" he shouts over the noise of the engines.

"They're the tail fins of aeroplanes that didn't get off the ground," says the Flight Engineer.

The Wellington is loaded to its limits with fuel for the long flight to Malta. The Flight Engineer stands up in the cockpit, holding the throttles open as far as they'll go. My father pushes hard on the brakes as the engines come up to full revolutions, the aeroplane shak-

ing so much now that it feels as if it will come apart. Then he lets go and they charge off down the runway.

Algeciras Bay races closer and closer and then they lift off and skim over the watery wrecks. My father realises he's been holding his breath. He takes the aeroplane up into the haze, circling slowly round the Rock. An hour out of Gibraltar they're caught in thick, cold cloud. One of the big Bristol Pegasus engines starts to cough, the other develops a miss-fire. It's carburettor icing again, something they learned about the hard way just two and a half weeks ago at Portreath. They limp back to Gibraltar, losing height all the way.

It's necessary to go to a place to see how the world turns about different axes for different peoples, how a change in physical orientation impels different cultural effects, how all this can change your point of view. There are weightlifters in the little gymnasium at La Salle School from India, Sri Lanka, Wales and Malta—joined briefly in a brotherhood of competition and common interest. But Malta is also at the centre of other spheres. Back at the Holiday Inn the television brings in snowy pictures of Italian game shows from Sicily, and the news in French from Tunisia. More ominously, two Libyan gunmen flew in the week before I came here and shot up the airport terminal with automatic weapons. Malta is, after all, south of Tunis and Algiers, close to Ghadaffi's Libya. Britain's influence on the island is reflected in subtle, arcane details like the tidy concrete roads and roundabouts, the shapes of traffic signs and white-painted bollards at the roadside, the fact that cars drive on the left. But despite the political strains of recent years, it's easy to sense the affection which remains on this island towards the British. Even the young ones know that people like my father came here during the war, and shared in Malta's adversity. During the wartime bombardments, the Maltese and the British developed a partnership of transcendent spirit, and in some un-articulated way this affects the way that the people I meet treat me all these years later.

The people here are too pale and olive-skinned to be Arab,

and yet too relaxed to be Italian. Like the Turks they seem to stand on a cusp where eastern and western civilisations meet; half-forgotten remnants of past empires like the Carthaginians, or the Phoenicians; missing their place in the world, searching for a context. They live on an isolated island, yet it stands at the centre of ancient worlds; an ocean crossroads caught in a time shift and seeking today to re-set its clocks, if it can only establish what time zone it should be in. The Malti language is Arabic in origin, but it has borrowed much that is Latin and Greek and Italian. It is written in Roman script, although to me it seems that the pronunciations bear little relation to the printed texts.

Pilot's Flying Log Book—June 1, 1942
Wellington DV607 – Self & Crew – Gibraltar-Malta – 8hrs 30mins
Soon after takeoff cloud closes in on them and blots out the ground. Darkness comes down early at these latitudes, and soon the only light in the cockpit is the soft green glow from the dials on the instrument panel. They're flying blind—this crew which is on its first big flight. But all the crews which left England the previous day are green, all of them young.

It's considered too dangerous for aeroplanes to transit Malta in daylight, and the bombers were ordered to leave Gibraltar in mid-afternoon so that they'll arrive in Malta at night. My father's crew carries with them a small cargo of cigarettes, and some luxuries, like soap and tea, for the beleaguered island.

Italy and Germany dominate the Mediterranean in 1942. Axis troops occupy most of North Africa, to the south of the route the nineteen RAF bombers have to take. To the north, German and Italian forces occupy France and Italy, Sicily, Sardinia and Corsica. Next door to Gibraltar, Spain is a hostile, neutral country which shoots at Allied aircraft that stray over its territory. Malta is more than eight hours flying time away, and almost completely cut off from the outside world. The little island faces constant day and night bombing raids from the Luftwaffe and the Italian Air Force flying from bases in Sicily—a scant sixty miles away. A year or two later, this time will become known as the Second Great Siege of Malta.

Down on the gymnasium floor a tiny bantamweight lifter from Sri Lanka is taking deep, deep breaths, his unblinking gaze fixed on an impossibly large barbell. He slaps his hands together, and chalk-dust floats up in the sunlight. My eyes follow the light to a high window which frames an old bell tower, its plaster cracked and pitted and white against the blue sky.

Cam Hill is the bomber's navigator, a Canadian from Kitchener, Ontario. Because of the cloud, he must calculate their course and position by dead reckoning, a notoriously inexact science in those days of inaccurate wind and weather forecasts. But it's the only method available to him; there are no radio beacons or radar to guide them. The navigator plots a course on the map, and gives out headings and directions based on forecasts of the wind speeds at the height they're flying, and on their ground speed, which must be estimated from their air speed. The weather and wind forecasts were made more than two hundred miles away, and they're hours out of date. The crew is very much on its own.

After they've been flying for three hours, a small break opens in the clouds below them.

"Cape Bon," says the navigator, pointing down at a rocky headland. It's only a fleeting glimpse, and the clouds quickly blot it out.

"Are you sure?" asks my father; he's wondering how this inexperienced navigator can be so certain about a landmark he's never seen before. Cam Hill shrugs his shoulders and hands him a new course.

They fly out over the Mediterranean and night comes down on them. They fly on and on into the darkness, and begin to think about their fuel running low. There will be no lights for them at Malta. The island is completely blacked out because of the danger of enemy bombing. They're looking for a tiny, dark island on an immense black sea, at night.

Hours after the Cape Bon sighting, the rear gunner spots lights on the horizon, far behind them on the port side—faint flashes

*in the sky, low down, in the north. It can only be Malta, under
an air raid.*

*If it were not for the air raid they would miss the island and fly
on into the Mediterranean night, eventually run out of gasoline and
ditch in the sea. No one would find them. It's what happens to ten
of the aeroplanes which left Lyneham the day before. Only nine out
of the nineteen make it to Malta. All the others disappear, with all
their crews: six young men in each aeroplane.*

At the Weightlifting, I am introduced to Paddy Stubbs, a di-
shevelled looking Englishman who has married the heiress to
the Littlewoods Football Pools fortune. Paddy is an important
patron of amateur sport in Malta. He leans over and confides
that he usually stays in bed on Sunday mornings. He holds his
coat closely about him as if he might still have his pyjamas on
underneath.

The announcer reads out the name of a Welsh contestant.
Sotto voce, Paddy simulates a singsong Welsh accent and gazes
down at the barrel-chested weightlifter on the floor below us.

"Do you think they call him Morgan the Snatch, or Morgan
the Jerk?" he whispers.

For a moment I wonder if he really wants an answer, this
funny man who cultivates the air of a rogue; generous and
witty; charming, almost in spite of himself.

*The landing procedure calls for them to somehow line up the bomber
with Luqa's unlighted runway in darkness. One small light—little
more than a masked flashlight—will show itself when they are ac-
curately positioned. Then, when they're straight on, and close in on
final approach, a Duty Officer on the ground shines a beam called
a 'Chance' light straight down the runway in order to give my fa-
ther a visual. The Chance light is switched off in two seconds, to
avoid attracting enemy bombers. The air raid is still going on.*

*Landing in these conditions calls for precise and careful flying,
and my father is drenched in sweat by the time the aircraft slows
down on the runway. A truck drives alongside the bomber with a*

sign written in faint, luminous paint on its back—'Follow Me'. One
of the ground crew hoists himself up into the aeroplane and directs
them to the far side of the airfield. Here they can refuel, ready to
depart before sunrise—as soon as they can get away again.

But the air raid increases in ferocity and they have to leave the
aeroplane and take cover. By the time the Luftwaffe departs it's too
late for them to refuel and take off for Cairo. When they climb back
into the bomber at dawn to collect their bags they discover that the
cartons of cigarettes they brought to Malta have all disappeared.

When the weightlifting is over I wander through Sliema's nar-
row streets, and catch a bright yellow bus into Valetta. Out-
side the bus's windows, the city's architecture unfolds
influences from around the Mediterranean, echoes of past civi-
lisations and passing conquerors etched through its stonework.
This island has known well the cultures of Greece and Rome,
of Phoenicia and Carthage. It has seen the Crusades, and it was
a battleground for the Knights of St. John long after those
bloody wars had supposedly ended. Napoleon came here two
hundred years ago and evicted the Knights of St. John, and for
a short time Malta became a French colony and staging post.
Then the British came and drove out Napoleon in his turn, and
the island became a British colony, tidy with whitewashed
walls and administrative order.

Most of all, though, I want to explore this place where my
father briefly came one black night in 1942, at the height of
Malta's blitz. Memories are long here, and the Maltese people
remember well the soldiers and airmen who came here from
across the Commonwealth during the war. My father used to
say he wanted to come and live here when he retired. But he
never came back. After a life spent overseas I think he was hun-
gry for an English life. He went home instead.

Valetta's streets are narrow, and most of them slope steeply
up from the sea. A soft sea breeze brushes my face, and dries
the washing hanging on lines strung between the buildings.
Instead of sidewalks, steps climb the hills beside the narrow

roadways. A cat flits through a shadow and disappears into a doorway; a horse pulls a carriage through a road-end farther down the hill. Above my head, an old lady opens a window and leans out to shake a tablecloth. Her little balcony is Venetian, its wood and glass slowly crumbling away in a decaying, Mediterranean way. The atmosphere is soporific, the languorous domestic sounds that drift down into the street in perfect tune with the distant reflected light that illuminates it—as if time itself has become somehow bemused, as if it could easily be reversed.

The next night, they're about to taxi out for takeoff when they're ordered to wait for two passengers they must take with them to Cairo. After a while, a woman and a young boy are brought out in a truck, and they climb hesitantly into the aircraft. There is no place for passengers to sit in an operational Wellington, and so the woman and the boy perch uncomfortably on a narrow canvas fold-down bed intended for wounded crew.

The bomber is not pressurised and it becomes very cold during the flight. The two passengers endure it in silence. Neither of them speaks at all, not a word to any of the crew. My father thinks they're frightened out of their minds.

Like all my father's flying log entries, this one is spare, barely informative.

June 2, 1942
Wellington-DV607 – Pilot "Self" – Malta to Kilo 17, Cairo – 8hrs 50mins

Down at the bottom of the hill, at the very tip of Valetta, beside Fort St. Elmo, I come upon a small museum. Inside the museum stands what looks like a shrine to George Beurling. It contains some of his effects, a few souvenirs from his pockets, a blue RAF uniform with the 'Canada' patch on its shoulders.

'Buzz' Beurling was a young farm boy from Verdun, in Quebec, and he was stationed in Malta at the height of the blitz. Well known for his disdain for order and authority on the ground, Beurling was incredibly well organised in the air. He was an exceptionally accurate shot, and he became one of the top scoring Allied fighter pilots of the war. During his time on the island he endeared himself greatly to the Maltese people. Beurling was resourceful as well as brave. He took great care to align his Spitfire's eight machine guns so that the streams of bullets would converge at two hundred and fifty yards, instead of the more normal three hundred yards. This brought rewards for a pilot with his skill, but it involved great risk, and required precise flying. He developed intricate formulae to help him calculate angles in his head, help him shoot down more enemy aircraft than anyone else. The people who flew with him thought he was the best deflection shot they'd ever seen.

One morning, after a successful dogfight over the city he flew the length of Republic Street upside down below the height of the rooftops. The street is so narrow that there can't have been more than a few feet of clearance on either side of his wingtips: at three hundred and fifty miles an hour, a fraction of a second away from disaster. The Spitfire's big Rolls Royce Merlin engine must have made a tremendous racket and frightened the life out of everyone in the street below.

Beurling's other nickname was 'Screwball'. Now he's part of the island's fabric: a figure as important to Malta as any of the revered Knights of St. John. In Canada, he is virtually forgotten.

Because of Beurling, I decide to walk up Republic Street to see what it looks like, this main street of Valetta, the island's capital. It's a thin, constricted thoroughfare, which climbs up the spine of the city's narrow peninsula, reaching in a straight line from the fort at its tip all the way up to the thick-walled bastion at its base. The street is lined with fashionable shops, teeming with shoppers and hustlers, cars and carts and delivery trucks. Republic Street is the commercial centre of the city, the buildings on either side of it four and five storeys high, all in the same state of gradual disintegration as much of the rest of Valetta.

From where I'm sitting at a small street café beside the sea wall, Grand Harbour unfolds a profusion of inlets and jetties and wharves. These bulwarks around Grand Harbour are massively thick and fortified. High explosive German bombs were unable to topple them, and it's hard to imagine what possible effect cannonballs could have had on them in more distant times.

Sitting up here, it's not difficult to picture the navies of the colonisers refitting their ships under these sun-bleached walls. Phoenician traders and Greek triremes once sheltered in these protected bays. Napoleon's Men-o-War and Royal Navy aircraft carriers alike have stared up at the chiselled stone blocks of Vittoriosa and Senglea.

The rich black coffee is energising, and when it's finished I walk quickly up to Floriana to catch a bus out of the city. Except for two old ladies with string shopping bags, the yellow bus is empty as it winds along narrow roads between dusty houses. Half an hour later the driver stops at the bus terminus, at a place called Mosta. It's hot here and airless, and I'm surrounded by acres of waste ground. Two boys are picking their way carefully through a spiny hedge of prickly pear, both of them as grey and dusty as their landscape. A raucous group of school children is kicking a ball around, puffs of dust rising in the midday heat from their feet as they run. The children have attractive tan-olive skin and dark hair. Two hundred yards away lie piles of breeze blocks and terracotta tiles, the beginnings of a housing development.

Beyond all this, across a mile of rocky fields, the ancient citadel of Rabat rises up on a hill, with a single, small cloud balancing on top of a minaret. Rabat is the main suburb of Mdina, the medieval capital of Malta, and it lies in the centre of the island. The narrow, shadowed alleyways of this ancient town are Arabian, and cleverly designed so that even on the hottest, windless days the air moves, and by moving, cools. These same design features also provide security from attack by funnelling invaders into tight, restricted spaces, and offering defence in depth. These combinations, these clever architectural influences of Muslim and Christian and Jew, are also found among the remnants of Mudejar planning and design in Spain, in places like the Barrio Santa Cruz in Seville, as I was to discover a year or two later.

A few days after leaving Malta my father is flying with a completely different crew, gaining operational experience. The Duty (including Results and Remarks) is printed neatly in red ink in his flying log, as per the King's Orders for operational flights. It's as terse and uninformative as his other entries. **Operations. Troop Concentrations. Sidi Barrani-Mersa Matruh.** *Bombing tanks and infantry, risking the vicious 88's—the anti-aircraft guns that Rommel's Afrika Corps used to such deadly effect.*

The bus carries me back to a bay near the hotel, and I get off beside a statue of a man wearing prominent boots. It's my last evening in Malta and the weather breaks. By dusk, high, running seas are dashing themselves against the esplanade, a rising wind flinging sheets of spray over cars and people and shop fronts. A small waterfront café near the hotel offers a warm seat behind a picture window where I can watch these Mediterranean elements at play. The food is good, the wine gentle and forgiving.

Doors

The weather along the most southerly of Scotland's two north-facing coastlines is so fine and reliable that the War Department built a number of airfields here during the war. They were training fields, far away from the guns, where they could teach young pilots to fly. Two of these airfields lie near the old market town of Forres.

Forres, and the village of Findhorn three or four miles to its north, sits on a narrow coastal plain blessed with temperate weather the envy of communities hundreds of miles to the south, in England. There are more clear flying days each year up here in the northeast of Scotland than in any other part of the British Isles.

Only two military airfields remain now on this coast, both of them used by surveillance squadrons of RAF Coastal Command for Air Sea Rescue, weather flights, and training. These are the bases at Lossiemouth and Kinloss. In 1943 and 1944, these airfields each had a number of subsidiary, satellite stations in order to keep up with the demand for new pilots, because of the high attrition rate among operational crews. Balnageith Farm, barely a mile west of Forres, was one of these satellites. You can still see the remains of its old Air Force huts from the Grantown road, and more of them lie down the lane which cuts across the farm to the main Elgin-Inverness road. This is where my father went after he'd finished his tour of bombing operations, where he taught young pilots the same age as himself how to fly.

South of Balnageith Farm the hills rise up gradually towards the cold, treacherous Cairngorm mountains, the land more barren and less populated as it rises, the weather and the air currents unreliable and dangerous. By 1943, RAF Bomber Command was conducting virtually all its operations at night. The casualties from daylight bombing earlier in the war had been disastrous, and the twin-engined Whitley bombers from those days were no longer suitable for operations. They were used instead for flight training, but there wasn't a lot of room to lift a loaded Whitley off the grass strip at Balnageith Farm.

One autumn evening one of the instructors from 19 OTU is scheduled to take off with full fuel tanks on a routine night-flying exercise. Flight Lieutenant Alf Doors has two student pilots and a rear gunner on board. Doors is the most outspoken of all the instructors about the condition of the airfield; he's been complaining about the short runway for a long time.

"Someone's going to come to grief on that fence if something's not done about it," he grumbles to the other instructors in the Mess. "It's far too high, and the trees behind it ought to be cut back."

The other instructors think Doors is a moaner. "I wish he'd shut up about that fence. He's giving me the willies," mutters a new Flight Lieutenant, who's only been on the station for a week.

"Don't pay any attention to him," says another. "He's been on about that fence for so long that no one takes him seriously any more."

Everyone on board the Whitley is a trainee, except for the Instructor. There is no Navigator. The aircraft isn't scheduled to fly anywhere, simply to do a couple of hours of 'circuits and bumps'—takeoffs and landings.

The Whitley roars across the field into the gathering dusk, tak-

ing a long time to stagger into the air. As it lifts off, its wheels clip the fence at the end of the runway. The instructor feels the vibration as the undercarriage catches the barbed wire and rips out three fence posts and part of the hedge. But he only becomes aware of the size of his problem when the undercarriage sticks half way up. Alf Doors knows then what has happened, and he knows they're in trouble. If he can't get the undercarriage up or down, things will be very messy when they land.

Meanwhile the other instructors have all finished flying for the day and they walk up to the Mess for a drink. Some of them have been detailed for early cross-country flights in the morning. One comes in late and tells the others that Alf Doors is just circling the airfield, not doing any landings. They pick up their pints of beer and wander outside to look.

"He's got something stuck in his wheels," says one of them, squinting through the twilight.

"Christ, it's the fence," says another.

They stand for a long time outside the Mess staring up at the lone aeroplane, discussing Alf Doors' plight, sipping their beer.

"He can't dump his fuel either . . . there's no fuel jettisoning pipes on the Whitley."

It's much too dangerous for Alf Doors to try and land the aeroplane with the tanks full of highly explosive aviation gasoline. One spark from a belly landing could blow the aeroplane into little pieces. The watchers outside the Mess know all this, and contemplate the options.

"He'll have to stay up there until he's used up his fuel," says one.

"That'll take him a while," mutters another. "He hasn't got a Navigator on board either. He can't even go anywhere without a Navigator."

They ponder this as it grows dark, and they watch the black aeroplane circling against the stars and think of the excruciating boredom of flying round and round the airfield all night, hour after hour.

"Might as well go to bed then," says the new Flight Lieutenant. "It'll take him eight or nine hours to burn his fuel off. He won't be landing before morning."

"Might as well have another pint before we go," says another.

They leave Alf Doors and his green crew outside, circling the starry sky, and walk back inside the Mess. When they finish their nightcaps they go off to bed.

When they wake up in the morning Alf Doors' engines are still droning away, the Whitley still circling the airfield. They dress and check the time and walk back to the Mess for breakfast. Each of them has calculated when Alf Doors will have to make his belly landing. There's still plenty of time for breakfast.

After the RAF's bacon and eggs and baked beans and tea the instructors make their way down the short hill to the airfield to watch the landing. They know Alf Doors has been up all night; that he'll be tired and bad-tempered. He's probably been sitting at the controls himself, afraid to trust the crippled aeroplane to any of his students; circling for hour after hour, waiting for the sky to lighten in the east.

Eventually the petrol gauges tell Alf that his aeroplane's fuel tanks are nearly empty. He lines the Whitley up with the airfield and comes in low and slow, just over stalling speed, with full flaps on and the undercarriage wheels jammed halfway down—and yards of wire and fence posts trailing below.

The aeroplane touches the ground and pancakes and skitters crazily across the airfield, ripping open the earth. The metal buckles and tears and rends the morning air with teeth-grinding noise. Almost before the battered aeroplane has stopped moving, and long before the dust has settled, the hatches burst open and the students and the instructor are out of it and sprinting like hell for the huts in case the remains of the fuel and the gases in the tanks ignite.

An auxiliary fire truck chases after the aeroplane and sprays water over the smoking wreckage. The watchers puff at their pipes, counting off the running crew, shouting encouragement as they charge across the field.

The sea lies cold and wild and grey-green to the north of Balnageith Farm, beyond mile on mile of sandy dunes and uncluttered beaches. The village of Findhorn stands here, at the edge of the Moray Firth, once a small, wealthy fishing port and now home to the world famous Findhorn Foundation. This quasi-religious Foundation arouses the suspicions of locals—its adherents speak to plants and grow the biggest cabbages in Britain. Big four-engined RAF Nimrods packed with electronic surveillance equipment take off over the Foundation's eastern fence from the air base at Kinloss, and head out over the North Atlantic and the North Sea on patrol.

The Findhorn River, full in springtime of snowmelt-clear water, carves its way down from the Cairngorm mountains and empties into Findhorn Bay. It's a peaceful place, with a picturesque harbour just inside the narrows, sheltered from the open sea. Sailboats bob at anchor offshore, their masts nodding and curtseying in the swinging tides.

The bay loses most of its water at the low summer tides and lies flat and sandy, channelled with streams and rivulets. Sailboats sit up on their keels or rolled over on their sides, and the bay looks then as benign as a child's paddling pool; as if it might be possible to wade across its length and breadth even when the sea fills it with water. It doesn't look deep enough to drown anyone, but the bay has seen its share of tragedy.

A young Pilot Officer called Cook is based at Kinloss during the winter of 1943-44. He's a New Zealander and he's just completed a tour of operations flying night bombers over Germany. He's lived through the flak and the night-fighters and the tiredness and strain, and now he thinks he's going to live forever. Sometimes Cookie drinks too much.

One night Cookie walks down to Kinloss village with a couple of friends from the airfield Mess. My father wants to join them but he's been detailed as Duty Officer and that means he's got to stay on the base. It's a dull chore and he's annoyed at having to miss the party so he tries to make a swap with someone who's off duty, but no one will do it.

Cookie and the others drink beer in the pub and probably some whisky as well and then they go out for an excursion on Findhorn

Bay in a rowing boat. Soon after they leave the shore a storm blows up and they lose the oars. The chop rises and the boat begins to fill up with water and they decide to try and swim for shore. It isn't far but Cookie can't swim very well and he drowns. My father would have drowned too if he'd been with them. He can't swim at all.

Cookie's grave lies among a small group of service graves in the shade of the ancient, ruined cathedral by Kinloss village. His headstone says nothing about the way he died. It simply gives his name and rank and his dates, and invites no conclusions beyond the fact that he died on active service. There is nothing to suggest waste. He was twenty-four.

The old airfield at Balnageith Farm is bright with wheat when I drive past it on a summer's day. There's not much left now to show that aeroplanes ever flew from here. A couple of chicken coops have the curved, black corrugated metal roofs of pre-fabricated wartime huts. What remains of the old living quarters are used as cattle byres, and for storing feed. Down on the flats, where the old airstrip used to be, I can just see the edges of an old concrete 'hard-stand', serving as a base for a pile of steaming silage.

More remains nestle in a small pinewood on the west side of the Grantown road, overgrown with brambles and spindly scrub trees. I climb up a small rise to a pile of bricks which was once the Mess, and gaze out over the farm. There are few other signs of all those people and the lives they lived here, hardly anyone left who remembers the energy and purpose that built a small, temporary military community here and lived its occasional dramas such a long time ago.

Alf Doors? He was the best man at a local wedding a few weeks after his long night flight over Balnageith Farm. Nine months after that wedding, I was born.

Belfast

On an early spring morning in 1988, a helicopter sits in the opaque sky above the Falls Road. It floats up there all day and night, five thousand feet above the city. The helicopter is painted a dull, sky colour, but it's the noise that makes you notice it; invasive, like a washing machine full of old boots rattling round and round and round. The people who live below never look up at it; pay it no attention at all.

But it's hard to ignore, and I stare up at it, wondering about the people inside, what they're doing. Are they gazing, hunchbacked, into high-powered cameras, heat imaging instruments and radarscopes? Or is theirs a more old-fashioned operation, with binoculars and road maps? Is it an easy, sought-after job, or do they feel exposed up there all by themselves, like ducks sitting in some kind of celestial shooting gallery?

In the end I decide the reality is probably more mundane. They are, of course, sitting on top of the Catholic area watching for signs of disturbance: secure and invisible inside their metal gunship but paradoxically observable for many miles around. Whether it's the Catholics or Protestants who cause trouble is neither here nor there to the British Army. But it seems to me as if the helicopter is singling out the Catholic area for its attentions. It's the symbol of a common oppressor, and if it is ignored by the people below, it is at the same time a focus for the city's resentments. There are many people in the streets below who'd wish for the kind of weapon that could bring the helicopter down.

I've come here for an important business meeting, and the hotel I've been booked into is ringed by a ten-foot high fence topped with razor wire. Every thirty yards or so the hooded lens of a powerful spotlight stares down from a high tower. The only way in to the hotel is through a hut set into the fence itself, so that you go in a door outside the fence and come out inside the compound. There are two, and sometimes three, men in there—occasionally a woman as well.

Inside, one of the men is sitting at a desk. He greets me politely. He's wearing a nondescript grey suit. His eyes are flat and empty. His arm rests lightly on the desktop. His partner stands warily off to one side, blocking the door out of the hut on the hotel side.

"Can I see your passport please?" It's not a request, and I won't get any further than this if I don't show it to him.

He thumbs through the pages, lingering over the big green and red stamp which reads *Ceskoslovenske Vizum*. I know what he's thinking. They make Semtex in Czechoslovakia; both sides here are fond of using this plastic explosive to blow things up.

Once, in the small town of Clifden on the west coast of Ireland, when I was going to meet my friend Susan I stumbled by mistake into an IRA bar. Waiting outside I could hear the 'crack'—the Irish pub chatter—rising and falling in a hubbub of great animation. Cigarette smoke curled under the door, wreathed out from windows glowing with convivial warmth. It was a cold night and I was sure she must be already waiting for me inside, a pint of Guinness standing on the bar with my name on it. I pushed the door open and went in, and in that instant of the door opening every voice in the place fell silent and every eye in the place turned to stare at me. I nearly fell down such was the power of it. I went on with a great effort for I could see Susan wasn't there. In the short transition from the door to the scarred black wood bar I saw that everyone in the place was male; that nearly everyone in the place was wearing a black leather jacket.

I walked up to the bar and asked for a pint of Guinness. No one spoke, not even the barman. He pulled the tap and the sound of the beer running into the glass was seditious and hypnotic and the only sound in the whole place. There was complete silence while I paid for the beer and took a drink of it. Then the door opened and Susan came in and one or two of the men recognised her and knew that it was all right and all of them started to speak again.

"What's your name?" the security man asks casually.

I tell him, resisting the urge to ask if he can read. He's only doing his job.

"Address?" The questions are correct, delivered in a quiet voice, on the edge of boredom. But firm.

"Where have you come from?" He nods his head slightly when I tell him.

"And how long will you be staying here, in the hotel?"

The questions go on.

"Have you got friends in Belfast? What's the purpose of your visit?"

He finishes off with a question about the Czech stamp in my passport. "When did you visit Czechoslovakia, sir?"

"Last Christmas."

He nods. "Uh-huh." He turns the page towards me. "Can you explain why the date stamp says October 30th, sir?" His finger rests on the incriminating line—'30. X. 1986'.

"I don't know. That's probably when they approved the visa. If you look closely you'll see that it was issued in Montreal." I point at a line above the date. "I had to send my passport off to the Czech Embassy in Canada to get it."

The answer seems to satisfy him and he smiles. His eyes remain hooded. This hotel has been blown up once before. He doesn't want it to happen again, not on his watch.

As I turn away he says, "What were you doing there, sir?"

"Pardon?"

"In Czechoslovakia. What was the reason for your visit there?"

"Oh. We went there for Christmas—to see the place that Good King Wenceslas came from."

The other man takes a step forward and asks me to stand up straight and move my legs apart. "Hold out your arms," he says. He pats me down carefully for concealed weapons: small of the back, armpits, inside leg, calf, biceps, forearm. If anything arouses his suspicions, they'll do a strip search.

He steps back and grunts. The formalities are over. I walk out of the hut by the other door into sunshine and find myself inside the compound. I feel as if I've escaped from a cell I've been in for a week.

Inside, the hotel looks like a place under siege. The carpets are worn, the wallpaper scuffed, the paintwork scratched and marked. The staff are lethargic and move around as if they're wearing lead boots. The whole establishment wears an air of dowdy respectability, like a place which has known better days, but has now been reduced to a billet at the front lines.

As night falls, the outside of the hotel and the grounds inside its caged perimeter are lit by white arc lights so that it feels not like a hotel at all, but more like Stalag Luft IV. The dining room smells vaguely of cabbage. The food at dinner is overcooked in a wartime British sort of way, the vegetables boiled to a pastel blandness and the beef grey and anaemic. The dessert is soggy and the coffee lukewarm. Outside the window the night is like day up to the chain link fence, the fields beyond held off by an inky blackness.

In the morning, the centre of Belfast is grey and empty. A few pedestrians hurry along with their eyes fixed in front of them. No one stops to chat by the shops, and no one parks their car in the street any more. If the security forces don't blow it up as a suspected bomb plant, then someone else will probably put explosives in it. To make sure there are no foreign wires or packages stuck onto the chassis, people poke mirrors on the end of long sticks under cars before they start them up. The people who live here have long ago grown used to the indiscriminate nature of events relating to the Troubles. It's second nature to check everything out, whether they have religion or not, whatever their personal distance from the conflict. No one in Belfast is neutral. One of the most terrifying things about the Troubles is the knowledge that both sides make frequent mistakes.

Our lunch meeting is held at a genteel golf club in the countryside at the edge of Belfast. The dining room is buzzing with conversation. It's an exclusive place, like Bruntsfield in Edinburgh or Uplands in Victoria, full of its own formalities and culture. The walls are hung with real paintings, not prints. There's not a spare seat in the place. There's not a woman in the place either.

My companions must be people of influence to have a seat here at all, never mind one by the window overlooking the eighteenth green. Willie and Duff are two upright Ulsterman. Duff's the tough one, and generally steps into a discussion first. But his gruffness belies an intelligent, thoughtful man underneath. Willie is generous and quick, with crow's foot lines around his eyes from smiling. There's steel in him though, and you can see it whenever the talk strays anywhere near the subject of Roman Catholicism, for the existence of Catholic people is a constant that worms its way somehow into every subject. The banter of these two men employs a kind of casually racist language that slides seamlessly through conversations, accompanied by qualifiers like " . . . now I'm not racist" or "I'm not sectarian mind, but . . . " The lunchtime discussion depresses me, shows me how insoluble the problems of this place really are. Where I live their comments would be considered bad taste, discriminatory and ignorant, even criminal. What can I make of it, sitting here with two otherwise decent people who are faultlessly correct with their observations in all the other traditional areas of discrimination?

Later on I'm listening to the BBC. The Irish writer Roddy Doyle (or is it Coim Tobin?) is saying, " . . .it's not easy for us, you know, to generate and perpetuate this sectarian thing. It's not as if there's a mark on any of us, or anything like that. We're not even different colours, so we can't tell the difference between each other—between Catholics and Protestants—just by looking. This conflict's something we've had to work very hard at . . ."

A lightness comes over me as the Manx Air flight lifts over the green Ulster countryside and sets course for Douglas. The ground drops away under the wing, taking with it the drab airport terminal and its police and soldiers and armoured cars. The aeroplane passes over the south side of a city lying serene and grey and silent in its spring haze, smoke slanting tidily from its chimney pots. Far off to the north, a tiny speck is hanging in the sky at about the same height as us, hovering steadily over the Falls Road.

Following Edward

Duck ponds lie across the face of Flanders like a rash, as if everywhere the water is waiting underground to overflow the land. This countryside still shows the scars of the Great War, its landscape marked with strange undulations. Once these peaceful ponds were shell holes, craters where soldiers sheltered.

After the autumn ploughing, chalk slicks stain the surface of the fields, tracing the zigzag lines of old trenches. There are graveyards here, tombstones standing thick as corn where the young soldiers fell: in the corners of fields, in villages, beside streams and woods and farmyards. Perfect rows of crosses stretch over hillsides: black ones for the German dead, white for our side. There must be more crosses here than any place on earth.

Flanders and Picardy are pockmarked with cemeteries; surprisingly close together, separated by a field or two on the ground, by years of bloodletting in the history books.

Sanctuary Wood, Vimy Ridge, Mount Sorrel, Beaumont Hamel . . . Passchendaele.

These names are chiselled onto lichen-covered monuments in towns and villages across the breadth of Canada; familiar to mothers and children and old people; the names of places where resolve and courage were stitched into the fabric of a young country.

Old German fortifications, grey and crumbling now, still guard the harbour at Calais. The rotting concrete weeps moisture, and mould and weeds grow from cracks between the bricks; shrubs sprout from long-silent gun ports. We want to get away from the coast before we stop for lunch, and so we point our green Citroen at the hills, towards Boulogne.

I was sixteen when I walked down this road with my friend Charles. The German defences at Calais were in better shape then, looming dark over the harbour, looking as if the soldiers might still be inside, sleeping.

Old pillboxes survey the Straits of Dover from the hills, and ships pass like toys across the surface of the sea. My companion, Em, and I keep to the N1 through Montreuil and all the way to Abbeville, and cross the river Somme at Pont-Remy.

We stop to buy food at Poix, a neat little white and black village beside the Route Nationale I; bread and cheese, wine and processed meats. The field we choose for our picnic is plump with ripening wheat, latticed with red poppies as if it has been arranged by Renoir, or Sisley. We sit on a bank brimming with wildflowers and contemplate it all.

Charles and I walked the hill road from Calais to Boulogne with only one short ride from a passing farmer, who sat us up on top of a trailer full of hay. We detoured through a small coastside village called Wimille (named, we thought, after a famous French racing driver) because Charles wanted to buy a cigarette lighter. At the edge of Boulogne we waited out a rainstorm in a wood and afterwards couldn't get anyone to stop to give us a ride. In the end we set out for the railway station and took a cheap train to Amiens, riding in an old third-class SNCF carriage on hard-slatted wooden seats. We didn't know anything about this war then, this Great War. We were interested in other things. French girls, red wine, the fat Gauloises cigarettes.

Amiens spun us out through its leafy suburbs onto ruler-straight country roads lined with tall Lombardy poplars. We inched along all afternoon, always moving towards the next bend in the road, each one an hour away: walking in hope, hour after hour. But the next bend never delivered its promises, just another long stretch of dead straight road and more poplar trees, and a solitary car passing by every hour or so without ever stopping to give us a ride. We walked for thirty kilometres, and towards evening we reached Poix.

It's a warm day. Poppies nod hypnotically among the wheat stalks and skylarks rise above us, singing far up in the blue sky.

We have to move because we pitched the blanket on an anthill.

Wounded at Beaumont Hamel

Canadian shrubbery is planted all around the car park at Beaumont Hamel in the valley of the Somme—salal, maple, some pine. A deep-chested caribou, cast in blackened bronze, stands on top of a mound at the crest of the slope, surrounded by neat, sub-alpine rockery plants. The sun is fierce.

The Newfoundland Regiment was destroyed here on July 1st, 1916.

The killing field falls gently away to a small copse. Sheep are grazing. The sun beats down and the air is thick with flies, and no-see-ums which bite like tiny piranhas.

When the soldiers were here the air buzzed with bullets. The Newfoundland Regiment was wiped out in less than thirty minutes.

The field is open. There is no cover. Two ravines fork into its base from a single stem at the foot of the slope. This was called

'Y' Ravine. Even an amateur soldier would see little profit in sending men over such ground to attack machine guns dug into the sides of the ravine.

It is hot. I take off my shoes and socks and listen to the gentle, tearing noise of sheep cropping the grass. It is peaceful, dreamy; on this high summer day, seventy years on, this place presents no dangers. Everything is forgiven, most of it forgotten. I walk down the hill to a lone tree. It is a skeleton, bare as midwinter, stuck with red poppies centred on small crosses made of popsicle sticks. Some of them carry messages.

"Never Forget"

"I'll always remember you Johnnie"

"I wish I'd known you Grandad. With love . . ."

This is the Tree of Death. Once it was an apple tree and bore fruit. Then this whole area was pulverised by shellfire and machine gun bullets. The tree died, and became petrified.

A sharp lick of pain stabs through my foot: blood soaks onto the grass, my blood. I drop onto my knees and feel the wound with my fingers. The blood makes them sticky. Slowly, carefully, I pull out a piece of ragged metal no bigger than a shirt button, but sharp around its edges like a scalpel. It is such a tiny piece to have caused so much pain, spilled so much blood.

All over this field thick, intertwined grasses cover old shell holes and disguise detritus, expired ordnance; the garbage of war. Shrapnel and barbed wire hide in the undergrowth. Screw pickets lie at angles, pitted and rusting. Once they held coils of impenetrable barbed wire, and funnelled the Newfies into the muzzles of the guns.

My shoes are up at the caribou monument. I make my way gingerly back across the field, checking each footfall. The Newfie boys who crossed this place had no such latitude, forced to maintain a steady, prescribed military walk when their wits screamed at them to run, through flying razor shrapnel the size of dinner plates; red hot, jagged metal as big as roof slates, window panes, kitchen scales. More than anything else, the men who fought here needed generals who could read maps, understand the most elementary aspects of terrain, cover, camouflage, stealth.

It's said that a hundred men died for every yard of ground in the Somme valley, which would mean that a mile cost roughly one hundred and seventy-six thousand men. The field at Beaumont Hamel is about a hundred yards across. Seven hundred and thirty-three men were lost here in half an hour—less than that demented average—and they failed to take the objective, a ravine with no military value, in the Valley of the River Ancre. It was detached, careless slaughter engineered by Generals who were decorated after the war with baronetcies and estates and medals; no mistakes admitted and no enquiries into the heedless carnage. Endless death was the accepted face of war.

My shoes are sitting between the hooves of the Newfoundlanders' caribou, which continues to gaze nobly across the battlefield. The handkerchief I tied round my foot is red with blood. There are band-aids in my bag but it seems churlish to apply them to my little wound. I fold the handkerchief and tie it on again.

The Newfoundland Regiment was under British command in the Great War. Newfoundland didn't become part of Canada until 1948. Ironically, Remembrance Day is observed in Newfoundland each year on July 1st in recognition of the slaughter at Beaumont Hamel. The rest of Canada celebrates Canada Day on that date—with fireworks and street parties.

Vimy Ridge

Slag heaps and collieries dot the landscape as far as we can see, stretching all the way back to Lens. The grey slate roofs of the old French mining town of Beauvry rise out of nearby fields, on the edge of the Douai plain. As it grows dark, glow-worms illuminate the reeds along the canal bank beside our campsite;

the houses by the lock gates pretty with climbing vines, noisy with cats.

Em and I pack up our tent, pay the attendant for the two nights we've stayed here, and drive off towards Vimy Ridge. We're approaching it from the east, from the German side, where it climbs steeply out of the plain above the city of Lens.

Cemeteries sprout on all its slopes, tucked into all its corners. The one at Neuville St. Vaast is enormous; rows and rows of crosses reaching through the trees, across fields. Most of the crosses are black, marking German dead. They make tidy patterns no matter which angle you study them from.

Bois Carré cemetery lies below the village of Thelus, near a small memorial cross in a field. It's a Canadian graveyard, planted with Douglas fir and sorrel, pine and salal and maple: a peaceful place, well tended and welcoming.

We stop at the start line for the Canadian assault on the Ridge, right beside a new motorway which curves busily away to the Channel ports. Cars and heavy trucks speed past.

The Canadian Divisions were brought up to this section of the front after the French and the British had tried unsuccessfully for two years to capture the Ridge, at a cost of nearly half a million men.

A gentle incline curves up to the crest on this western side. The ridge dominates the surrounding countryside and it's not difficult to see why the Germans held it for so long. Any defender would have wonderful fields of fire. The Canadians astonished everyone by capturing it in a few hours on an April morning amid unseasonal snow flurries. It was an unbelievable, magnificent feat—of arms, courage, intelligence.

Now, in sunshine, the ridge lies benign and pastoral under a sky swollen with stacked, rumbling clouds. A sunken lane leads off between wheat fields towards Arras. We lay a blanket down in a field on the soft slope, and set out a picnic. It's peaceful up here, warm and deserted, the air still. It's like a place off the map, at its most useful in war when it commands all the surrounding countryside. The motorway snakes away below but we can't hear the traffic, only the rich song of skylarks and the calls of nameless field birds.

We're sitting in the line of the 3rd Battalion advance on that cold morning in 1917. Bullets flew like hornets where we're eating our sandwiches, through air thick with shrapnel, black with deafening shell bursts. This is ground that Em's grandfather crossed; a place he never spoke about after the war.

When we've finished our lunch we drive up to look at Farbus Wood, a thin copse on top of the ridge beside a lane which falls down the back of the hill to Lens. Four old concrete bunkers stand twenty yards apart from one another at the edge of the trees. They've been well shot up, pockmarked and scored by bullets and shells. Rusted reinforcing metal rods poke through the crumbling concrete.

The bunkers are used now as cow byres, and littered with straw. Em and I climb inside and peer out through the gun slits, and see for ourselves how easy it would be to defend this place; how simple to pick off anyone within two or three hundred yards.

Our friend Arthur fought here when he was only seventeen. Even though it's a lifetime away he remembers these four bunkers when we tell him about them a month later. I can see his mind going back as we talk to him; know that it's just as hard for him as it is for us to reconcile the old man he's become, with the youth who was on that ridge.

Walter Allward's fine stone monument to the Canadian soldiers stands on the crest of the ridge, looking out over Lens towards the rising sun. It is vast, imposing, classical . . . and yet strangely delicate. Students from Trent University in Ontario work here as guides during the summer. One of them explains that the French government gave the ridge to Canada after the war, as a gift of appreciation. This place is Canadian territory now. The maple leaf flag flies over Parks Canada picnic benches and grassy craters and re-constructed trench systems. The firesteps in the trenches have metal shields for snipers; flat, steel plates with a tiny slit for aiming. The trenches are amazingly close to each other. An average athlete would find the enemy lines well within the lob of a baseball, or the toss of a hand grenade.

It's a strange feeling to stand here in France, in Canada.

Vimy Ridge lies at the edge of the great chalk basin which surrounds Paris. Chalk is soft and porous—easy to excavate—and the area is honeycombed with miles of tunnels, hacked and chiselled by miners from Northumberland and Lanarkshire, Nova Scotia and Cape Breton. Fresh troops and supplies were brought up to the front this way, undetected and safely.

It's damp and musty underground, gloomy and dark. Water drips from the ceilings. Some of the tunnels are flooded, tangled with relics of twisted metal and rusted equipment, as if no one has been down here since the soldiers left. Some of the soldiers sculpted images with their bayonets on the pastry-white walls while they waited for the signal to attack: initials, a heart with an arrow through it, a flower with petals, cartoons; a relief of a page from the Bible, a maple leaf. Notes to loved ones. The messages wait, frozen in the dirty yellow light, great with tension.

Much of the ridge is closed to the public, overgrown with brush and brambles. Barbed wire fencing is hung with warning signs, *'Danger de Mort'*. A student guide explains that so much explosive was thrown at the ridge during the four years of war that it has never been possible to clear it all. The forbidden areas are laced with thousands of unexploded shells.

It's a gentle place now, informal and un-military, where maple trees make shade from the summer sun. It feels like Canada.

In the dream, I'm fighting with a young German soldier on the Ridge, stabbing him over and over with a bayonet, but he won't die. I rip at his windpipe with my hands. He stares at me with big, child's eyes.

I wake up soaked in sweat and pull back the flap of the tent.

A wheatfield-yellow sun is rising over pyramid coal bings, and the long waving grasses of the Douai plain.

Two young Alsace Germans join us for breakfast. They tell us that they come from one of the mining towns along the Franco-German border, an area that has changed hands for hundreds of years through wars and treaties. It's part of France now, they explain, although most of the people there speak German.

Em and I drive up to Notre Dame de Lorette—another place of great killing. The French lost more than a million men on this ridge, which mirrors Vimy, across the valley. We walk among endless rows of crosses up here, and see that each cross marks four graves. From the top of the high, bleach-white tower which stands at the centre of this massive graveyard we can see over all the surrounding countryside: a haunting vista of peaceful farmland and cemeteries. An ossuary lies at the base of the tower, an enormous pit full of the bones of unidentified soldiers; guarded by sad old men in blue berets.

The four Canadian Divisions were well officered and resourceful. The British High Command discovered that they nearly always accomplished what they were asked to do, and so they used them repeatedly as spearhead troops in the Great War.

Em's grandfather, Edward, was a young infantryman in the Canadian First Division. After the assault on Vimy Ridge he went to fight at Hill 70, on the other side of Lens.

No signposts mark Hill 70 today, but we manage to find it by carefully comparing the new *Guide Michelin* to old maps of the area. Hill 70 is not really a hill at all. It's so flat that the French built an airfield on one side of it, a supermarket complex on the other. Only prairie boys would make sense of a hill like this, or a good tactician like Arthur Currie, Canada's best General of the war.

We walk across the supermarket's parking lot to some waste ground, and the remains of an old chalk quarry overgrown with bushes and nettles, flowering hemlock and wild grasses.

These old diggings were at the centre of a vicious, uncompromising battle in 1917 and the white chalk ran red with blood. Thousands of soldiers died here.

There is nothing here to show it, nothing at all.

On the far side of the plain, we're standing beside a signpost pointing to a village called Poelkapelle. I feel suddenly cold, as if a winter wind has just combed my bones in this summer place. There's nothing around, just a crossroads surrounded by wheatfields: red poppies at the side of the road.

"I don't like the sound of that name." I'm whispering. My knees have gone. I'm shaking for no reason at all, my own voice coming to me from a long way away, from the other end of a long, long tunnel.

"Why not?" asks Em.

"I don't know. I don't know. It gives me a bad feeling, sends shivers through me. I can't explain it, but . . . if I'd been here then, it's where I would have died."

I know this.

Passchendaele

A windmill stands on Gravenstafel Ridge, beside the valley of Passchendaele. From its base we can see more of the surrounding countryside than we could before. In war, this would be an important place. This ridge is not a feature of the terrain, like a hogsback in Shropshire or a hill in Cape Breton. The land here is flat to my untrained eye. But these folds and mounds and shallow vales would give cover to prairie boys tracking spring jackrabbits with a twenty-two, looking for advantage in tiny undulations.

We're gazing over a shallow valley, peaceful and long-shadowed at the end of the day. Sheep nibble the tufted grasses. It is not a real valley, more of a depression. It doesn't cover a large area, only a few hundred yards. Green and verdant, it has been well fertilised. This was the killing ground of Passchendaele, the apogee of the ineptitude and futility of that awful war. It is a name still spoken softly by old people.

Edward came here after Vimy and the carnage at Hill 70, to fight through mud and noise, across the backs of rotted corpses.

In 1917, the artillery bombardment here was so intense and prolonged, and it so pulverised the land that it altered the gravity of the place. The barrage wrecked and then reversed the natural drainage of the land, creating a quagmire which sucked down thousands of soldiers. Many of them were never found.

The Germans had good fields of fire from the rising slopes opposite. A casual glance at the terrain shows that any attacker must be completely exposed for two hundred yards or more. The German machine guns were sited so that each one was covered by others; if one post was knocked out, at least two more came into play. In this way their well-positioned guns commanded the whole valley.

It was a tactically clever defence in depth, but it came straight out of the German Army handbook and it was well known to the Allied commanders. Nevertheless they forced wave after wave of troops across these long open fields towards the echeloned machine guns. Where movement was possible at all, the sucking mud slowed it to a crawl. The result was murder, and the guilty were the Allied Generals, the German machine gunners simply the instruments of slaughter. Well over half a million men bled into these fields.

What did the German soldiers think as the young English, Scots, and Canadian boys were driven to suicide in front of them? What did the doomed think? Did they find nobility in it? Or poetry, like McRae in the watery ruins of Ypres down the road? Or were they too numb with cold and wet and fear?

The German army lost relatively few men at Passchendaele. Most of their forces stayed in the rear during the battle, waiting in case the Allies made an unexpected breakthrough. As long as they were well supplied with ammunition, only a few defenders were needed at the gun pits to stem the tide of khaki soldiers.

The names of the farms and properties in this little valley are innocent enough, many of them English names, which sound strange in this Belgian landscape. Vine Cottage. Crest Farm. Tyne Cot. They leave clues to the dead.

Thin lanes cross the battlefield like veins; grails and shrines sit beside them at corners and crossroads, grown over with wild roses. The land is recovered now, the farms prosperous and well worked, the soil rich with blood and bone.

An old Englishman wanders silently among the white crosses.

Sanctuary Wood

Monsieur Schier is pale and overweight. He sits on a stool behind the counter in his souvenir shop and barely moves; he only speaks when we ask him questions.

This land, he explains when we ask, has been in his family since before the First World War. His grandfather built this little museum on his shattered farm in 1919 when he realised that the survivors were coming back to see where they'd fought and where their friends had died; where their lives had been so utterly changed. Some of them, unable to explain the madness, brought their wives and mothers to see for themselves. But they found that this didn't help to explain anything at all . . .

Monsieur Schier's grandfather saw that there was money to be made from this sad business. He put up signs and built a small café and made sure that the old trenches and dugouts on his land were not ploughed over and planted. Like the grandfather, the son and the grandson have left things untouched. Cows stand in the field next to Monsieur Schier's museum. Mist lies in the hollows, concealing the creatures' hooves. The countryside here is barely above sea level.

Sanctuary Wood has grown thick with undergrowth over the years. Brambles climb broken telegraph poles and tug at sagging wires. The only things which grow here are weeds; stinkwort, nettles, brambles, chickweed. The old earthen ramparts have collapsed under the gentle onslaught of rain and the weathering of time, and the banks are slippery with mould. Rain puddles in the bottom of the trenches; it rusts abandoned metal and broken pieces of corrugated shelter, slowly washes away the old dugouts, erodes the narrow, musty tunnels.

Monsieur Schier's museum is full of artefacts and compellingly gruesome 3D photographs which must be viewed through a stereoscope viewer, with a lens for each eye, like binoculars. The photos are plated on glass; some of them are cracked. Monsieur Schier has hundreds of them.

In the pictures, bits of bodies are scattered around like pieces from a lunatic's jigsaw puzzle. In one, the front legs of a horse hang from the branch of a tree, neatly crossed. An arm lies on top of some sandbags. Stringy, splintered countryside stretches as far as the lens can see, in a wasteland of mud and water. The people in the photographs look like the vegetation around them—shattered legs like shattered tree stumps, a dead, clawing hand like the root of a bush. It's almost possible to imagine the hellish racket that must have accompanied it all: the shaking of the ground and the hailing of earth and stones and shrapnel. Or the stench. This is the stuff of a lifetime's nightmares. How could it ever be explained to someone who wasn't there?

Monsieur Schier's pictures have never been published. They are too horrible for the people of today.

There are no other visitors to the museum while we are here.

"It has not been a good summer," says Monsieur Schier. "There is too much rain. Besides, nearly all the old soldiers are gone now."

It rains all night.

✦

Charles and I knew nothing about this Great War when we passed through Picardy. We walked on, that summer, towards the west—into Normandy and relics from a more recent conflict—Caen, St. Lo, Coutances, Avranches, Rennes . . . Falaise. Falaise, where the air smelled strong and sweet for weeks in the high summer of 1944 from the composting flesh of German divisions caught in the savage crossfire of Poles, Canadians, Brits, Americans, and from above, the bombs of the air forces.

The Falaise Gap, a more recent carnage; a reaping of the whirlwind. The end the same though, as it is in wars: the end of young men and women—and glimpses perhaps, of ultimate knowledge, fleeting.

The Ardennes

Bonn is full of politicians. The Bundestag is winding up its affairs before the Christmas break, and every hotel room in the city is taken. The German parliamentarians make sure they turn up in the capital for the season of parties and fairs.

I've forgotten what it's like to drive on roads with no speed limits. The Germans call the road between Bonn and Cologne 'the Racetrack'. It's like Indianapolis. The speedometer of the rented Volkswagen winds through 180 kilometres an hour and cars pass us as if we're standing still.

Our friends own a small hotel on Filzengraben, a quiet street near the centre of Cologne. They take us up to a special guest room in the attic, high up under the sloping roof. The window frames the rooftops of the city and Rhine barges churning up the river against the current. At the far end of the Kaiser Wilhelm Bridge, the number 4711 flashes out in yellow neon.

"What does it mean?" asks Em, gazing out of the window. "4711."

"It's another name for *eau de cologne*," says Ulrich. This is Ulrich's hotel, his city. "The recipe for it was given to a man called Muhrens on his wedding day about two hundred years ago, by a friend of his who was a Carthusian monk. Back then it was known as *'aqua mirabilis'*—miracle water—because it was such a refreshing stimulant. I used to think the number was something to do with its chemical formula, but it's not. It's simply the street number of the place where they manufactured it."

The black gothic spires of Cologne's great cathedral—the *Dom*—reach high above the city, dominating everything. The cathedral received sixteen direct hits in the bombing raids during the war. But it survived the bombs and was virtually the only recognisable structure left at the end, standing up in a desert of grey rubble like the ancient, scarred warrior symbol that it is.

Close by the cathedral, in the *Domplatz*, an old man rests on his knees, bent almost double, scratching an image in coloured chalks on the grey flagstones. We stand and watch him, admiring his skill. Every few seconds he holds a crumpled postcard up to the light of the shop windows, checking it against his sketch. It's a picture of Piccadilly Circus. The old man is dressed in a tattered *feldgrau* greatcoat, his hands mottled with chalk dust, his face pallid and unshaven. Some pfennigs lie scattered beside him on the ground. A line of yellow chalk marks one cheek like an old battle scar, and he looks every bit as gothic as the *Dom* nearby.

"He looks as old as his coat does," I whisper to Em. "Look at it; it's an old German Army greatcoat from the war."

It's after five o'clock, almost dark. We're standing in the middle of throngs of Christmas shoppers hurrying across the square to catch the stores before they close. Commuters stream out of the nearby *bahnhof* and scuttle off down neon-lit pedestrian streets, racing to get home for dinner. No vehicles are allowed in this part of the city. No one pays any attention to the old pavement artist. He comes from another time, a different age.

The centre of Cologne is designed for people and not cars, and this gives the city an unhurried sense of civility. The

Neumarket lies at the edge of the pedestrian area. Hundreds of stalls, cheerful with Christmas decorations, have been set up here for the festivities.

The *Neumarket* is like a town within the city, with a busier pace to its surroundings. Music spills out of loudspeakers, competing with a brass band and the rattle of clockwork toys, and tapes playing Christmas carols. Beeswax candles hang from awnings; there are toy trains, mannequins and dolls, games and racing cars and balsa-wood aeroplanes on tables and counter-tops. Hot chestnuts are roasting on open braziers, and spicy *gluhwein* bubbles in pots beside fresh chocolate and toffee apples, all lacing the air with exotic odours. Children drag parents excitedly from one stall to another, and the place is jumping with a gypsy liveliness.

The timber-frame houses and shops in Cologne's *Altstadt* look as if they've been here for hundreds of years. But the city's old centre was completely devastated during the war. The old, dry wood burned like matchsticks under the onslaught of Allied incendiary bombs and nothing was left of it by 1945. Now the Germans have rebuilt it as it was, with a care and attention to detail which is almost a national characteristic. In a corner of the *Altstadt* the ancient stones of the church of Gross St. Martin are scarred and scratched from thousands of shrapnel splinters. Gross St. Martin received several direct hits during the bombing and the church was completely flattened. The congregation began to restore it in 1946, after the war was over. They retrieved as many of the original stones from the rubble as they could, and began to piece them together like an infernal jigsaw puzzle. They numbered and coded the stones and bricks, the remains of doors and window frames, slates and pieces of the steeple, and metal and as much wood as had survived the fires. Now this beautiful Romanesque church is open for worship again, and Em and I stand inside it, wrapped in its silence, bathed in the light of the church's exquisite new grey and red stained-glass windows. The glass is elegant and reverent; the past, present and the future blend together across the coloured panes with a poignant simplicity. A display of black and white photographs in the church lobby tells us the whole astonishing story.

We walk down the riverbank beside the sullen, brown Rhine and come upon a small, smoky-beamed *gaststatte* with the unlikely name of 'Heller Skeller'. A sandwich board outside it is offering a dinner special at a low price. We go inside and sit down. A waiter appears right away, takes our order, and disappears into the back of the restaurant. Suddenly, a patron jumps to his feet and runs out the door clutching his throat. He staggers across the riverside walkway and vomits over his shoes, onto the grass. A woman runs after him, and stands awkwardly with her hand on his shoulder while he shakes and shudders and barks painfully into the night.

The little scene is daunting, but we're already committed. The Wiener Schnitzel I've ordered turns up seconds later, and I inspect it carefully. The waiter hovers nearby, sensing that we're nervous. The man who was ill outside, he explains, got a fish bone stuck in his throat.

"Oh, the poor man," says Em sympathetically. But I find this news reassuring, and the food is excellent.

The moon rises slowly out of the river from the southeast, outlining the flat span of the *Severinsbrucke,* laying a bright path across the slow, mud-brown water. It's a big, white winter moon, and as it climbs it touches the steel cables of the bridge one by one. By the time it leaves the last cable and sets off into the inky sky, the moon is a thin, cold silver plate.

I glance at my watch. It has taken twenty-seven minutes for the moon to rise from the horizon and clear all the *Severinsbrucke's* cables.

A few days later we rent a black Volkswagen and take a country road out of Cologne towards Euskirchen. The road winds through pretty little towns like Munstereifel, Blankenheim and Stadtkyll, passing quaint church steeples and Hansel and Gretel houses, aiming for the hills. Near the village of Losheim we come upon lines of weathered concrete dragons'-teeth, and thread our way carefully through them. These are the old border tank traps, for this is a road well known over the past century to Bismarck, Schlieffen, von Runstedt, Mantueffel.

The crumbling eyesores stretch away along the sides of fields and the edges of woods, coil like snakes over the crests of hills—sinister and lichen-covered and brambled; once part of Germany's feared Siegfried Line. After the war, there were simply too many of these dragons'-teeth up here in the Losheim Gap to eliminate, which is why so many of them still remain.

Bismarck's forces came this way to attack France in 1870, and we find several conical metal posts from that Franco-Prussian conflict spaced along the Luxembourg border. Forty-four years later, Schlieffen was the military genius who drew up plans to outflank the Allied armies by attacking through here at the start of the Great War; plans which ultimately caused the trench lines to push out all the way to Switzerland, and led to a bloody war of attrition.

The Losheim Gap was well known in 1940, when its name sent chills through the French and Belgian troops up the road. Von Runstedt's *blitzkrieg* campaign in the spring of that year caught the Allied military planners napping. His swift armoured thrust through the Ardennes outflanked France's Maginot Line, and his troops raced on to the Channel ports in northern France and Belgium.

Four and a half years later, in the midwinter of 1944, von Runstedt dusted off Schlieffen's plans once again, out-thinking the Allied military minds who had chosen to defend this sector with only a pair of weak and inexperienced army divisions. Most of the Allied Generals thought the hilly Ardennes countryside to be much too restrictive for a modern war of movement.

This was the route followed that Christmas by Jochen Pieper's SS Panzer Kampfgruppe—the shock spearhead of the German attack which came to be known as the Battle of the Bulge. The SS made mincemeat of the understrength American forces in this sector, most of whom had been sent up here for a rest.

We stop the car on top of a high ridge in the Eifel mountains and gaze out at a great rolling swathe of eastern Belgium, a vista of shadowed valleys and hillsides sprinkled with picturesque little towns and villages. Woodsmoke from hearth fires sits blue and dusky in hollows, and narrow lanes wind among fields of sheep and grazing cattle.

"It's difficult to believe isn't it," I suggest to Em, "that we're looking down on what has been one of the main European battlegrounds for hundreds of years." This beautiful place, where the borders of five countries come together.

The road drops down through Honsfeld to Bullingen, and on to Murringen. Over there, I tell Em, on that hillside, stand the villages of Krinkelt and Rocherath—killing grounds where the fighting at Christmas 1944 was particularly bloody; where a pair of understrength companies of the US Second Infantry Division faced a prolonged and ferocious assault from the Twelfth SS Panzer Division—the notorious *Hitler Jugend*—who had executed captured Canadian troops a few months earlier in Normandy.

The killing of prisoners took place here as well, and the rumours of it grew until trained men became frightened, and began to think of the place as Armageddon, and did the same thing back to the enemy; and so no quarter was given, and executions were coldly carried out on both sides.

The children in the villages look tough and wild, and they stand and stare at us as we drive slowly through. Sheep and deer dot the mole-hilled fields which roll out of the forest. The light is soft and yellow, the sun low, creating a haze which shuts off the farther distances, forcing you to concentrate on what is immediate. Shafts of sunlight slant down from the clouds, painting the fields.

Inside the forest the trees are well spaced, the ground dry underfoot, with little underbrush. Most of the trees are fir and some of them lose their needles in wintertime. We pass a group of men cutting Christmas trees and loading them onto trucks. In one place there are beech trees, their leaves fallen onto the ground in a rich golden carpet.

A poignant memorial stands mossy and neglected beside the road.

"*Toi, qui s'arrete ici . . .*" it states. "*You who stop here—this is the place where the inhabitants of Faymonville suffered the murderous fire of the Germans during the Von Runstedt offensive in December 1944.*"

Most of the road signs here have been scratched over, so that Ambleve now reads Amel, which is the old German name for the town. Half a century after the war, German-speaking Belgians have begun to re-assert their identity.

In 1940, and again in 1944 the Belgians here hung swastika flags from their windows and greeted von Runstedt's troops and helped them.

This fragmented country, already struggling with the differences between its Flemish and French speaking people, was even more deeply split after the war. German-speaking Belgians were greatly mistrusted, and they kept their heads down for years.

We pass through countryside that is marshy all the way to the bleak, moorland crossroads at Baugnez. Another memorial stands here. A hundred US Army Artillery GI's, overtaken by the speed of Jochen Pieper's advance, were disarmed and herded into a field at these crossroads just before Christmas, in 1944. The SS soldiers lined them up in ranks, as if they were going to inspect them. Then they shot them. The memorial is lonely and damp, this shoulder of hillside swept by a cold wind.

"Let's go," says Em. "Let's find a town with some good food and wine, and a warm room for us." I nod in agreement. What took place here all those years ago was so murderously casual, so easy and banal that it defies proper explanation—certainly in peacetime. It still haunts this place, and people like us who stop here.

We drive slowly into Malmedy, a country town of winding streets in a valley at the base of hills below the *haute fangen*— the high moors. It has been a long day, traversing a landscape which barely manages to conceal its memories; where we can sense that much, much more lies just beneath its surfaces.

The Hotel du Centre offers us bed and breakfast for twenty dollars a night. The place is clean and spartan, its linoleum floors echoing our footsteps as we walk down the corridor to our room. Across the street, framed in our small window, lies the town square. Beside it, the car park at the Scotch Inn is packed with expensive cars. The rim of countryside around the town is hazy and remote. As the sun sinks into the hills we follow our noses down the road to a café with red-chequered tablecloths. Its *prix du jour* menu advertises fresh mussels and vegetable soup and *pommes frites*. The soup is earthy and strong, the mussels cooked in wine with subtle suggestions of anise and thyme. The food and these peaceful surroundings contrast with the rustic violence of the countryside that we've travelled today, and we find it difficult to make sense of it. So we eat, deep in thought, retreating inside ourselves, digesting more than the fare on the table between us, our silences much longer than our conversations. Knowing perhaps that this place is fragile still.

It is not an easy thing to speak of this, not even to each other, and it's harder still to bring ourselves to ask questions of any of the people here. Memorials and wartime tales fill this part of Belgium. The crossroads at Baugnez, the Hotel Moulin at Ligneuville nearby—where more American soldiers were shot in cold blood by Jochen Pieper's SS troops. It is almost impossible in today's Europe to see this as a place of such transcendent inhumanity. The tranquil present gives the lie to the past, makes it hard for us to reconcile the enormous changes that have occurred here in such a relatively short space of time.

In the morning we make our way over the hill to the valley of the Ambleve River, which rushes, cold and swollen, through the village of Stavelot. Red brick houses line a narrow street by a bridge. A cobblestoned road winds up the hill on the other side of the river to a square where a lively country market offers clothes, vegetables, fresh bread, even furniture for sale. A lady wrapped in scarves sells bags of peanuts from a stall. She smiles as she hands a bag to Em, says *"merci"* in a cloud of warm breath in the cold air.

In this pretty village, on December 19th, 1944, the SS herded Achille Andre, Henri Delcourt and nineteen other men into a tiny eight-by-twelve-foot wooden shed beside the bridge. They padlocked the door and set up two MG42 machine guns outside. Each gunner fired a belt of ammunition through the thin clapboard walls of the shed, and then the officers went inside and with Luger pistols finished off the men who were still alive. When they'd finished shooting, the SS soldiers piled straw around the hut and set it on fire. Miraculously, eight of the Belgians managed to escape from this carnage.

> *"Ami, entends-tu*
> *les cris sourds du pays*
> *qu'on enchaine?"*

A few miles away, La Gleize sits up on the shoulder of a hill above the river. This pretty village marks the furthest advance of Pieper's troops, who were chronically hampered by a lack of fuel and ammunition in that far-off winter campaign. One of Pieper's huge Tiger tanks still sits in the tiny village square beside the church in front of the school, scarred and gouged from artillery strikes which failed to penetrate its thick armour. Children chase each other across the street and play around the schoolhouse. Smoke from a garden bonfire drifts over the tank.

A small memorial stands at the side of the road in the village of Cheneux, honouring a handful of soldiers from the US 82nd Airborne Division who died here. Max Bruch's Violin Concerto is playing on the car radio as we drive past, knitting the seasons together, bridging time, celebrating life. Like the music, this countryside is achingly beautiful, its peaceful, rolling hills cared for and cultivated over centuries. Two foresters are at work in the woods, selecting trees to harvest. A hawks sits up on a fence post, another walks in a field.

> *"Ce soir l'ennemi*
> *connaitra le prix du sang*
> *et des larmes."*

After the war Jochen Pieper was tried by the Allies for the crimes committed by his troops in this campaign. Ultimately, he was acquitted. Later, he went to live in the village of Traves, in eastern France. His house was firebombed in the summer of 1976 and he was killed. The French police were never able to discover who had done it.

In the evening we turn away from a frosty sunset, back towards the old, concrete dragons' teeth.

It's a cold morning at Bliealf in the Eifel Mountains, back at the German border. In the *gasthaus,* we're served breakfast on a spotless white tablecloth, our boiled eggs perfectly done. The coffee comes with condensed milk, and rectangular sugar lumps wrapped neatly in paper. We are the only guests. Outside the windows a thick mist holds visibility down to twenty yards, revealing only the merest hint of bushes and trees, which change their shapes as the fog thickens and dissipates.

The crumbling dragons' teeth of more old tank traps line the road to Grosslangenfeld, winding off into the murk, moss covered and forbidding. Clervaux steps up from the river, dominated by its twelfth century chateau-fort. We've crossed unknowingly into Luxembourg, passed through the infamous Siegfried Line. There are no borders here now, but the people of Clervaux are unfriendly until they realise we're not German.

The air is arctic. Icy-thick hoar frost coats the trees. Barbed-wire fences, hung with clumps of sheep's wool, disappear into the mist. Crows stand in fields scrubbed bare by winter winds.

Bastogne is a busy, regional centre and big articulated trucks hammer through the middle of town, jolting us into the present for the first time in days. It is easy for a traveller to live in the past in this part of Europe.

Bastogne was completely cut off by German Wehrmacht and SS forces, and besieged for days at Christmastime in 1944, but the 101st Airborne Division, which was holding the town, refused to capitulate. The powerful German advance floundered against dogged American resistance at this important crossroads, and lost much of its steam.

In front of the rundown Hotel le Borges a brightly lit Christmas tree dominates the Place McAuliffe. This is Bastogne's main square, named after the American General who led the defenders during the siege in 1944. Trucks rumble through it all evening and into the night. All the cafés display menus in their windows, and we make our inspections on foot.

The Cafe Leo looms out of the fog, a converted old railway car on the Rue du Vivier. Tonight's speciality is meatballs and *pommes frites* with a *picquet* of *vin rouge. Prix Compris.* Inside, the youthful staff operates at a gallop, dashing among the packed tables. The food is passable.

After the meal we walk back to the hotel. Small Christmas firs, decorated with ribbons, hang from the walls outside the stores. An icicle falls in the still, cold air from the branches of the big Christmas tree in the Place McAuliffe, tinkling to pieces on the sidewalk like an expensive crystal glass. It makes me jump.

The next day is the day the old soldiers walk the boundaries of Bastogne to commemorate the lifting of the 1944 siege. An old, grey-haired man sits at breakfast in the Hotel le Borges, wearing paratroop boots and the 'Screaming Eagles' patch of the 101st Airborne Division on his combat jacket. A young woman sits with him.

"Make sure you're wrapped up warm, Dad," she says kindly. "It's very cold outside." She leans forward and adjusts his scarf, pulling it gently under his chin.

He looks sad and doesn't say anything, out of place now in his military fatigues in this modern town; someone from another time, with a daughter who was not even imagined in those far off days.

The streets outside are jammed with shoppers and traffic. The Christmas tree in the market square is covered with red, purple and white balls and hung with glittering diamonds and squares. The mist is thicker than ever, hazing the lights and coating the bare trees with the glaze ice that climbers call '*nevé*'.

The main road that runs north and east from the city of Luxembourg to Brussels is the N4. It deviates little from ancient tracks and paths tramped and ridden by traders over the centuries. The road was improved and straightened by the Romans, and some of it was paved in the early years of the twentieth century. Today, it is gradually being replaced by a massive new autoroute, the A4, which promises swift passage between these two great centres of a united Europe.

On its way north, the old N4 hugs the Luxembourg/Belgium border until it turns sharply westwards at Bastogne. Rippled snow and stubbled earth cover the fields, and we follow the road across open, windswept farmland and rolling moors until we come to the Ardennes forest near Herbaimont. There are few settlements on the highway after this and the road runs straight and fast from the big intersection at Barriere-de-Champlon towards the old market town of Marche.

About halfway between Barriere and Marche the N4 drops down a long slope into a bowl rimmed by hills. Down here, the road is sheltered from the winds and the valley sweeps around us, lush and green. Beside the highway but separated from the traffic by a low concrete wall, stands a row of cottages, a filling station and a café. Across the fields to the north, a village straggles untidily up a shoulder of countryside to the top of a hill. A small stone church sits up on a mound by itself, overlooking the crooked village street. A thin brown stream runs along beside the main road, and there are railings on the bridge.

This is Bande; a place etched in the memory of the Belgian people.

It's late afternoon when we turn off the N4 here, and trace a narrow road through the fields to the village of Grune. The lane bends around hedges and barbed wire fences until it reaches an aged, half-ruined chateau. Cobblestones pave the lane beyond the towered gates of the chateau and lead on to a cluster of low-roofed farm cottages, and a little church. We stop in a tiny square by the church and get out of the car to stretch our legs. A faded Belgian flag hangs limp against the church wall beside a stone memorial. Wilted flowers droop from glass jars. The cobblestones are plastered with farmyard mud. Tractor tracks peter out at the last house and a staunch farm gate closes off the lane.

A face appears at the window of one of the cottages, and disappears behind a lace curtain when I look up. The lane doesn't seem to have a name. I walk slowly to the corner. A door opens in a house to my left. An elderly woman moves stolidly into her doorway. She crosses her arms and stares hard.

"Pardon madame, mais . . .?" It's as far as I get.

"Vous etes Allemand?" Her narrow eyes flick over to the black Volkswagen. I follow her gaze. The car has German licence plates.

"Er, non madame. Canadien."

She watches me carefully, but she doesn't move and says nothing more. It's hard to tell how old she is. She's very straight and thin. Her hair is grey, brushed back from her face, but not tied at the back. It falls to her shoulders in the style of a much younger woman. She wipes her hands slowly on a blue print pinafore. A small cloud crosses the sun, and the air feels stretched and tight.

I try again. *"Pardonnez-moi, mais . . ."*

"Canadien?" She splits the syllables like the Quebecois do and pulls the door close behind her as if someone might be

listening. She takes a step out of the doorway. "Why do you drive a German car?"

"Oh. I rented it in Cologne." I'm careful to pronounce it as the French do; not *Koln*, like the Germans.

She studies me further. "Ah, I see." She nods her head slowly, up and down. "Cologne is a long way from here. "

Then everything changes, and she surprises us by asking if we'll come into her house for a cup of coffee. The kitchen is small and warm; a thick rug covers most of the flag-stoned floor. A pot steams gently on an old black stove and the room smells of woodsmoke and coffee.

Helene Detry-Gustin was a young woman in December 1944 when the Sicherheitsdienst—the SS secret police—came to her village. The SD rounded up all the men in the neighbourhood, including three of her friends from Grune. Then they shot them. Only one young man escaped.

"Some of them," she says, "were shot outside, against the churchyard wall, where the little memorial stands now." She points through her front window. The tragic spot is right there, across the cobbled street. The cross we can see is part of the everyday life in her village; it commemorates real events, not ceremonial obligations.

She goes on. "The day they shot the men in Grune the Germans took us all down to Bande on the main road, to the cellar underneath the tobacconist's shop where they had shot the others and laid out the bodies. They forced us to look at them. It was a warning to us."

Outside it begins to rain. A soft drizzle slowly rubs out the fields and clings to the window panes on a cold northeast wind. The wind soughs under the door with a peculiar, low whining sound, like a child crying, as it used to do at my grandmother's house in Edinburgh. Madame Detry-Gustin stands up and moves across the room. Smoke puffs out from the grate when she opens her back door. She brings in a log and places it beside the fire. It is nearly dark now.

The smoky kitchen and the oil lamp, the sounds and the peaty, earthy smell of the room work with her voice to move time backwards. It's not an unpleasant sensation; it is even seductive. But it's unsettling, and very, very far from the world that Em and I live in.

Madame stares out of the window.

"It is all peaceful now." She indicates the dim fields sloping away to the forested hills. "But it wasn't like this fifty years ago." She glances up at a small crucifix on the wall. "We had to be careful every moment. We had to watch what we said and who we said it to. We couldn't move around like we can today, not in this part of Belgium. Everywhere we went there were checks. We needed papers for everything. Coupons for food, for fuel, for clothes."

She turns away from the window. "There isn't a family here that was not changed by the war; that doesn't still feel the effects of it in some way today. I don't think it was the same in North America. There are many of us here who have not forgotten."

Em and I drive slowly down to the village of Bande on the main road, to visit the place Helene spoke about, the place with the old tobacconist's shop.

Most of the men were young. Some of them were children. The Germans lined them up in rows at the side of the main road as if they were going to march them away. Three rows of them. It began to snow.

The soldiers made the men hand over their personal belongings—watches, rings, wallets, jewellery—then they took them across the road one by one to the hole in the ground which was the burned-out cellar of the tobacconist's shop, next to where the Café de la Poste had stood. There they shot the men one by one in the back of the neck so that they fell in among the charred and tangled beams.

One of the young men saw tears running down the cheeks of the tough SS Sergeant who was about to shoot him. He punched him as hard as he could in the face and leaped over the stream and ran off across the fields through the falling snow, chased by a hail of bullets. He was the only one who escaped. His name was Leon Praile.

It was Christmas Eve, 1944.

The old tobacconist's shop is still in ruins, a shrine now. The cellar is almost pitch dark, the air inside chill and odourless. We light a match and it helps us to find a light with a time switch, illuminating a crucifix and a small altar draped with coloured ribbons. Photographs of the dead are set into a stone slab, thirty-two of them, surrounded by flowers. A plaque in front of a sculpted peasant-figure carries their names.

It is a place of the dead, and no one else comes to it while we're here. But the memory of it is alive for people in this part of Belgium to whom these events remain almost as immediate as the day they happened. The fresh flowers tell us this, and the passion with which the old lady Helene spoke of it to strangers.

It's a sad, sad, desolate place. We leave, conscious of the German licence plates on our rented car. Sharing somehow the shame of it.

Paris In December

Paris is like an armed camp after student riots and a terrorist bombing a few days ago. It's 1986, but the police are just as edgy and short tempered as they were during the 1968 riots—which heralded the beginning of the end of de Gaulle's time in power.

Today, the paramilitary CRS are everywhere in blue quilted coveralls and funny, forage half-hats, most of them wearing flak jackets and nervously fingering Uzi sub-machine guns. Grey buses and vans are parked up side streets, dozy with relief shifts of sleeping CRS men waiting to take their turn on the streets. Every few minutes a police van tears past with its lights flashing, siren blaring. The city looks weary and run down and sad.

But this is Paris. Turn around on any street and the mind races with history and imagination. Paris won't stay tired like this for long.

I push a pile of francs over the counter at the metro station and say, *"Un cachet, s'il vous plait"*.

The lady behind the glass gives me a funny look.

"Un cachet?" Her eyebrows rise. A smile tugs at the corners of her mouth. "You have to go to the *pharmacie*," she says in

English. "A *cachet* is an aspirin." Reverting back to French she says gently, *"Je pense que vous voulez acheter un carnet monsieur."*

"*Ah oui,*" I agree hastily. *"Je veux acheter un carnet s'il vous plait.*" Em catches my eye, grinning widely.

The ticket lady hands me a *carnet*, a small book of tickets, and smiles and the passengers waiting behind me smile tolerantly too. Parisians are kinder to visitors in winter.

At the Gare de Lyon we're told that the administrative part of the SNCF, the French railway system, is on strike. It's impossible to make reservations. Hunched shoulders, shrugs, upraised palms. Nothing can be done about it.

The Place de l'Opera stands busy with traffic at the meeting of seven streets, bordered with extravagantly painted hoardings sheltering new construction projects. The Opera itself rises grandly across the square, the heart of classical culture in France.

On a sultry summer night two years later, I sat across this square and watched the apprentice dancers from the Paris Opera Ballet perform in the glass-domed Palais Garnier. I watched enthralled inside the brilliant crystal palace while these talented teenagers mesmerised an intimate audience of family and friends. Throughout a performance of exquisite delicacy and colour a tumultuous thunderstorm raged overhead, directly above the enormous glass roof. Lightning crackled across the Paris night and I tried not to think about the miles of steel holding all the glass panes together above us: a perfect lightning rod.

The French Ministry of the Interior, in the narrow Rue des Saussaies, was the headquarters for the Paris Gestapo during the war. The CRS are all around it today, holding rifles and tommy guns, standing in shop doorways, lounging on street corners. Groups of them are moving through the gardens on the other side of the street, drifting like shadows under the trees. They cultivate an image of toughness, an air of unpredictability beyond the studied discipline of the gendarmerie or the army.

The Gare d'Orsay, beside the Seine, has been restored and re-opened as an Art Museum. The last train left here years ago and now the old station is choc-a-block with paintings by Pisarro, Sisley, Monet, Renoir, Matisse. We walk past huge sculptures of dinosaurs and triceratops, and pass through the turnstiles.

Darkness falls as it does in France, with little space between day and night. We walk outside onto an upstairs balcony and the city is laid out magnificently in front of us like a stage-set in strings of white light against a black backdrop. A whirling funfair of multi-coloured lights spins round in the Tuileries Gardens across the river. The cathedral of Sacre Coeur sits up on its hill like a marble sculpture, with beams of searchlights cutting the black sky above it. The scene is breathtaking, the movement of the lights making it look as if the cathedral is floating up into the night sky; we don't notice the biting wind coming off the Seine.

Despite the strike our train leaves punctually from the Gare de Lyon at midnight. Our sleeper is expensive, but it's a well-appointed little apartment. The sleeping cars in France orient the beds up and down the train, so that your head or feet lie towards the engine—unlike British sleeping cars, which place their slumbering passengers across the train. All through the night the uneven rocking of the train makes it difficult to sleep.

Nice

The grey pre-dawn light reveals houses that are plastered Mediterranean white, with tile-red roofs. We're stopped in the station at Avignon. By the time we draw in to Marseilles the sky is heavy with drizzle. The train to Nice leaves at eight o'clock, sliding around mottled white and green hills, heading into a cold sea wind. Outside the compartment window the Cote d'Azur unfolds beside a grey-blue sea.

Monsieur Plouchiers' farm rushes past, where we camped near La Ciotat four summers ago, living for a week or two in an arbour at the corner of his hayfield, fattening ourselves on the produce of his land—fresh tomato and basil, grapes, corn and cucumber. Up there on the hill stands the red stone building where we went to buy the rich Provencal wine, dispensed in industrial quantities through a hosepipe into a five gallon container.

Great grey derricks tower over the naval dockyards at Toulon, and then the train heads inland through low hills before drawing back to the coast at Fréjus. The hills are briefly sandstone and we pass by St. Raphael at the water's edge, and then we're speeding along the corniche below the woods of the Esterel massif. The land rises steeply from the sea along here, set with narrow clefts and indentations. The railway line twists and turns above the shore, diving through tunnels, down cuttings, across the high Antheor viaduct.

The Résistance tried many times in 1943 and 1944 to blow up this stretch of line, attracted to its deep cuts and the chance to block the tracks with tons of blasted rock. It was an important supply route for the German armies fighting in Italy and defending the southern edges of the Alps.

The RAF's elite 617 Squadron mounted three major bombing operations against the high viaduct at Antheor in an effort to cripple the line, the last one on the night of 12/13 February 1944. Two of 617's pilots made daring attempts to mark the target with flares for the rest of the attacking force. Mickey Martin and Leonard Cheshire flew their big, four-engined Lancaster bombers low down the cramped, steep-sided valley time after time, their wingtips scudding round dangerous outcrops and buttresses. Martin's aeroplane was badly shot up by the fierce anti-aircraft fire and his bomb aimer was killed. Cheshire kept at it, and made seven attacks that night on the bridge; a feat of great bravery. But the Antheor viaduct, scarred and chipped by shrapnel and bomb splinters, survived the war.

Beyond the bulge of the Esterel a small coastal littoral runs past La Napoule, Cannes, Juan les Pins, Antibes. Rows of suburban houses dot once-forested hillsides, and car parks and supermarkets have spread like a blight. This is the heart of the Riviera, incredibly changed since I first came here, when I was a boy.

I made an innocent mistake that summer in front of my new Dutch stepmother by whistling a piece of music from a school hymn as we drove up into the hills from Cros-de-Cagnes. We already had a difficult relationship, even though we'd only known each other for a few weeks. My father had brought her to my grandparents' house near London, where I was staying for the Easter break. It was the first time I'd met my father for six or seven years, and I didn't know who he was until my grandmother introduced us. Then, days afterwards, my new stepmother turned up—a surprise to everyone except my father. He'd met her in Delhi, where he'd been posted. His new wife; signed, sealed, delivered. We didn't like each other from the start.

"That is the German national anthem," she said angrily, banging her fist on the car's dashboard. "You must never make that music in front of me again." She appealed to my father for help, but he stared at the road and said nothing, holding tightly onto the steering wheel of the rented blue Simca.

It was dry and hot and the hills smelled of pine resin and lavender and thyme. Old men in blue overalls with Gauloises dangling from their mouths argued over *boules* in the dusty square at Rochefort-les-Pins, and the door to the *boulangerie* was made of stringed beads which clacked together whenever customers came and went.

One morning I found a scorpion in the bathtub, scuttling helplessly from one end of it to the other, its lethal tail balanced delicately above its back. My newly discovered father pumped our water every day by hand from a deep well, and in the white heat at midday the sound of the crickets sat right at the high-pitched edge of consciousness. At night, I fell asleep among shadows from the flickering flame of a wick floating on a piece of cork in a glass of water and oil.

At Nice station we find that our friend Jacqueline has booked us into luxury accommodations at the Hotel Beach Regency on the Promenade des Anglais. John Rebman, the manager, comes down from his office to greet us in the plush, marbled foyer and reassures us that there will be no charge for the room, thanks to the generosity of the Nice Tourist Board. Jacqueline is the head of the Tourist Board, and she has pulled some strings, called in a favour. It's a generous thing to have done. After a shower we find that it's warm enough to sit out in the sun on our balcony and gaze at the sea.

Nice is really two distinct cities—an old and a new. The old quarter belongs to a different culture than the rest of this part of France: to a different culture even than the rest of the city. The people in these tight streets are Nicoise, a mixture of Piedmont Italian and Savoie French. They're fiercely *separatiste* and from time to time they mount independence campaigns. The streets in the old quarter are so narrow that you can touch the buildings on either side if you stretch out your arms. Alleyways lead into tiny squares with fountains and cast iron benches, and reveal old churches and cafés. Butchers' shops and bakers' are tucked away among studios for potters and painters and all types of artisans.

A little girl in a café by the harbour asks me for help with a drawing she's working on, and I give her a Canadian pin for her coat. We could explore this place for hours. Kids on motorbikes scoot up and down the muddled lanes, and sandal-footed children dash about, looking like urchins from another century. Little dogs scratch at café doors while their owners sit inside drinking coffee. Washing dangles from windows. The people here greet each other in the streets with handshakes and kisses, no matter how many times they've met already in the day. It was like this when I lived in Portugal, when I stayed on Plouchiers' farm, whenever I've visited Spain or Italy—a lovely southern European custom.

Two elderly ladies run a café cheerful with red-chequered tablecloths, in one of old Nice's tiny squares. We fill ourselves up with thick lentil soup and steak and spaghetti and *vin du pays*. Church bells begin to ring. Three children run past the window with a roman candle, just as we're finishing off some chocolate cake. A garbage truck squeezes down the lane.

Nice is a city of many nationalities—Tunisians, Moroccans, Algerians, Italians—people with olive-tanned Mediterranean complexions. Here and there, plaques on the walls commemorate the bravery of their fathers, mothers, uncles and aunts during the war, with the words *"Mort pour la Patrie . . . "*

✦

The next morning the wind is warm, and we walk the long, elegant curve of the Promenade des Anglais to the centre of the city. Beside us the Baie des Anges is whipping up with white-caps. Fresh flowers and fruit are on sale in the market. Ducks sit in cages waiting for buyers, and string bags hang nearby for the buyers to carry them off in.

Up on the hill above the old town a waterfall is blowing rainbow spray on the wind. We warm ourselves with creamy *café au lait* at a restaurant beside the chateau at the top, and sit down behind a glass screen and gaze out over the rooftops of the old town. Nearby, cypress trees and cactus stand beside pathways inlaid with mosaic patterns, enhancing the city's ancient Greek and Roman connections. Em visits a stainless steel automatic toilet which looks like a science fiction time-travel machine, and only just manages to escape before it automatically sprays, cleans and disinfects itself.

In the evening, Jacqueline brings her staff from the Nice Tourist Bureau to the hotel for Christmas dinner and invites us to join them. The piano player sings an Italian love song called 'Marguerita'.

The sun rises crimson and orange over a still, blue sea. We take a taxi to the station, and catch an early train from Nice to Monte Carlo and Menton. The guard at Ventimiglia on the Italian border scratches himself and looks lost. He's gazing vaguely up and down the platform, winding and unwinding his green flag. One of his front teeth is missing. Italy looks poor from here, and dirty.

A big man with a flowing moustache slides into the compartment. He begins right away to speak to us in English, and tells us he has travelled all over Canada, New Zealand and the United States.

"In Italy," he says, "only poor people travel on trains. They never close doors behind them and they make a mess of the toilets. Not only that," he adds gloomily, "they push and kick their way into compartments and take up all the reserved seats."

He asks us where we are going. We tell him we're travelling across Italy, to Austria and then Czechoslovakia.

"Don't go to Venice," he says, and his face clouds over. "Venice is spoiled. Too many tourists go there now. It is hardly even Italian any more, all the signs are in English and German." He stares at us mournfully. "Portofino. That's where you should go if you spend any time in Italy. It's much nicer." He jumps to his feet and rushes off to close some doors as the train slows for a station.

Italians are noisier than French people. Our large Italian friend was correct. Train travellers here do what they want to do. They barge into First Class compartments with Third Class tickets. They smoke in no-smoking areas. They talk a lot. A voluble couple sits in our compartment from Genoa to Milan, where they're supplanted by a trio who talks all the way from Milan to Verona.

Outside the window the Po Valley unwinds, broad and flat. Cold, impassive mountains rise up in the northern distance, the landscape full now of small livestock farms instead of the fruity vineyards which were layered along the Mediterranean coastline.

The Gondolier

The train to Vienna speeds us across the flat north Italian countryside. Treviso and Portaneno fall behind us. The sun touches the snowy-topped Alps with yellow light. Zigzag roads climb the flanks of foothills which rise straight out of the northern plain. A hard frost lies like fresh-milled flour dust on the fields. Rows of small, spaliered trees wait for spring, and a stream steams with wispy vapours. All the livestock must be inside; the fields are bare and deserted.

The train climbs slowly into the mountains. Haystacks stand in fields at Carnia, and we pass a horse with his head down. The valley steepens and rugged peaks tower overhead. A cart on the platform at Tarvisio offers sandwiches for sale.

A smart, blue-uniformed ticket collector slides the compartment door open and steps in, and hands us a neat, printed schedule. This train, the schedule tells us, is called *The Gondolier*. The schedule goes on to list all the stations along the route to Vienna, with our exact times of arrival and departure.

As we move on towards Austria, the architecture outside the window is changing subtly into something alpine and quaint. Onion domes take the place of church steeples. The people who live up here are used to winter; firewood is stacked neatly beside the houses, skis stand in tidy racks against walls. A Christmas sleigh sits under an awning. The villages look clean, better organised somehow than the towns down on the plain.

Beyond a summit the train descends through snow-covered fields, past the tracks of hares to the town of Judenberg. A herringbone ski pattern etches a slope opposite the platform, the star-stick shapes of bird's footprints, dog paws.

Tens of thousands of Cossacks who had fought half-heartedly for the Wehrmacht surrendered here, in this peaceful valley, to the British Army at the end of the war, trusting themselves to an innate British sense of honour and fairness. But none of them knew about the secret Yalta Agreement between Roosevelt, Churchill and Stalin; that all Soviet citizens were to be repatriated to Soviet custody when the fighting had stopped.

The British tricked the Cossack leaders into separating from their men, and then disarmed them. They penned nearly fifteen hundred Cossack officers in a specially constructed compound a few miles down this valley at Spittal, and then told them they were to be repatriated to the Russians in the morning.

The Cossacks hated the Russians, who had displaced them from their traditional lands north of the Caucasus twenty years before; they had only taken up with the Germans as a matter of survival. The Cossacks had no illusions about what this 're-patriation' would mean for them.

The devastated Cossacks held an Orthodox church service at five o'clock in the morning, the singing "quite magnificent" according to a British officer who was there. They knew what would happen to them when they were handed over to the Russians. The British soldiers knew too, and so did the British government of the day.

At least a dozen Cossacks committed suicide before the British soldiers managed to force them into the trucks which drove them up to the border at Judenburg. More Cossacks killed themselves by leaping into the deep boundary gorge near the station, as the soldiers forced them onto the bridge and over to the waiting Russians.

The British soldiers couldn't see what was happening in the territory controlled by the Russians on the other side of the river gorge, but all through that night and into the next day they could hear bursts of gunfire. It was the sound of Soviet firing squads dispatching the troublesome Cossacks, and it was accompanied by the singing—as one witness said later—of the most beautiful male voice choir he'd ever heard.

The stationmaster stands on the platform at Judenberg, resplendent in his red cap and black cape. We cannot see the tragic gorge because the station buildings are in the way, and there is not enough time for us to leave the train—to make our own small recognition of these events. The station clock ticks off the seconds. The train begins to move at the precise moment indicated in the schedule in our compartment.

The forced Cossack repatriations went on for two more weeks. Next to go were the common Cossack soldiers, the rank and file, and the rest of the 'train'—the women and the children. For this was not an army, it was the wandering exodus of a people. Like the European armies of the eighteenth and early nineteenth centuries, war to the Cossacks was a communal business; their families went with them, carting along most of their possessions.

During these chaotic post-war months the Cossacks had been living in a kind of diplomatic "no man's land" between the Allied armies, for this was one of the places—like the River Elbe, and Berlin—where the western and eastern Allies had demarcated their territories, their zones of control. Stateless and uncertain, the Cossacks had simply stopped where their war had ended. Once here though, they had gradually established—for the first time in years—schools for their children, churches, newspapers, supply distribution systems; the first trappings of a settled existence.

This second wave of Cossacks refused to obey the orders of their British custodians to march peacefully over to the Russian lines, and the young men formed a protective circle around the women and children. Then, on orders that came directly from the highest offices in London, the Argyll and Sutherland Highlanders attacked the unarmed prisoners. A number of Cossacks were killed by the Argylls; others committed suicide, some with their whole families. Many threw themselves into the swollen river and drowned.

In the end, with the Scottish soldiers on the verge of mutiny at such craven orders, the Argyll's Colonel refused his Brigade's command to use more force.

It's not known how many Cossacks died that day on the British side of the bridge, but it was almost certainly several hundred. Altogether, some fifty thousand Cossacks were forcibly repatriated to the Soviets during this shameful passage of European history, most to execution, the rest to a deathly exile in the Siberian prison camps. It's a story that has been quietly swept aside, invisible to all but the most dogged of researchers, the tragic story of a few short weeks in this part of Austria in the spring of 1945, a tale of international power politics at its moral nadir.

Old haystacks are scattered across the fields at Knittefeld; a ruined *schloss* sits up on a hilltop. Once again, it's difficult for us to equate this peaceful, central European valley with such heart-breaking events, almost impossible to accept that the British and American governments were complicit in such things. Harold Macmillan was British Minister-Resident, Mediterranean Theatre, in the spring and summer of 1945—the Foreign Office official with responsibility for ensuring the repatriation of the Cossacks. But this tawdry, heart-breaking episode did not become widely known in Britain until long after he'd served two terms as British Prime Minister in the 1950's and 60's. When these events did eventually become public knowledge, Macmillan—in a television interview in 1985—vigorously defended the actions he had taken.

✦

The river running down the valley floor beside the train is wide now, and black, whereas a short while ago in the mountains the streams were glacially green, and clear. A man with a rope around his chest pulls a child down a lane on a sled. It starts to snow, the sun a dash of paintbrush red in the sky to the south.

We have to make a brief stop in Vienna. Friends have told us that it's the best place to acquire a visa that will let us travel behind the Iron Curtain. Western visitors are rare in Czechoslovakia, particularly in mid-winter, and visas are difficult to obtain. It's more than three years before the "velvet revolution', and the Russians are still firmly in control of Czechoslovakia. We want to spend Christmas there; we want to see what life is like in the land of Good King Wenceslas. We've heard too that Prague is one of the most beautiful cities in Europe, and quite unspoiled by tourism. Besides, Em is going to have a baby and we think it might be a long time before we'll have adventures again, a long time until we'll be able to travel on whims.

The clerk at the *Cedok* office—the Czech state tourist authority—in Vienna's old city centre checks our identification documents with exaggerated care, asks questions and re-checks our visas. After a long examination she's satisfied, and explains that she cannot issue us visas unless we first book half-board at the Hotel Garni in Prague. We have to pay in advance, she explains firmly. She takes our money and shuffles it disdainfully into a drawer under her desk. The train to Prague, she says, leaves right after lunch.

Christmas Behind the Iron Curtain

The train edges slowly across a barren No Man's Land, past wire barriers, a ditch and a moat, and a stretch of land which has been so levelled and cleared that it looks as if it might be a minefield. We come to a stop out in the open. Outside the window of the compartment there's nothing but an undulating white landscape. Czechoslovakian guards and Customs men climb aboard. The first man who comes in to our compartment is an Immigration Officer. He tries to speak to us in Czech, and Italian. Then he tries a German dialect we can't understand. We're no good at any of these and test him with English and French. He smiles politely and leaves.

A young soldier comes in, wearing army fatigues. He doesn't look at any of the passengers, doesn't acknowledge our presence in any way, and starts right away to give everything in the compartment a thorough going over. He kneads the seats and armrests with vigorous fingertips, runs his hands along the curtain rails and drops down to his knees and peers all around the floor at shoelace level. We watch him with interest. His examinations take about a minute and a half, and he doesn't say a word to any of us.

As soon as the searcher has finished a third man comes in

and asks us to show him our passports and visas. He checks them carefully, even holds a page of Em's passport up to the light. He speaks a little English and as he goes out he grumbles about the behaviour of a group of American girls in the next compartment. The ticket collector comes in next. Our tickets, he tells us in German, only carry us this far. We must now pay the fare from the border here, to Prague. We're not sure whether to believe him or not. But there's nothing we can do about it and so we hand him the money he wants. In the end he leaves, annoyed because we've paid for our tickets with Austrian Schillings instead of Czech Crowns.

The train stops at Tabor to collect more passengers. It's 10:30 p.m. We doze fitfully without a blanket to warm us, curled up uncomfortably against the seeping cold.

The train slides into Prague station at midnight and decants us onto a cold stone platform in a draughty, barn-like hall. A furtive man in a black leather jacket and brown corduroy trousers approaches us and asks if we need a taxi. When we shake our heads, he asks if we want to change money. We've been warned about black marketeers. The people at the *Cedok* office in Vienna told us we'd be thrown in jail if we had anything to do with them. We tell him to go away.

All the passengers from the train seem to be waiting in line in front of us at the taxi stand. There's no sign of any taxis. Everyone looks tired and pasty-faced, resigned to a long wait. We wait for half an hour. Two taxis turn up and the line shuffles forward a couple of feet. It doesn't look as if any more taxis are coming, not at this time of night. Later, we discover that all the taxi drivers in Prague are paid a regular salary, so hardly any of them work after five or six o'clock. According to the map the *Cedok* lady gave us in Vienna, the Hotel Garni doesn't seem to be too far away, so despite the intense cold we decide to start walking. Em is six months pregnant and we have two heavy bags to carry, but there doesn't seem to be much of a choice. We could easily wait here all night for a cab.

We walk down deserted streets, and over a railway bridge. It's hard to read the map properly in the dim streetlight. The cold freezes my nostrils with every breath, and works its way down into my lungs like a punch in the chest—a still, penetrating, razor cold. The buildings are increasingly derelict and seedy as we descend towards the river. The bags are heavier by the minute. It starts to snow.

After an hour of fruitless searching along pitted cobblestoned streets among tumbledown tenements and warehouses, we decide that the map must have confused us. The road we want is not where we think it is because of the way the map reads at the page-fold. It's nearly two o'clock in the morning, and we haven't seen another soul for a long time, and we're very aware of the fact that we're in a foreign country with rules of conduct that are quite different from the ones that operate where we come from. For all we know there might even be a curfew on civilians here.

A sodium-bright backlight etches the roof of an apartment building against the night sky and we make our way, stiff and cold, up a rutted street towards the light. The light is coming from the Sokolovska metro station, which stands closed and shuttered in the middle of a big, empty plaza. Two stern soldiers with sub machine guns and Russian fur hats walk round a corner, a teenage girl beside them. The soldiers stop, right hands on the straps of their Kalashnikovs. We must look strange to them. They look very ominous to us, and so we quickly show them our map. Only the girl speaks any English. She explains in a mixture of German and schoolgirl English that we must take a tram down the street for four stops, and that will bring us to the Hotel Garni.

The girl and the soldiers leave us to wait at the tram stop. Big snowflakes float languidly out of the black sky. The long street is completely deserted in both directions, the silence complete. Then a tram rattles across a set of points in the distance, and a moment later a single light appears out of the gloom and sways down the darkness towards us. It occurs to us that we should probably have dealt with the black marketer at the station after all. We have no Czech money to pay the fare. But the tram has no other passengers and the driver doesn't seem to care.

It's 2:30 when we reach the Hotel Garni. The hotel stands all by itself, like a big warehouse on a winter prairie, on the far side of a great white expanse of parking lot. We drag ourselves through deep snow to the front door. It is locked; the place is closed for the night. We stand there shivering, peering through the plate glass door. Everything is dark inside, everyone asleep. Then we hear a faint, irregular buzzing sound through the glass and we can just pick out the night porter in the dim night-light, stretched full length on a sofa in the lobby, snoring. We hammer on the door, but the man doesn't move, snores on, oblivious. We keep hammering and a girl in a dressing gown pads through a thin shaft of light, crosses the lobby and lets us in. The night porter snuffles in his sleep as we creep past.

The girl is half asleep, her hair disarmingly tousled and wild. She rubs the corners of her eyes with bunched knuckles, and says in halting English that she knew we were coming. She takes us upstairs in a rickety elevator, then down corridors of patched, threadbare carpet. We collapse into 2012, a tiny ship's cabin of a room with two bunks at right angles to one another. In minutes, we're asleep.

The telephone rings in the night. A mysterious voice at the other end says something in Czech and then hangs up when I reply sleepily in English. In the morning it takes me a while to realise that it wasn't a dream, so deep was the sleep I was in—and then it feels unsettling, as if the authorities are checking up to see that we are where we're supposed to be.

Breakfast in the hotel dining room is spartan; cold hard-boiled eggs, processed meat slices, dry toast without butter. The maitre d' is a tall, straight-backed man with lank, fair hair. Even though it's only just after seven o'clock in the morning, he's wearing a black dinner jacket and bow tie; in fact we never see him dressed any other way the whole time we're here. A livid red scar bisects his cheek, as if he has once fought a duel with swords. He's formal and distant, but there's an indefinable air of sadness about him. After breakfast he opens up a little. He takes us over to the hotel's main desk, and in halting English helps us to buy vouchers for our meals, and tram tickets.

The Number Three tram takes us in to the centre of the city. It's Christmas Eve but there's no joy in the air, no street decorations or colour in the shop windows. The passengers on the tram are bundled up in dowdy clothes, worn greys and blacks, as if they all shop at the same second-hand store. No one speaks; there is none of the chatter of the trains in Italy, none of the banter of the tramcars in Vienna. All of the passengers keep their eyes still, and stare at the floor, or at the back of the person sitting in front of them—anywhere but at each other. None of them acknowledge us at all. I catch one old man stealing a glance at the red maple leaf insignia on the back of my gloves; we're sure they know we're foreigners from the west.

The tram fills up and Em starts to stand up to offer her seat to a frail old man who has just got on, but the elderly lady beside her suddenly clutches her arm, forcing her to sit down again. The old lady does this without looking at Em or speaking, without making any sign that she's seen her. Perhaps she's noticed that Em is pregnant; thinks that it will be embarrassing for the old man if Em gives up her seat. To Em it's a clear connection, a small sign of empathy.

Wenceslas Square lies at the heart of Prague, and flows down the slope from the Czech National Museum, near the railway station. This wide, renaissance boulevard is lined with old hotels, empty shops and threadbare trees. Presiding over it all is a magnificent statue of the Good King mounted on his charger; beneath him is the entrance to a subway station, and some public toilets. A succession of men approaches us here, one after the other, almost all of them clad in leather jackets and corduroy trousers as if it's some kind of uniform. All of them want to change money. Some of the moneychangers, the woman in the *Cedok* office in Vienna told us darkly, are even *agents provocateurs* in the pay of the police.

On this Christmas Eve, forty years after the Soviets first occupied Czechoslovakia, Wenceslas Square is a bleak and heartless place. The shop windows are virtually empty. Most of the stores are closed; the few that are open are deserted, bare shelves gaping, except for one or two specialised establishments offering goods for sale in foreign currencies. Police and army personnel in field green uniforms are everywhere, walking two at a time down the centre of the sidewalks, cruising up and down the boulevard in green and white Skodas and smoke-blowing Trabants. Each car contains two or three cops who scan the faces on the sidewalks as they drive past. There's hardly any traffic except for the police cars and the rickety red and yellow trams skating gingerly down the icy streets. There's not a hint of laughter in anyone, no Christmas music, no bells or chimes or unexpected noises. No one smiles. It could be a crime to laugh or shout here or to make eye contact with strangers. Em and I say hardly a word to each other as we walk down the hill, and when we do speak we converse very quietly, as if we're afraid to disturb the uneasy equilibrium of the place. It's a subdued and cowed city, a long way from what used to be the lively heart of bohemian creativity, so brilliantly expressed in literature and music.

At the foot of Wenceslas Square we come upon a young man with long, stringy hair taking garishly painted Christian icons out of a battered suitcase, and placing them on a black cloth on a collapsible table. He seems well practised; it only takes him seconds to set up his little stand at the entrance to the metro station. They're not great art, these tiny plaques of long dead Byzantine saints, but from the reactions of the people around, it must be rare to see them in these times. Passers-by slow down, glance quickly around for police, and stop to look. More people stop. In minutes the young man is surrounded by a small crowd, the people at the back standing on tiptoe, everyone glancing constantly over their shoulders, tensed and poised for flight.

Despite the crudity of the work, some of it is quite beautiful, the icons delicate, spare, fine-featured, predominantly blood red in colour. Holy. Transactions take place swiftly. Money moves from one person to another as if by sleight of hand. Everyone knows that a crowd like this will attract official attention, that the police will arrive any second and close him down. The crowd's movements are rapid and jerky, as if we're watching an old black and white film. A siren rises and falls, people melt away. The young man folds everything up in a flash and vanishes into the darkness of the metro station.

A line of people stands outside a bookstore down the street. Two women are loitering outside the *Cedok* office next door. One of them asks if we're looking for a place to stay, speaking quickly out of the corner of her mouth as we walk past. Her English is passable and educated, but she has the manner of a prostitute and we walk past, trying to ignore her, feeling her shame, desperately sad. Their behaviour and body language tell us that these people are frightened, and we're afraid we'll cause them trouble if we speak to them.

The metro station at the foot of Wenceslas Square is clean and bare and lined with tiles. Statues of important Party people stand deep underground, and the station's cavernous walls are hung with red Socialist-Leninist banners. An empty train takes us under the river to Leninova, on the south side of the city, where the streets are wide and spacious, and lined with squat grey apartment blocks. All the buildings look exactly the same, as if each one of them has been squeezed out of a rubber mould. All the streets are empty. We're standing in the middle of an urban steppe. A tram clatters across points at a nearby road crossing. The passengers inside it are staring straight ahead, as if the world outside the tram windows doesn't exist. Em is astonished at their apparent lack of interest. "We could be standing in a scene from George Orwell," she murmurs.

This district of Leninova sits on a hill on the east side of the Vltava River, and we're making our way towards the *Hradcany*—Prague Castle. The wind whistles down the broad streets and I start to envy Em the old winter coat she bought at the Salvation Army shop before we left Canada. It's made of thick wool, and its previous owner probably discarded it, not because it didn't work, but because it was so long out of fashion. The wind slashes through my thin windcheater as if it doesn't exist. We pass three boys playing street hockey in a tiny bare concrete park beneath a gigantic statue of Koniev—the Russian general who cut through Czechoslovakia in 1945, decimating German armies on his way to Berlin. In their patched woollen sweaters, the hockey players look just like kids in Canada, and seem just as impervious to the cold.

We're walking the margins of the district of Holesovice, very near to the place where Reinhardt Heydrich was assassinated on a sunny morning in May, 1942. Heydrich was one of the most feared men in the Nazi hierarchy, the main architect of the 'Final Solution' for Europe's Jews, which was promulgated at the infamous Wannsee Conference in January, 1942. Hitler had appointed him *Reichsprotektor* for Bohemia and Moravia with orders to stamp out rising Czech resistance. As soon as he took up his office in Prague, Heydrich declared martial law and initiated a time of terror across the country. His first act was to order the execution, without trial, of three hundred and ninety four Czechs accused of treason. Soon after that he set up the Jewish ghetto—in effect a concentration camp—at Theresienstadt, in Terezin, to the north of Prague. Most of the Jews who were shipped there were moved on sooner or later to Auschwitz-Birkenau, Chelmno and other Nazi extermination camps. Heydrich's courts carried out hundreds of executions, usually on the flimsiest of pretexts and without proper trials. He very quickly earned the nickname, 'The Butcher of Prague'.

Two British-based Czech SOE agents, Jan Kubis and Josef Gabcik, were parachuted into Czechoslovakia to kill Heydrich. They selected a spot where his car had to slow down at a steep corner on the way to his office at the *Hradcany*. Gabchik stepped out into the street and tried to fire his Sten gun, but it jammed. Heydrich stood up in the passenger seat and drew his pistol, whereupon Kubis tossed a small anti-tank grenade at the car. It went off, fatally wounding Heydrich and damaging his green Mercedes.

Heydrich's wounds didn't seem at first to be life threatening. But his condition was deceptive, his injuries painful and slow acting and he died a week later from blood poisoning caused by pieces of upholstery which had been blasted by the grenade into his spleen.

The Germans retaliated massively for Heydrich's death. Within three weeks they'd caught the assassins and executed thousands of innocent people. One of the Czech patriots came from Lidice, and so the Germans shot all the men in the village, and sent all the women off to concentration camps. Seventy-nine of the children in Lidice were killed, the rest taken away for adoption into Nazi homes, for what the Germans termed 're-education'. Every building in the village was blown up, and the rubble bulldozed flat, the town erased from the map as an example to the Czechs.

The street climbs up from Holesovice on slippery cobblestones to the *Hradcany*. A young soldier guards the gate. His eyes are watery, his nose is red; he's bent almost double with the cold. The Czech flag flutters from the castle roof, signifying that the President is at home. St. Vitus' Cathedral, one of Europe's great classical structures and part of the castle complex, is closed for renovations. We pass through a broad courtyard and walk the Street of the Alchemists, where sixteenth-century chemists reputedly tried to turn base metals into gold, and where three hundred years later, Franz Kafka wrote short stories at Number Twenty-two, in the house where his sister lived.

At the end of the street long, wide steps curve down towards the snow-spattered, red-tiled roofs of the old town. Someone has sprinkled salt on the steps to melt the ice. We make our way carefully down, easing ourselves out of the biting wind. The streets at the bottom of the hill are cobbled and narrow and lined with severe grey embassies and government ministries. Huge metal-studded, wooden doors shut off interior courtyards, and plaster flakes from the walls of the buildings. A Belgian flag flies over one broad, black portal; next door to it flies an Indian flag.

This central European cold is unlike anything we've ever experienced. It sweeps down from the Arctic, gathering an icy agility from the steppes, slicing like a surgeon's scalpel. Em says through gritted teeth that the Czechs must have invented something to neutralise such appalling cold, some kind of restorative antidote, and seconds later we notice that a lot of people are going in and out of a certain basement door at the far end of the street. Clouds of smoke pour out into the chill air every time the door opens. Although none of the pubs in Prague seem to have signs, this kind of activity looks promising. As we come up to it we can see windows thick with dirt, lit from inside with a warm glow. We descend some steps and enter a small, square room with a scattering of wooden chairs and tables. It is indeed a little pub, with people standing at a bar, and others sitting at tables.

A waiter bustles past and delivers drinks to a nearby table. On his way back to the bar he mutters over his shoulder to us that the place is now closed. But then a young man weaves his way past us to the toilet. He's wearing a neat blue sweater with the logo 'Kingsbury RFC'.

"Rugby club!" I exclaim hopefully. We're chilled to the marrow of our bones; never before have we needed a drink so much.

"Yes?" he replies, squinting slightly as if he's asking a question of his own. I ask him if he can help us get something to drink. This is Emanuel.

Emanuel tells the waiter right away to bring us two glasses of *slivovic*, cutting him off when the waiter starts to argue. When the waiter goes behind the bar to fill our order, Emanuel explains that we've stumbled upon Sparta Prague Rugby Club's annual Christmas party. A dozen members of the team are here. "You must come and sit with us," he says.

The surly waiter brings our *slivovic* to the table and bangs the glasses down on the tabletop. Emanuel won't let us pay, and his team-mates won't hear of it either. We drink the *slivovic* slowly, savouring every rich, plum-brandied drop. It burns its way down to my boots, sets my insides on fire as it cauterises each one of the frozen passageways inside my body. Slowly we relax, overtaken by the warm fug inside the room.

All the time we're chatting with the Sparta Prague rugby players and savouring the *slivovic,* the little pub's customers are emptying out into the street. The waiter starts piling tables and chairs in the middle of the room, irritably resisting the blandishments and bribes of the rugby players. It's Christmas and he's closing the pub. Maybe he has a family to go home to. A few minutes later, all of us are out in the cold street.

George, one of the *Sparta Prague* rugby players, has a week's worth of stubble on his face. He's pleased when Em tells him that unshaven faces are now the fashion for men in North America. He's wearing a dark blue ski jacket, open to the wind, a sweater, and a checked flannel shirt underneath. He tells us he's coming to the end of his rugby-playing career, and he's started studying to be a lawyer. "It is a difficult thing to do when you're thirty-five," he says. "It's a lot of work, a long time after I thought I was finished with studying." He wants to talk about books and writers. Em tells him she spoke recently with Josef Skvorecky, the brilliant Czech writer who lives now in Toronto.

George's English is not very strong, and the two of them speak at cross-purposes on this for a while. When he finally grasps what Em has said, he doesn't believe her. "This cannot be true," he says in astonishment. "Skvorecky is dead. We were told this a long time ago."

Em assures him that he is not, that he runs a small Czech language publishing company with his wife, the actress and writer Zdena Salivarova, that he teaches at a college in Toronto, that Skvorecky's writing is just as compelling as it ever was. George is visibly cheered by this news. Then he shakes his head and sighs, "But it is so sad that Czechs cannot read him any more."

Three years later, I'm standing at the entrance to the Street of the Alchemists, the street where Kafka used to write, in the heart of the *Hradcany*. Now another writer, the Czech playwright, Vaclav Havel, is the much-loved President of the newly liberated Czechoslovakia. On this sunny spring afternoon I'm watching a bizarre little scene as Havel's chauffeur drives the Presidential limousine slowly across the same small square I walked across when I was here before. The chauffeur is using the big, black Russian Zil to brush back a crowd of reverent tourists who are trying to touch Havel's little Renault, a personal gift from President Mario Soares of Portugal. The chauffeur drives the Zil slowly but firmly into the knot of people until they disperse, then he backs the limo across the square to its parking place and sits there waiting until he has to do it all over again. The Presidential chauffeur has little else to do, for Havel doesn't travel in the Zil at all. He loves his little Renault and drives it everywhere himself. Someone has stuck a big red heart on its windshield, love-notes are scrawled in lipstick across the rear window, and affectionate messages are pasted down the Renault's sides.

Czechoslovakia's new President remains a man of his people, a security man's nightmare, often dropping into the local pub on his way home at night to the same small apartment in the centre of Prague that he's occupied for years. He refuses to live in the luxurious Presidential apartments in the *Hradcany*, which are maintained now only for visiting heads of state.

Emanuel tells us that he has to go home, and we arrange to meet him the next day. George waits with us for nearly an hour at the tram stop on a raw, exposed corner by the river, the wind sweeping down the valley, keening through the electric wires above our heads. When the tram finally comes I'm so stiff that George has to help me on board. He doesn't climb on himself though, and waves goodbye to us from the stop. We watch him from the back window as he trudges off into the gathering dusk. He has only waited with us to make sure we're all right.

On Christmas morning the sun is shining. I go downstairs and set about trying to change some money at the hotel's front desk.

"How much do you want to change?" asks the desk clerk in a mixture of German and poor English.

I wave some bills at him. "About fifty Deutschmarks." I'm thinking of the official exchange rate of 6.85 Crowns to the Dm, which will give me about 340 Czech Crowns, enough to see us through the next few days. I drop the German notes onto the counter top.

The desk clerk deftly covers the notes with a tourist map of Prague and slides the map and the money beneath the counter. His eyes flit quickly round the room. He fiddles under the counter for a few seconds, then brings up the tourist map and places it on top of the counter in front of me.

"I don't need a tourist map," I explain patiently. "I've already got one. I want to change some money."

The clerk stares at me for a demi-second, and then his eyes move around in his head as if he's about to faint. But he quickly gets hold of himself, reaches out a finger and thumb and surreptitiously peels back a corner of the tourist guide to reveal an enormous pile of Czech bills. He covers them up again.

It suddenly occurs to me that I'm being inexcusably slow, that the desk clerk is functioning on an entirely separate wavelength, and then I'm almost overpowered by a sense that everyone in the lobby is staring at the back of my head. The desk clerk's eyes are rotating in his head alarmingly. I start to sweat.

It's clear that the clerk wants me to leave. I pick up the tourist map and head quickly for the elevator. When I count the money in the privacy of our room I find that he's given me more than six hundred Czech Crowns, twice the official rate of exchange. I've unwittingly become involved in a black market transaction.

We're waiting for George by the statue at the top of Wenceslas Square. It's early afternoon. Green and white police cars are cruising slowly up one side of the street, down the other. One car circles past us four or five times, slowing down each time. The policemen inside stare hard at us. It seems to me that they must have got wind of the recent financial transaction at the hotel and are just waiting for the right moment to swoop. Em tells me not to be silly. We search the nearby Metro station for George, and hang around for an hour, but there's no sign of him.

Now we're cold again, and disappointed that George hasn't come, so we retire to the Hotel Europa to warm ourselves up with coffee. The Europa has a classic pre-war, nineteen-thirties feel to it. The café inside the hotel is like an old-time coffee house, overlooked by a balcony with polished wood railings, the ceiling supported on stout, panelled pillars, music hall chairs arranged haphazardly around marble-topped tables.

A man in a leather coat stands up from a table by the wall, moves to the table next to ours and sits down. He's trying to listen to our conversation. We lower our voices. The air of paranoia in this city is so strong that we're sure that George has been warned off by the police. We're probably being watched as well. The money-changing transaction at the hotel might have something to do with this too.

Then a scruffy, short man walks right up to our table from the other side of the café, and addresses us in English. Without waiting for a response he pulls up a chair and sits down and carries on talking as if he's known us for years.

"I used to live in Canada," he says, "I was a postman in Toronto for nineteen years. When I retired I got a letter from Pierre Trudeau, congratulating me for my long service." He chatters away like this for several minutes, like an old friend. We're very suspicious and we don't know what to make of it.

He tells us his name is Gerry. "I know Toronto as well as I know Prague. I wore out about thirty pairs of shoes on the city's streets." He chuckles easily. "Now I get my Canada Post pension cheque in the mail every month. It's only about five hundred dollars, but it's plenty for my wife and me to live on in Prague." He winks at Em. "I can change the dollars on the black market for three times the official rate." He leans back in his chair and chuckles loudly. I glance nervously round the room when he mentions the black market but nobody seems to be paying us any attention.

When we've finished our coffee, we say goodbye to the ex-Toronto postman and take the metro down to the *Dvorakhalle* beside the river. The *Dvorakhalle* is Prague's Opera house, a magnificent building with legendary acoustics.

Reinhardt Heydrich, the SS *Reichsprotektor* for Bohemia and Moravia was scanning the city with his binoculars one evening from his office high up in the *Hradcany*. His eye fell upon the roof of the Dvorakhalle, which is adorned with the statues of famous composers. He spotted something up there that he didn't like, picked up the telephone and ordered the people in charge of the opera house to remove the statue of Mendelssohn by the next morning. Mendelssohn, of course, was a Jew.

The frightened manager told his workmen to climb up on the roof and get the job done as quickly as possible. When they got up there, one of the workmen turned to the other and pointed out that the Manager hadn't told them which one was Mendelssohn. The other workman suggested that everyone knew Jews had large noses, so they'd just have to find him that way. In the gathering darkness they felt their way carefully round the perimeter of the roof, feeling the nose on each statue.

Eventually they found a statue with a much bigger nose than any of the others and duly toppled it down into the street below, where it smashed to pieces.

In the morning Heydrich went to his window and scanned the roof of the Opera house through his binoculars. He froze with anger when he saw Mendelssohn still standing up there. Then he came to the gap with the missing composer. The workmen had destroyed Wagner.

There are other oppressors in Heydrich's offices in the *Hradcany* now, but on this Christmas afternoon the *Dvorakhalle* is the site of a Bohemian folk concert. Em has found out about it and she's insisted that we come here, but it seems as if half the people of Prague are hurrying here as well. In the crush inside the lobby we somehow manage to buy the last two tickets. Among all the teeming people we even find the correct seats. Every single seat in the concert hall is taken, and people are standing, lining the walls. The hall is full of children; in keeping with an old Bohemian Christmas tradition, every one of them has brought a little bell to ring.

Twelve musicians and six singers stand up on the stage, waiting, all dressed in traditional Bohemian costume. The audience falls silent as the red-jacketed Concertmaster steps to the front of the stage and raises his hands. The children watch him, spellbound. He will indicate when they can ring their bells he explains. We can tell this from the hand signals he makes to them, the nodding and shaking of his head. When he's finished his instructions he gives them a small respectful bow and turns to face the musicians. They begin to play. Not a child makes a peep until the Concertmaster directs them to. When he turns to face them and drops his hands to give the signal, they respond. The sound they make is like the tinkling of water droplets; like the sound of sunlight passing through mist.

At the end of the concert the Concertmaster quietly makes an announcement. A lady sitting beside us lets out a gasp, and reaches in her pocket and pulls out a handkerchief. The audience rises to its feet with great solemnity and heads are raised up in a single movement, with a collective intake of breath.

We stand as well, and in whispered English we ask the lady beside us what is happening. Her eyes are misty.

"We are going to sing our national anthem," she says, " . . . our national anthem." She doesn't look at us at all. "It has been banned for a very long time."

The anthem begins carefully at first and the audience sings uncertainly, not as if they've forgotten the words, more as if they're unsure of the consequences. But their confidence slowly builds and the voices swell and join and gather force and the power of it causes the crystal chandeliers hanging from the *Dvorakhalle's* great concave ceiling to tremble. It is a wonderful sound, the sweet singing of these voices, perfectly in balance, poignant and thrilling and unimaginably uplifting. We gaze around the hall, wishing we knew the words to such magnificent music. Tears are running down everyone's cheeks.

As we walk along the riverbank after the concert, swans drift past on the water. It is nearly dark. People are flitting like shadows in and out of a church beside the Charles Bridge. We know that religious observation is not condoned by the communist authorities, and we've been told that overt celebrations of Christmas are not allowed. We decide to see what is attracting the people inside.

The church is the Church of St. Francis and when we step inside the door it feels more like a crypt than a place of worship. The only light comes from tall white candles, flickering in the icy draught from the door and throwing shadows around the walls. Despite the cold air the place smells musty, as if it has been closed up for years. A steady procession of people winds over to one corner of the church, and we follow them there. In the corner, on top of a broad platform spread with straw, stands a nativity made out of carved and painted wooden pieces. It looks very, very old.

There are old people in this line, and young people, parents and grandparents. Most of them have brought children with them. Some of them seem simply curious; others are quite overcome. Right in front of us a middle-aged woman drops to her knees, tears coursing down her cheeks. Everyone, and especially the children, speaks in hushed voices, and the air in the place is full of magic and mystery and reverence. As we move away from the little scene a man explains that the St. Francis Nativity is a priceless medieval work of art and religious significance. "The priests hid it away during the war," he says quietly. "They were afraid it would be stolen by the Nazis, then after that, by the Russians. This is the first Christmas that the Nativity has been shown for more than forty years." The children gaze at it in wonder. They have never seen anything like it.

The length of the Charles Bridge is lit by ornate streetlamps, which glow like gaslights, giving us a sense of a time before politics and expediency. People walk quietly up and down, stepping through the pools of light, stopping from time to time to greet acquaintances. A young man stands beneath a statue in the middle of the bridge, playing his violin, a piece from the exquisitely lyrical *Romanza* in Dvorak's Czech Suite, the notes sweet and clear and brittle in the sharp air. A scarf is wrapped around the musician's neck, a battered hat on his head, his hands protected from the cold by fingerless woollen gloves as they move swiftly across the strings. An Irish Setter trots past him with its head high: a dash of red, cocky, sure of itself. A man in a faded yellow jacket whirls a child around in a circle by her arms. We cross the bridge as if we're part of a winter scene in an old postcard, feeling as if we're walking back through the ages, greeting the fates, encountering the muses.

Gerry, the Toronto postman we met at the Hotel Europa, has left a message for us at the Hotel Garni. He will come in the morning with his wife Vera, to take us out. At 8:30 on the dot they're waiting in the lobby, both of them about five and a half feet tall; Gerry with a round face and light hair; Vera dark and plump and cheerful. Both of them seem nervous, but they insist that we come with them to their apartment in Wenzigova for breakfast. Vera drives us there at speed in an old, smoke-blowing Skoda, picking her way through the quiet streets, dodging trams and parked cars. Their apartment is like an old Glasgow tenement, grey stone and four storeys high, and Vera leads us up worn stairs to the first floor. The doormat is a worn bathmat. The front door opens into a tiny kitchen, and Vera ushers us past the stove, into their living room. The whole of one wall is taken up with a huge photo-wallpaper scene of the Canadian Rockies in autumn, filling the room with silver birches, orange-yellow leaves and snow-topped mountains. A woodland stream tumbles all the way down to the carpet. A big, bright porcelain tiger sits off to one side on a table. Gerry drops into an armchair beside the electric fire and Vera retreats into the kitchen.

In a minute we can hear the sound of frying, then Vera rushes out with plates of cakes, cookies and biscuits. A few minutes later she swings through the door again with a huge platter of fried eggs and a jug of coffee. Gerry apologises while she sets out this enormous breakfast. He's sorry, he says, that he hasn't been able to buy a traditional ham for the occasion. Instead he brings out a bottle of *Palinka*, a powerful Hungarian cherry brandy with no colour to it at all and the consistency of diesel oil. He pours out a glass of it for Em, and a bigger one for me. "To wash down the eggs and cakes," says Gerry. It's far too early in the day for something as lethal as this, but it would be hugely impolite to turn down his hospitality. Gerry looks at Vera, the *Palinka* bottle in his hand. She wisely shakes her head, and pours herself a glass of orange juice. Em pats her pregnant tummy and shakes her head regretfully.

"Perhaps I could join you in a glass of orange juice," she says to Vera.

We raise our glasses and drink to Christmas, and to the liberation of Czechoslovakia. Gerry throws back his head and knocks his *Palinka* straight down. I take a sip of mine, anxious to get it over with. It immediately brings tears to my eyes, and sends explosive vapours up my nose that make me want to sneeze. It knocks the breath out of me, and I wait apprehensively to see what it will do, hoping that the eggs will provide my digestive system with an adequate cushion. As it burns its way down I speculate for a moment whether it goes for the brain first, or the knees.

Vera pours us coffee and we sit back exhausted and contemplate our empty plates. Vera brings out an exquisite lace doily she has made and presents it to Em as a gift. Gerry tells us that he opposed the 1948 'revolution', which is what the Russians called it when they took over Czechoslovakia after the Second World War.

"I didn't really mean to," he explains, "I kind of like the quiet life. But we had some German prisoners working on our farm and the Russians complained that we were giving them too much to eat. I tried to explain that the work was hard and they couldn't do it without decent food. The Russians wouldn't listen, and about that time they started shooting some of the German prisoners on other farms, so I helped my ones to escape.

"They were no more than boys," he continues. "I didn't like the Germans during the war, but these kids were just kids. I got them some civilian clothes and then I helped them to get to the border and saw them safely into Austria.

"A few years after that, in 1951, a friend told me that the Russians were looking for me and they were going to throw me in jail, so I decided it was time for me to leave Czechoslovakia too. I made it to the border all right, but the Austrian Border Police caught me and wanted to send me back. Things were very tense then; it was about the time when the West started talking about the Iron Curtain. But I'd kept the address of one of the young German soldiers I'd helped, and the Austrians eventually agreed to telephone him with a message from me. I was very lucky. The call worked, the German remembered me, and the Austrian authorities let me in to the country."

Gerry holds up the bottle of *Palinka*. Em shakes her head, Vera heads for the kitchen. I tell him I'll join him in a small glass. The sun has cleared the tenements across the road and is pouring in though the windows of Gerry's flat. We clink our glasses together. The *Palinka* goes down easier this time.

"When I got to Vienna I went straight to the Canadian and Australian Embassies and applied for emigration papers. The next day, because I was stateless and didn't have any money, I joined the French Foreign Legion. They put me down for service in Indo-China. A few days before I was to be shipped out to the Far East, my Canadian immigration papers came through, and I managed to persuade the French to let me go. I was lucky, because for the French, Indo-China—Viet Nam as it became— was a real mess. Within two or three years they'd lost the war there, and a lot of Legionnaires were killed."

Vera asks if we'd like to go for a drive in the country. "Karlstejn Castle," she says. "We'll go there. It's about forty kilometres from Prague." Soon she's piloting the little Skoda down country roads like a rally driver, whizzing through winter-scoured villages, past clusters of tiny, garden-shed-like dachas in the wooded hills, down the valleys of the Vltava and the Berounka. The churches out here have bulbous steeples, onion domes, like the orthodox churches in Austria, but the towns we pass through seem deserted, as if the inhabitants have all gone into winter hibernation.

The four of us walk up a narrow street from the car park, past crooked, timber-beamed houses to a village square with a horse trough. A young boy is practicing ice hockey skills on the road, batting an old tennis ball against a wall, trapping the rebound with his stick, spinning and shooting the ball hard at a bale of hay. An old, crippled lady works her way painfully over the slippery ground with the help of two sticks. A horse leads a cart carefully down the icy lane towards us, the teamster's hand hovering over the brake lever. The castle towers above it all, partly covered with scaffolding. When we reach the top of the village Vera asks an old man something in Czech. He tells her that the castle is closed for renovations.

We make our way down to the car park and Vera drives us back to Prague and drops us at the Hotel Garni. We thank them for their kindnesses and tell them that we'll write. The telephone rings minutes after we reach our room. It's George, the rugby player who's studying law. He says he's waiting in the lobby with a Christmas parcel for us.

Solemnly he presents us with a package of Czech folk music records wrapped in crushed brown paper. It's a generous gift and unexpected, and we have nothing to give him in return. Then Em has a thought, because it is she who had the conversation with him the other day about literature. She runs upstairs and brings down a poem she wrote when we were in Luxembourg, and gives it to him. She reads some lines from it.

Love, we stand in a grove of birches, we pull our coats tight
against the wind. Bullets fly backwards
into the mouths of our guns.
This is the picture to step in:
now we are part of the land.
—Marilyn Bowering, 'Native Land'

George lets out a long sigh when Em finishes reading. I can see that he is touched. He collects himself and explains that he must now go off to work, but first he telephones Emanuel and arranges a place for us to meet him.

At seven o'clock Emanuel is waiting for us outside a church beside the river at Stare Mesto. A lovely blond woman in a short white and tan fur coat is waiting with him. Emanuel shakes Em's hand, then mine, and then introduces the woman he's with as his wife Blanka. Her English is better than his, although she seems shy about speaking it.

Emanuel's Kingsbury Rugby Club sweater has gone, replaced by a dark blue coat over what looks suspiciously like a suit. "I want to show you something," he says, turning towards the church. "There are two nativities inside this church, both of them very old. It's not that I'm religious," he adds quickly. "I'm too old for that. But I just wanted to see them. Perhaps it's because yesterday was my fortieth birthday." He gives us a quick grin and takes Blanka's hand. "Forty makes you think about things."

He leads us through the door of the old Romanesque church of St. Anthony. The basilica soars high above us. We can tell that the vaulted ceiling is decorated generously but the light is so poor in here that it is difficult to make out any figures, or scenes. A simple, roughly carved Nativity is set among the pillars, the holy family with wooden sheep set out in front of them, a relief of green hills and sky behind. Deep inside the church we come upon a second Nativity.

This one, explains Blanka, is made of more traditional Czechoslovakian figures; a man carrying a caged bird, women in biblical costume, a figure carrying loaves of bread. "It is a novelty to have these things in the open like this for people to see," she says. "We've never seen them here as long as I can remember."

We walk back out into the street. "I was very involved in 1968—in the Prague Spring revolution," says Emanuel. "There was a lot going on, marches, protests, some fighting. But it all fell apart when the Russians came here with their tanks and their soldiers. Now I've told my sons that the best thing they can do is to marry a girl from the west. I think it's the only way they'll ever be able to leave Czechoslovakia." He stops at the door of a rundown restaurant. "For me, it is too late." He says this in a matter-of-fact way, without sadness or self-pity.

Inside the darkened restaurant we talk, and eat goulash stew and dumplings. Emanuel tells us that he's a qualified international rugby referee, and sometimes he's asked by the International Board to referee important matches in Western Europe. "It always takes months to get travel permission from the authorities here," he says, "and they never allow me to take Blanka, or either of the boys."

George comes in, straight from his shift at work. We eat a hearty meal in an old bohemian stage-set, with wallpaper peeling off the walls and the lights flickering and dim. All through the meal we're wondering if the lights will go out. The tables are rickety, the chair legs uneven. An *art nouveau* pilsner advertisement is etched in stained glass on the ceiling above our heads, a sign of better times. When we've finished, George insists on paying the bill—George, who is visibly poor.

"You can't do that," I tell him. "We'd like to treat you to dinner—after all you've showed us around the *Hradcany*, you've brought us presents . . . you must let us do something."

George shakes his head. "When I come to visit you, then you can pay," he says. No matter how hard we try, we cannot contribute a penny.

Blanka has to leave us after supper, and the rest of us take a tram back across the river and get off at a stop beside an ornate, baroque theatre at Namesti Republica. The tramlines shine black on the road as we walk through the old town's cobblestoned streets to Wenceslas Square, gazing in the empty shop windows. The streets are virtually deserted, the streetlights dim as if they're only receiving a fraction of the electricity they need—the effect like gaslight. Our footsteps echo against the walls, and the old buildings loom above us in shadow. It feels as if time has been distorted, as if we have drifted back a hundred years.

At a pub called Pinkasu we sit at a table in a crowded upstairs room, and order beer and coffee, and *slivovic*—for the cold. The waiter is over-worked and harassed, the café-pub crowded and noisy.

An old man hears us speaking in English, and leans across from the next table to tell us about his time in England during the war. "I knew about trains so they made me a train driver. But I was also a highly trained fighter pilot. Even though they were terribly short of pilots, that was somehow less important to them. It was more than a year before they let me fly a Spitfire." He grins. He's wearing a battered leather hat on his head, a heavy coat as big as Em's, his big hand wrapped around a glass of dark beer.

"That would be the English," I tell him. "They don't trust people from other countries."

The old train driver–pilot nods. "Yes," he says. "It was like that for a lot of Czechs, for the Poles too. They didn't let us fly until it was nearly too late."

"I've read about it. A Canadian pilot called Johnny Kent wrote a book in which he said the same thing. He flew with a squadron of Poles. He thought they were the best pilots he'd ever seen."

The old man nods again. "Yes," he says. "We'd already fought the Germans. We weren't afraid of them. They'd occupied our country, and it made us very angry. Our anger made us better in battle than they were."

Outside in the cold night we wait again for a tram, until Emanuel loses patience and waves down a passing car driven by someone he says he knows. We're driven off to the Hotel Garni in style, but I notice that Emanuel gives the driver some money when we get out.

Inside the hotel the bar is doing good business, open this late for the first time since we arrived, supported by two more busloads of Hungarians from Budapest. Emanuel has had a bit to drink, and when three young Czech men enter the bar in black leather coats he starts to berate them for wearing the same clothes as the secret police. "You should be ashamed of yourselves," he tells them, and some heads turn at the bar, and stare. "What are you trying to do? Eh? Look like the Russians?" They're simply young men trying to look cool, but for Emanuel the leather coats seem to stir memories with dark overtones. It occurs to me that he might be living dangerously, and I pull him away. These men could be police, or black marketeers— they could be anyone. In either case, they'd be unpredictable. George says that he has to go, and the two of us steer Emanuel out of the bar and into the night air. But I notice as we leave that the men in the leather coats are looking a bit sheepish after Emanuel's onslaught.

George has to work early in the morning, but he tells us he'll come and collect us in his van and take us to the railway station in time to catch our train for Cologne. Emanuel has to work too, and says he'll try to come to the station to see us off.

In the morning the maitre d' greets us at breakfast with a smile for the first time. He wants to talk about Canada and asks us where we live. "The only places I've been to in Canada are Montreal and Gander," he says. His English is better than I'd thought.

"Gander?" Em's father comes from Newfoundland; she's always open to such connections.

"Yes," says the maitre d'. "It's where Aeroflot refuels on the way to Cuba. I've been to Cuba twice but they never let us get out of the plane at Gander. I've only seen it through the window." He shakes our hands solemnly when we leave the dining room, stands at the door and watches us get into the elevator to go up and pack our bags. He seems sorry to see us go.

George calls up to our room at twenty past ten. We're ready to leave, and make our way with our bags down to the lobby. George looks tired, as if he can hardly keep his eyes open.

"I didn't get home until very late," he explains, "then I had to get up and go into work at five to service my van." He hasn't shaved and he's wearing a set of grubby blue overalls. He insists on carrying Em's suitcase out to his rickety yellow van, which must be more than twenty years old—perhaps thirty. It moves crabwise down the street when he engages the gears, and the transmission sounds as if it might give out at any moment. The brakes squeal at the slightest touch. George drives nervously, touching the brakes whenever a car comes towards us, and we realise that this lift to the station is probably something he's not supposed to do.

The train is standing at Platform Two. George struggles down the narrow corridor with our bags. When we reach our compartment he makes an odd, formal little speech, standing very erect with his hands stiffly at his sides. "It has been good to meet you my friends . . . a good thing to see you here in Prague. It has been good for us to hear about the world outside. But now my friends . . . my dear friends, I must go back to my work. I hope we will see you again in Czechoslovakia one day. We will wait for you to return."

His words are so heartfelt that we don't know what to say. We tell him that he and Emanuel have turned our stay here from an experience filled with apprehension and suspicion, into something memorable and unique, something we'll never forget. We watch from the carriage window as he makes his way down the platform and wonder if we'll ever see him again.

"Do you think," wonders Em, "that he'll finish his law studies?" I shake my head; I don't know. At the top of the stairs George turns and waves, and disappears from view.

The clock ticks slowly towards 11:20. There's no sign of Emanuel and we begin to realise that he won't be coming. We're sad because it's Emanuel more than anyone who has lit up Christmas with his optimism and thoughtfulness, his instinctive understanding of what to show us, what to explain. The train starts to move off down the platform.

Suddenly, springing up the steps two at a time from the concourse below, dancing onto the platform, comes Emanuel; blue jeans, grey check jacket, more or less the same clothes he's worn since we met him. We shout. He runs the wrong way, towards the engine. We shout again. He stops, scratches his head and looks up and down the train. Then he sees us and in a moment he's running alongside the compartment, reaching up to shake our hands. "Ciao," he says grinning, falling back as the train gathers speed. We watch and wave until we can't see him anymore, both of us knowing that we'd have been sad to have left this city without seeing him this last time.

The train dives into a tunnel and brings us out beside the slow brown river. Two swans with long graceful necks fly overhead. Prague falls away and the sun shines in patches on villages. It starts to snow again. A farmer trudges across a field of stubble with three sacks on his back. A hunter with a rifle walks carefully along beside a hedge. Children are cleaning snow off a pond for skating. Karlstejn Castle appears in the train window.

✦

Three years later, a small hawk hunts the runways at Prague's airport. It is a wonderful flyer, its aeronautic ability mesmerising. The aeroplane's baggage is being loaded by hand onto ancient, rickety carts. I note the battered trucks, the peeling paintwork, the mail in threadbare sacks. But the Russians have gone, and the Czech airline has just ordered the new European Airbus. It will burn less fuel, carry more passengers than the old Illyushins, bring technological change. People are starting to paint the city's buildings, repair railings, manufacture lawnmower parts so that they can cut the grass in the parks. The French have started building a grand new hotel beside the Vltava in the centre of the city.

There is laughter now in this place. It is hard to believe.

The land around Pilsen is forested with birch and fir, the trees encrusted with snow on their north side. The train works its way up towards Cheb and stops in the middle of a desolate landscape of snow and ice. It is snowing so hard now that it's difficult to focus on still objects. Green-uniformed Customs men come on board with soldiers who immediately start searching the train. A soldier crawls up the corridor checking the ventilation covers. "Here we go again," mutters Em. "Do you think he's looking for people in these tiny spaces, or contraband?" The Customs men are brisk and efficient. Attaché cases hang from straps around their necks, opening out cleverly to make a shelf they can write on. One of them carefully removes a part of our visas and asks if we have any Czech currency. Maybe it's because we're about to return to Western Europe, but none of this is nearly as intimidating as it was the first time. Or maybe it's because we've spent a little bit of time in Czechoslovakia and seen how the people there quietly resist the bullying of the state. The soldier finishes checking the vents and pulls on green overalls. He jumps out into the snow and begins to inspect the underside of the train. We're running an hour late.

A gigantic concrete watchtower sits on top of a hill outside the carriage window, marking the border. We've watched it draw closer for miles. The train slowly eases its way past three formidable, twelve-foot high fences which run across clearcut countryside as far as we can see. Thinly camouflaged guard platforms stick up every two hundred metres. The train rumbles over a deep anti-tank ditch, past strange grey boxes mounted on poles among the fences. "What do you think they are?" asks Em.

"I don't know. Maybe they're sound and motion sensors. The British Army uses them in Ireland; the Russians probably use them too."

We stop at a gap in the fence and wait while several young soldiers in quilted fatigues check beneath the carriages. One of the soldiers stops his search to make a snowball. He throws it at one of his comrades; it explodes on the back of the young soldier's head. When they've finished searching we move off down a cutting, past another high fence which runs like a slash of black ink across the white, frozen landscape. Then we're in the station at Schirnding on the western side of the border, and everything is suddenly bright and cheerful. Christmas trees are everywhere, decorated with bells and fairy lights, the village houses like gingerbread houses, a floodlit church steeple, all of it encased in luminescent hoar frost. The railway station is spotless, the stationmaster waiting in his cape.

The change is astonishing, and palpable, as if someone has added stereophonic sound to an old silent film, or just invented colour. The train spends an hour here with West German Customs and Immigration, but the officials are polite and courteous, and they don't search under the train or check the vents.

The fast *Intercontinental* carries us northwards from Nuremberg. It's a first class train and we sink into the lush upholstery, telling ourselves that we've earned this comfort after the deprivations of the last week in Czechoslovakia. But we're very aware that we're able to leave the East; that we don't have to live like the friends we made in Prague. There's a knock at the door, and it slides open to admit a cheerful attendant carrying a tray with two steaming mugs of hot chocolate.

Berlin, Winter

Frankfurt station is a dingy, dirty place at night, deserted as an old aircraft hangar except for one or two drunks in the shadows. A half-hearted scuffle erupts in a dark corner behind some baggage carts, and quickly subsides. Two scruffy American GI's are talking to a pair of furtive civilians at the unlit entrance to the toilets. An aura of illicit trading hangs about the place; this could be the back streets of Detroit or Oakland.

A sleepy-eyed old lady sells stewed coffee and hot dogs from a cart. No one else seems to have any legitimate reason to be here. The train for Berlin is supposed to leave at 10:30 p.m. but it's difficult to get any information about it. It is three years before the modern unification of Germany, before the collapse of Erich Honecker's repressive East German government. Germany is still divided by barbed wire and minefields, and in Berlin, by the infamous Wall.

The train rolls slowly into the station at ten o'clock, and we climb on board. The GDR insignia on the dull green paintwork tells us that the carriages come from East Germany. Our carriage is spare and cold and looks about as comfortable as a cargo boxcar, not at all like the well-appointed *"Nuremberger"* we travelled on an hour or two ago.

As soon as we sit down, two men come in to our compartment. One of them is a big, bald-headed man in a knitted grey sweater. He takes a seat, pulls a sandwich out of his bag, takes a huge bite from it, and mumbles something to Em with his mouth full. It's impossible to understand what he's saying. She shrugs her shoulders and smiles at him. The second man is younger; dressed in a long brown coat, a black, woollen scarf wound twice around his neck. He has bushy hair and looks like a student.

The train pulls out of the station and takes us northeast through the darkness, past Hanau, Fulda and Bebra. It's almost two a.m. when we trundle slowly across the border at Helmstadt.

The train stops at the East German town of Gerstungen, just over the border. Six East German border guards stand on the platform about thirty feet apart, under bright floodlights. They watch the train, stone-faced, machine guns slung on straps at their hips, their breath forming little clouds which hang in the air like spun glass; all business. We stare back at them through the window. The atmosphere is brittle and threatening. Two officers confer inside a green hut, examining papers under a single yellow light bulb.

After a long wait the train starts to move, carrying us into the East German night. The Ticket Collector slides the door open and steps into the compartment. A jagged scar partitions his left cheek, as if someone has had a go at him with a broken bottle. He scans our tickets and then shouts something at me in German. He seems upset.

"*Nicht spreke Deutsche . . .*" I explain. It's as far as I get before the Ticket Collector interrupts, shouting in an incomprehensible stream of rapid-fire German, his voice rising as he works himself into a fury.

The student passenger in the compartment translates. "He's saying that you have the wrong tickets. These ones only take you from Frankfurt to the border, and we've passed the border now. He's telling you that the train can't go back, and you cannot get off." Impatiently the Ticket Collector interrupts again; I can't pick up a word of his dialect. The student listens and then continues. "The Ticket Collector is saying that you have to pay an extra charge."

"But we paid in Frankfurt for tickets to Berlin," I tell him.

The student nods his head patiently. "On top of the fare you paid in Frankfurt. Perhaps someone made a mistake," he adds sympathetically.

"How much does he want us to pay?"

The big, bald-headed man has put his book down and is watching intently. Outside the window everything is black; there are not even the lights of towns. The student speaks to the Ticket Collector, and then looks back at us. "One hundred and eighty Deutschmarks," he says.

It's a lot of money, about one hundred and twenty Canadian dollars. The whole affair is confusing. We don't know what to believe—whether this is a shakedown, or whether it's legitimate—but there's nothing we can do about it. We only have a few Deutschmarks on us, and so we offer the Ticket Collector the balance of the fare in Sterling and Canadian dollars. He shakes his head. We bring out our credit cards. He turns them over in his hand, frowns in puzzlement and throws them back at us and starts to shout again. The scar on his cheek turns scarlet. Suddenly he turns and stamps out of the compartment, slamming the sliding door behind him so hard that I'm surprised the glass doesn't break. I look at the student. The student shrugs his shoulders and picks up the heavy textbook he was reading.

After the departure of the Ticket Collector we catch some sleep. For some reason my left eye is hurting and I can sleep only fitfully, worried that the Ticket Collector might burst into the compartment at any moment with an armed guard. When I wake up we're at Potsdam. It's snowing a blizzard. Frost and ice cover the window in spider-web patterns; everything outside is white and arctic. Potsdam is a suburb of Berlin, but it's in the Russian zone. We move on past frozen lakes. It's almost

125

six a.m. The train comes to a stop at a station surrounded by a high concrete wall. We can't see beyond the wall and no one from the outside world can see into the station. Snow blows past the window, and drifts along the platform. The student and the bald-headed man are speaking in whispers. A soldier, wearing a fur hat which doesn't cover his red ears, stands right outside the window of our compartment with an Alsatian dog on a leash. He lets the dog off the leash and it prances and frolics playfully in the snow, a big, powerfully muscled dog the size of a small cougar.

Three soldiers walk down the platform through the snow, automatic rifles slung over their shoulders. They're young, kitted out in winter gear—snow boots, compact camouflage anoraks, gloves and toques. They look fit and efficient. Two older military men watch the train from the shelter of a hut. The soldiers keep us here for an hour and a half before they allow us to move out of the station, into West Berlin.

"They never explain," says the student. "They just seem to do everything they can to make it as difficult as they can for people to travel in and out of Berlin. Waits like that are standard procedure; I was once held up there for six hours."

We pass a series of frozen lakes at Wannsee and then move slowly into the station at Berlin Zoologische. The Zoo station is being battered by a howling wind out of the northeast, a wind that has flown all the way from the Russian steppes. The station is undergoing restorations, and the sharp winds have shredded the protective tarpaulin coverings. Snow blows in through open entrances, down the platform, drifts up against the wall of the ticket office. No one seems to care. We've heard that Berliners are used to discomfort and hardship.

We sit tired and hungry in the station restaurant, watching the blizzard through the window. Neither of us slept much last night, and my eye hurts even more than it did during the night. We order some breakfast from a languid waitress, and manage to chuckle at a man outside who's losing a battle against the gale, sliding slowly backwards down the icy sidewalk. The gale blows him towards a knot of people standing hunched over at the station entrance. One of them holds out an arm to snag the man as he slides past. The windblown man gives up the contest and joins in the wait for taxis that never seem to come. A few cars slither helplessly around in the snow. A big, green double-decker bus motors slowly past, the passengers invisible behind iced-up windows. It feels as if we've come to a city which has only just emerged from the Second World War.

Our boiled eggs are over-cooked and barely warm when they arrive, but the coffee is good and strong. It's enough to give us the resolve to test the weather outside, and to try out Berlin's public transport system. We have to find our way to Stieglitz, the Berlin district where we've booked a hotel room. Like most urban transit systems in Europe, the Berlin U-bahn is easy to understand. We buy a book of tickets and take line Nine out to the *Rathaus Stieglitz*, riding in yellow cars that are spotlessly clean. It's quite a contrast to the grubby East German train that has just brought us to the city.

Snow is blowing down the street outside the station at Stieglitz, piling up against the shopfronts. The *Rathaus* is the town hall for this district of the city and our hotel is nearby, a cavernous, characterless building which was once a department store. The corridors are about ten metres wide, and they seem spacious enough for a soccer match. But our room is big and comfortable, with a huge king-sized bed, and floor-to-ceiling windows. Better still, the central heating works, and the bath taps deliver steaming hot water. After a hot bath Em, sleeps until noon. When she wakes up, the pain in my eye is much worse.

She takes a look at it. "We'd better go out and find a drug store and get something to make it better," she says.

The girl at the front desk tells us there's an *Apotheke* round the corner from the *Rathaus*. The assistants at this local drug store inspect my eye and tell me that I should go to the *Klinikum*, that a doctor should look at it right away. They tell us how to get there by bus, and advise us to go to the nearby Deutschesbank for some money to pay for the treatment.

The heating system in the bank has failed because of the extreme cold; the teller so numbed that his fingers cannot flick the banknotes. It takes us half an hour to change a modest traveller's cheque. The pain feels as if a hot needle is being moved around in the corner of my eye, and it's increasing by the minute. Em is starting to get worried.

The Eighty-Eight bus takes us all the way to the *Klinikum*. A girl in a glass booth at the front door explains that the treatment for my eye will cost fifty Deutschmarks, and watches carefully while I count out the money. The elevator carries us up to the third floor and Em takes a seat on a hard wooden chair in an austere, lino-floored waiting room. A young doctor appears and tells me to step into his office.

"Ah, yes . . . I see," he says, peering into my eye. "Something has scratched the cornea and caused an abrasion," he explains in English. He tilts my head back and squeezes some drops into the eye. "It must hurt, but these drops will remove the pain." He takes my eyelid between his finger and thumb and stuffs a handful of ointment underneath it, then pulls the eyelid vigorously down and kneads it with his knuckles. "This will help it to heal," he says cheerfully. I can't believe the pain he's causing me. For a moment I wonder if he's done his training at a veterinary college instead of medical school. When he's finished knuckling my eye he tapes a patch of gauze over it and tells me to keep the dressing on for two days.

Em leads me across the road to the bus stop. The patch over my eye makes it difficult to gain perspective, to judge distances. The Eighty-Eight bus speeds us back through snowbound suburban streets to the *Rathaus* Stieglitz, and then we catch the U-Bahn up to Kochstrasse in the centre of the city. The lights of Checkpoint Charlie are right in front of us when we emerge from the U-Bahn station.

Checkpoint Charlie is a bleak, grey place. It's a break in the Berlin Wall, a crossing point between West and East, overlooked by glass-fronted watchtowers and cordoned into zig-zag lanes by red and white striped steel barriers. A dark green bus is passing through the checkpoint from east to west; another one is parked beside a barrier, waiting to be searched. Soldiers and Customs men come and go from a portable metal hut that looks like a construction site cubicle. The Wall stretches away on either side of the checkpoint, covered from top to bottom with brightly coloured graffiti. So much is written, so many images painted on the Wall, so many poems and quotations inked and jumbled together upon its face, that it's impossible to tell what its original colour could have been. The Wall is made of huge concrete slabs, ten or twelve feet high—about twice the height of a man or woman—with a rounded over-hang at the top to stop people climbing over it. The mass of the Wall hides the first two floors of a grey East Berlin apartment block which stands behind it, but over the top of it we can see a man working at a lathe in the third-floor window of what looks like a machine shop. Traffic comes and goes through the checkpoint, and we watch a small group of tourists hamming it up, snapping photographs of themselves simulating escape. The guards are not amused.

A narrow lane scattered with abandoned cars runs along beside the Wall in front of derelict flats, for the Wall here bisects a city street—like an untidy obscenity running neatly down its centre. The street seems to be as abandoned as the cars, which lie about without wheels or number plates. We follow a narrow band of trodden snow close under the Wall. An East German watchtower looms above the Wall, eerie and unnatural in the half-light. The bustle of Checkpoint Charlie recedes behind us, and dies away, leaving the soft silence of falling snow.

Em stops to rest for a minute in the doorway of a ruined flat. I take a photograph of her. When we see it after it has been developed a month later, she looks like a refugee in her Salvation Army coat.

Someone has run a white paint roller along the Wall, and amateur artists have filled in the stripe with more graffiti. Every inch of the Wall is covered with irreverent, colourful paintings and scratchings. Most of the art is too over-written by other etchings to make sense, and most of the language is German. But we come across 'Peace', 'No', 'Hola', an odd pair of shoes embedded onto the face of the Wall with a lump of concrete, thousands of signatures—as children might carve their names into a school desk or the trunk of a tree. "They came and did a little bit of shopping. . ." sits up under the curved lip of the wall—a complete non sequitur—although it might be a local comment on the parade of tourists to this place. A strange, skeletal sculpture of a man hangs by the neck high up on a broken lamp standard, twisting in the bitter wind, just as visible from the east side as from the west. But the confusion and the artistic chaos of it all makes it very clear to us, as we walk down this enormous outdoor art gallery, that the Wall carries the universal language of protest, and the sheer anarchy of it is uplifting; a caustic testament to people who refuse to be cowed.

The Wall continues on, running down the middle of streets, cutting them in two, slicing thoroughfares into cul-de-sacs, commuting wide, important pre-war boulevards to insignificant side streets. Two tattered buildings stand opposite one another like images in a mirror, hinting of past grandeur but riven now by the Wall. At one time they were the headquarters of Herman Goering's *Luftwaffe* on the Bendlerstrasse, a street that no longer exists.

We find ourselves standing at a corner of the Wall in an empty, windswept space, flat as a parade ground. At our feet lie a parallel set of steel tramlines, the grooves clogged with grit and dirt. A few yards away chipped granite kerbstones are set in a wide semi-circle. This was the PotsdammerPlatz, once the social and cultural centre of pre-war Berlin. "I've seen pictures of it," says Em quietly. "This was where a lot of the artists and theatre people used to hang out." Before the war, PotsdammerPlatz was a busy, congested place, like Picadilly Circus in London: the cultural heart of the city, full of traffic, lively with pedestrians and cafés and theatres, one of Europe's great meeting places. It's all wasteland now, scented with decay, soul-less in the biting wind.

And yet it all changes again. Only a few years on I'm looking at my friend Flanagan's photographs of a sun-drenched city square filled with people watching summer performances of music and street theatre, sitting at outdoor cafés and bars. High overhead among streaming banners and brightly-coloured ribbons, huge television screens are showing World Cup soccer matches. It is PotsdammerPlatz—most of its real estate owned now by Sony and Daimler Benz—risen in bright colour, with buildings of curved glass and steel, returned again to one of the important social and commercial centres of Europe. There's nothing in this photograph to suggest history or age, no vestige of tragedy or hardship or the desolation that we saw. This snapshot of the new Berlin, standing like an artifice that looks only to the future, is a creation of politicians and social planners and architects.

A man in a souvenir shack is selling cheap trinkets and key chains, postcards and pens. We climb onto a steel viewing platform nearby, which offers us an unimpeded view over the Wall. The sign at the top of the steps reads "Good for 90 Persons". On the other side of the Wall, the land has been completely cleared for hundreds of yards; it's utterly flat, without any features except for a few scattered high-intensity sodium lights that can turn the night into day. "Why do you think they did that?" asks Em.

"Probably to make sure they had open fields of fire for the guards," I reply. A steel chain-link fence stands twenty yards back from the Wall on the East German side; in some places they've built a second wall just like the main one. The Wall doesn't follow a straight line across Berlin. It turns and twists in accordance with the ceasefire occupation agreement the Allied powers made at Yalta, or the ones that the commanders made here, on the ground. From where we're standing on the platform we can see the eastern face of the Wall in several places where it takes a sharp turn. There's no graffiti on the east side of the Wall at all.

A man climbs the steps of the platform and joins us, staring over at East Berlin. "Canada?" he asks, gazing down at my ski gloves with the red maple leafs on their backs. His accent is English and he's wearing a fawn camelhair coat and brown leather gloves; brown shoes polished to a high shine.

"Yes."

We must look a bit odd to him; Em in her Salvation Army coat, and me looking like an impoverished pirate with a gauze patch over one eye and a knitted toque on my head, shivering in blue jeans and a barely windproof shell. But he doesn't comment.

"This is the British sector," he says. "The boundary here is actually marked by that fence." He points at a rickety metal railing that any ten-year-old child could pass through in seconds, about thirty feet in front of the platform. "But you don't see the Brits here very often. They only come when the Russians call them up to complain that someone's too close to the fence. Then they turn up in a Volkswagen van and tell whoever it is to get back." He's probably Army, off duty; or perhaps security, keeping an eye on things. But despite his English accent it's hard to tell his provenance; the English don't usually refer to themselves as 'Brits'.

A quarter of a mile away, a small green car motors across the white wasteland like an uncertain beetle. It stops, and two men climb out of it to look at something. The Englishman raises his hand and points at a spot near the car.

"That little mound out there," he says, "if you look carefully you can just see it. That's Hitler's bunker. The Russians say it's all blocked up now, but nobody over here knows for certain."

We stare out at the place where Hitler and Eva Braun committed suicide; where Magda and Josef Goebbels gave cyanide to their children before taking it themselves. I'm wondering why this Englishman has chosen to come here to this platform and speak to us. But maybe it's a bit like Prague, where the setting lends itself to twinges of paranoia. It starts to snow again, and I try to imagine what this desolate, depressing place must have been like when it was full of buildings—patterned by streets and houses and government offices—and animated by all the life that must have accompanied them.

We say goodbye to the Englishman and climb down from the viewing platform and follow a rusting fence into the Tiergarten, Berlin's old central park.

The first winter after the war was unimaginably harsh and the people of Berlin suffered an aching famine. There were terrible shortages of food and clothing and fuel. Most of the trees in the Tiergarten were chopped down and sawn up for firewood. The wood was so riddled with steel splinters from the bombing and shellfire that it dulled the saws. When the Berliners burned it in their hearth fires it crackled and spat out pieces of shrapnel as the metal heated up and expanded.

At the end of the war Berlin lay in ruins after years of bombing, much of the city little more than piles of rubble. There was no effective civil authority to maintain order, and what remained of Berlin's police force was unarmed. Marauding gangs, often made up of ex-soldiers from opposing armies and liberated prisoners, roamed the city. These gangs ran black market operations and prostitution rings, engaged in frauds and robberies. They were well armed, for the detritus of war was everywhere, and weapons were easy to come by. The gangs even held up Allied supply trains and looted them. Berlin became a city of rampant crime with an average of nearly two hundred and fifty offences—up to half a dozen of them murders—committed every day. The shortages of food, clothing, fuel—the basic necessities of life—were acute; in winter hundreds of people died from hypothermia, and for a time the city was gripped by widespread rumours of cannibalism. Wolves were seen in the outer suburbs, and warning signs were posted around the city's ring road.

West Berlin has been rebuilt since the war; the city has moved on, whereas large parts of East Berlin have been left just as they were in May 1945. The Tiergarten's trees have grown up again, and generous re-plantings have replaced the trees that were destroyed in the war and its aftermath. Berliners are proud of this park, and it must be a pleasant place in summertime, like Central Park in New York, or Hyde Park in London. A sign directs us along a path of deep, trampled snow to the Brandenberger Tor—the Brandenburg Gate. We follow the path through the empty woods. The sound of traffic, muffled by the trees, is indistinct in the distance, as if the city were many miles away. A corrugated metal Nissen hut and a concrete bunker loom out of the gathering dark. We can just make out a sign on a high chain fence. It states, "No Passage After 4 P.M." It's long after four o'clock, but a gate in the fence is open and we zigzag through a series of twelve-foot high anti-personnel obstructions made of wood and steel. A man in a green uniform comes through the trees towards us, with an Alsatian dog on a leash. Em stops in her tracks, startled. "God!" she exclaims, "We're in East Berlin."

But we're not. The policeman stares hard at both of us for a moment, and I'm conscious that the patch on my eye probably makes me look suspect. But the policeman is friendly enough, and explains that we can either go back the way we came, or follow a track along to our right. We take the track through the woods and soon find ourselves beside the Avenue de 17 Juni. We lean on the fence for a few minutes, relieved to see the city's lights far down the road. Off to our left stands the Russian War Memorial. An honour guard of Russian soldiers parades there twenty-four hours a day, the only armed Russian military personnel permanently stationed in West Berlin.

✦

During the Third Reich, this wide boulevard was called the East-West Axis. A few days before the end of the war, when Russian troops were closing in on the centre of the city, the desperate German defenders turned it into a makeshift airstrip so that they could maintain contact with their forces on the outside of the city; so that they might be able to receive supplies. A woman called Hanna Reitsch landed a tiny Feiseler Storch here on April 28th 1945, with the city burning all around her and the air thick with Russian flak and shellfire. One of the finest pilots in Germany, Reitsch brought General Ritter von Greim with her into the cauldron for consultations with Hitler. General von Greim was her lover. Von Greim found the meeting futile and frustrating; Hitler still harboured illusions about a counterattack to save the city, and refused to believe that there were no coordinated German forces left to undertake such a thing. Reitsch and von Greim were almost killed when they took off. The little aeroplane was hit several times by shellfire, and von Greim was wounded.

The city's defenders asked for the boulevard to be widened so that bigger aircraft could land with supplies and ammunition. But Hitler refused to allow his sappers to cut down the remaining trees beside the road, even though most of the trees had already been blown to bits. In a classic illustration of the fantasy world in which Germany's senior leadership was living, Albert Speer—Hitler's Minister in Charge of Armaments (and Re-construction)—also refused to allow the engineers to remove the ornamental bronze lampposts lining the boulevard.

"You cannot take down the lamp posts!" he said to the General in charge of defending the city, raising his voice above the racket of Russian shellfire. "I object to it. You do not seem to realise that I am in charge of the reconstruction of Berlin."

Forty-odd years later Berlin still projects an air of unreality, as if some of the chaos that prevailed at the end of the war has perpetuated itself. So much here seems artificial; the Wall; the whole idea that Berliners cannot move from one part of their city to another—that we can look at East Berlin but we cannot travel there; the absence of people near the border where we've been walking; the relics we've seen of grander times, and the sense that they bring of issues still unresolved.

It's gloaming now; dusk. Pale, gold-coloured light flows through bare, frosted branches as the path takes us back in amongst the trees. A man darts out of the woods, crosses the path to a tree and unbuttons his fly, stands there with his back to us for a long minute, and relieves himself. He finishes his business and disappears back the way he came, without noticing us. Now we can see through the trees that the golden light is coming from the Brandenburg Gate, from spotlights illuminating its magnificent stone columns. As we draw closer we can see that the ubiquitous Wall stands in the way, blocking off the Avenue de 17 Juni about thirty yards in front of the Gate. But the magnificent *Brandenberger Tor* dwarfs the Wall, so that we hardly notice it. On top of the Gate stands the Quadriga—a chariot, four horses and a winged driver bathed in soft green light. Em tells me that the whole classical structure is modelled on the Propylaeum in Athens—the entrance to the Acropolis. I can see why it upsets the Russians and the Poles, and wonder idly why they never blew it up. Although it depicts the Goddess of Peace it is undeniably aggressive, and faces belligerently eastwards toward Germany's traditional enemies. It has been recently refurbished by the Russians, and sits in a bed of fresh-fallen snow like an ornate wedding cake.

We climb the steps of a nearby viewing platform for a better view over the Wall. Two Russian soldiers in greatcoats, rifles slung over their shoulders, are patrolling the great gate's porticos, moving in and out of the pillars like wraiths. Behind the soldiers we can just catch a glimpse of the Unter den Linden, devoid of trees now, its buildings grey and ministerial, architecturally bland.

In the 1930's the Unter den Linden was one of the most magnificent avenues in Europe, lined with architecturally impressive buildings and framed by linden trees. Germany's most important government Ministries inhabited the fine buildings on each side of it. But the Unter den Linden was not just a centre of power like Whitehall in London; it was a social magnet too, like the Champs Elysees in Paris. This magnificent boulevard was badly bombed during the war—like the rest of Berlin—and when the fighting was over the Russians bulldozed it flat, even though the guidebooks say that much of it could have been restored. Now its architecture is like the architecture we saw in the district of *Leninova* in Prague; dull, blockhouse, *apparatchik* design, it hits the eyes like a punishment.

One of the Russian soldiers at the Gate stamps his feet. The east wind sweeps over the wall towards us. We turn away and walk to the Reichstag, which stands nearby, hard up against our side of the wall. Twin driveways sweep majestically up to its front entrance, and sculpted stone figures decorate its roofline. I've seen this scene before, in jerky old newsreels; Hitler driving up here in the Chancellor's black Horch, and getting out under the epigraph *Dem Deutscher Volk* chiselled in gothic letters above the great doors; then, in the last days of the war, Russian soldiers surging across the Reichstag's roof, and hanging the Red Army flag from one of these statues.

The reality is a bit disappointing. I know from my studies in European history that Europe's great cities competed fiercely in city works for international prestige in the latter part of the nineteenth century. In many ways it's possible to see how Berlin, with its grand thoroughfares, its great central park and the fine trees planted throughout the city—and particularly from the remnants of fine classical architecture that we've come across—might once have rivalled London or Paris; that it must have been laid out on the grand scale which was fashionable a hundred and fifty years ago. But, although it's impressive, the Reichstag is much smaller than the Houses of Parliament in London, or even the Chateau de Ville in Paris, and less spectacular than either of them. Colourful posters at the main entrance announce an exhibition of modern painting inside, but it seems clear to us from the care that has been taken with the Reichstag's restoration that it awaits a more important purpose.

On our way to wait for a bus to take us back into the centre of the city, we make a short detour to a small, threadbare wood right beside the Wall, in the shadow of the Reichstag. Sixteen white crosses are strung along a wire fence beside the trees, a poignant memorial to sixteen people who died near this spot trying to escape from the East. Each cross is etched with a name. Axel Hannemann was just seventeen years old when he was shot while he was trying to swim across the River Spree near here. Marienetta Jirkowski was eighteen years old when she was shot on November 22nd, 1980; Chris Gueffroy was twenty when he was shot through the heart by an East German border guard in February 1989, just a few months before the Berlin Wall was torn down.

We gaze at the dates on the simple wooden crosses at this makeshift memorial. It is all such a waste, so unnecessary, and at first it seems like just another fragment of the aura of artificiality which lies about this place. But as we turn away we catch sight of an elevated East German guard post, a soldier inside staring down at us, and we're reminded that we're outsiders, that the Wall and all it stands for—the splitting apart of families, the fear that surrounds it—remains terribly real for the people who live here.

By the main entrance to the Reichstag we wait, hunched against the wind, for the bus. Open fields stretch away to distant buildings across a park. A child romps happily in the snow while his parents stand nearby, shivering. When the bus turns up the driver greets us all like old friends. We make our way up the stairs to the top deck, which affords a good view although I can still only see out of one eye. Without any depth perception I find it difficult to distinguish reflections in the window from what lies outside, and the streets unfold beyond the glass like an invention. The bus driver keeps up a commentary on the intercom as we motor towards the city centre, provoking merriment among the other passengers, although we can't understand a word that he's saying. With just the one eye to see with, and the dim street lights outside, the houses flick past like a series of old, one-dimensional daguerreotype images, forcing me to refocus every time I shift my gaze. The pretty River Spree winds slowly past, lined on both sides with houses, and crossed by bridges. The bus circles the Siegessaule, which is topped by the winged, gilded figure of Victory—the great column that we saw far down the Avenue de 17 Juni when we were standing at the edge of the Tiergarten woods.

We get off the bus at the Kurfurstendam and descend beneath the ground to the U-Bahn station. A train comes and carries us off to Osloerstrasse, where we change to the southbound line for Linestrasse. We've seen from the subway map that this route runs under part of East Berlin. We want to see what it's like.

The train slows to half speed and the walls of the tunnel change from tile to bare rock. We move slowly through a deserted station decorated with lime green tiles, lit well, but completely empty. There are no advertisements on the walls, no people here. A faded board carries the station's name— BernauerStrasse. We know that our train cannot stop at these East Berlin stations, that this line is in use only because of the arcane series of trade-offs that have been agreed upon between the former Allies since the war. The stations are probably mined or booby-trapped, and certainly guarded in case escapers try to use them. Passing through these forsaken, dimly lit East Berlin stations is like being in a time warp. They've been left virtually as they were in May 1945, in the last days of the war, peopled by ghosts from another time. It's a strange feeling to sit in western comfort in this tiny time capsule and pass through these deserted places. But all around us the Berliners on the train are chattering away, taking no notice of it at all.

✦

These underground tunnels were used by desperate people trying to escape the bitter carnage above them in the last days of the war. Russian shock troops and German SS soldiers stumbled upon each other and fought spasmodically in the darkness while the final battle for Berlin raged in the ruined city overhead. Hitler's driver, Erich Kempka, crept down these grimy U-bahn labyrinths late on the night of May 1st, 1945 with a group which included Martin Bormann, Hitler's Deputy. Bormann was the object after the war, of extensive international searches by several governments anxious to bring him to trial. It was thought for many years that he'd escaped the city, until his bones were found, thirty years later, in a shallow grave up on the surface, not far from one of these stations.

The Rhine is high at Cologne, lapping the top of the embankment, spilling into the city's streets. The river has risen twenty feet since we saw it two weeks ago. At the Hotel Haus Lyskirchen, Pierot the manager tells us that the water level is up to 8.6 metres. When it reaches nine metres the street outside will be impassable he says, the hotel's parking garage flooded. At twelve metres the ground floor of the hotel will be under water. "It never used to get as bad as this," he says gloomily.

We don't know what to say. We're leaving here in the morning. We've seen the amazing amount of energy and industry that the Germans have put into rebuilding their towns and cities, into trying to move on to a future as different as possible from their past. We can only sympathise, tell him that we hope the river will show the city some compassion.

From our little room under the eaves the old city is timeless, the river running through it, brown with silt from the mountains. Beside it, the great black *Dom* towers over everything—impervious to Thousand-Bomber raids, political changes and altered states; symbolic of man's experience and spiritual need, of our questioning. Perhaps the truth of it is that the present and the past and the future are interchangeable here; that like the river, the present shifts in and out, shows us over and over again that it is just a passing thing.

Across the river, at the other end of the Kaiser Wilhelm Bridge, the number 4711 blinks its neon signal.

The Seville Diaries

Elgar on the Aeroplanes

Nimrod is playing over the sound system as we file on board the brightly painted Iberia flight in Madrid. The quintessentially English piece by Elgar, with its lugubrious rhythms appealing to mythical gods, and its associations with British colonialism, sounds incongruous in this sun-splashed Spanish aircraft. We're bone tired; this is our fourth aeroplane in twenty-eight hours. Travelling is a more complicated business now, because there are three of us; little Xan is two years old and she's come to Spain with us.

It's January 1990, and we're on our way to Seville to work on Spain's World Fair—Expo '92. The Fair is scheduled to open in two years, but it's already well behind its construction targets. I'm here to work with a Spanish-Canadian consortium which will design and build pavilions and exhibits, and undertake technical developments for the Fair. I'll be mainly concerned with marketing and client liaison. Canadian expertise has become a prized commodity at World's Fairs since the huge success of Vancouver's Expo '86; we're seen as having the world's most up-to-date experience with International Expositions.

Robert is waiting for us when we pass through the glass doors into the marble-floored Arrivals Hall at Seville's Airport.

Robert is a thin, angular Englishman who has worked for the Canadian side of the company for years. He speaks Spanish, and he's been here for more than a month as the company's advance guard, looking for office space, and temporary accommodations for the Canadian staff. I'm the second one from Canada to fly in, and I'll soon be followed by the rest of my colleagues.

"Did you bring any money with you?"

Robert's question catches me by surprise. He's watching me anxiously for a reaction, but then he collects himself. "Er, did you have a good trip?"

Robert is visibly relieved when I tell him that I've brought some company funds from Canada, but this first encounter should have been a warning to me. I met Robert in Vancouver before he left for Spain, and he told me then in his oblique, understated English way that he'd seen the Canadian company crash and rebuild itself more than once. But before I signed on as the head of marketing for this new consortium, GD, the company's President, assured me that our new Spanish partners had brought financial stability to the company, as well as the acumen to help us work in a foreign business environment. GD has flown over here many times to wheel and deal with various Spanish concerns and to finally set up the co-operative joint venture that we're now a part of. It will be a while yet before I find out that, despite all GD's assertions, the Canadian branch of the company still operates on the thin line between solvency and disaster.

Outside the airport terminal the flat countryside of the wide Guadalquivir valley is folded in a warm darkness. Cars whizz past the terminal on the auto-estrada. Robert commandeers a taxi. The driver stows our luggage in the trunk and Em and I collapse into the back seat. Soon we're speeding down the Avenida de Kansas City towards the city in a plush Mercedes. Robert sits in the front and converses easily with the driver in Spanish.

Robert has secured us a small residential apartment on the Plaza Ruiz de Alda, near the centre of Seville, in a modern building close to the railway station and the famous Plaza de Espana. Our Mercedes taxi takes us straight there, turning past brand new apartment blocks, and zigzagging through the plaza, which is jammed with parked cars. The hallways inside the apartment building are wide and paved with marble floors, but when we open the front door our apartment is freezing cold.

"Yes," says Robert unsympathetically. "Most of the heating systems in Andalusia are designed for summer temperatures which get up as high as 50 degrees Celsius, which means that they're quite hopeless in winter if you actually need any serious warming."

He helps us inside with our bags and then leaves us to explore. The apartment is small and impersonal, but it's spotlessly clean, with a living room and bedroom and a tiny kitchen and white-tiled bathroom. The walls are white and bare, and the floors are marble, which does nothing to diminish the January cold. Robert has told us that the rent is expensive, but that the company will pay it for two months until we can find a place of our own. Little Xan is fast asleep on the couch and so we go about unpacking, and set up her travel cot. It will do as her bed for a few months yet, until she grows out of it.

Seville Spring

In the morning we look down from our fourth floor window at children playing among the parked cars in the Plaza, and some old people sitting outside a café drinking coffee in the wintery sun. There's no food in the fridge and so we organise ourselves to go out to a small supermarket on the far side of the plaza to buy some groceries. The elevator is excruciatingly slow, and when we eventually step out of it we encounter a pleasant *portero* who inhabits the downstairs entry hall. He wears a blue uniform and sits by himself at a desk. He greets us politely in Spanish, and gets up from his chair to open the heavy glass doors for us. He doesn't speak any English. His main job seems to be to provide security for the apartment building. The *portero* carries a walkie-talkie on his belt, and occasionally while we're staying here we see him pull it out and speak into it with an air of casual importance.

Apart from the *portero's* desk and chair there are no furnishings in the bare, echoing entrance lobby or in any of the hallways, not even a potted palm. During our stay here we rarely encounter any other residents. It all suggests impermanence and transition, and makes us feel very unsettled, very much on our own in a strange culture. We need to find a place of our own as soon as we can.

✦

On GD's last trip to Seville, he and Robert negotiated the temporary use of a single, tiny office for our staff on the top floor of a building on the Avenida de la Constitution, near the Puerta de Jerez, a busy traffic circle in the centre of the city. The whole suite of offices on the top floor is owned by Francisco Rubiales, a local businessman. I've been working up there for a week before I actually meet Rubiales, and I find myself instantly unsure of him. He never actually looks me in the eye when we meet. He's a rotund man with a small moustache, and he's wearing a sharp brown suit and shiny brown shoes. Rubiales' English is poor and my Spanish is virtually non-existent at this point, so his demeanour might be a reflection of our general inability to communicate, but all the time we're acquainted I never manage to discover what his business actually is.

Unfortunately the whole top floor is barely large enough for Rubiales' own operation, and it becomes clear to us very quickly that our little space, with one telephone and one ancient fax machine, is not big enough for Robert and me to work in. To make matters worse our Canadian colleagues are now arriving in Seville on a regular basis—first Flanagan, our Technical Director, then Knowlton, the Chief Designer. GD himself flies in, and takes charge. He's a tall, fair-haired man and he stands out among the darker Spanish.

Rubiales' offices become impossibly chaotic as our numbers grow. Rubiales' secretary manages the main switchboard and she starts to become annoyed at the escalating number of telephone calls she's answering on our behalf. No sooner does one of us put the single telephone down than someone else grabs it to make a call. The fax works off the same line as the telephone, and because the telephone is in constant use we cannot receive or send faxes. As our staff complement grows and the tension rises, Rubiales makes himself increasingly scarce. We rarely see him in his offices any more, although we encounter him from time to time in the coffee houses in the streets below, and it seems to us as if he does much of his business in these places. GD holds a meeting with him and Rubiales allocates us a second office. We never discover the exact nature of the arrangement GD has made with Rubiales, but we think it must have something to do, on Rubiales' side, with expectations of future Expo business with us. From GD's point of view it's probably got more to do with paying minimal rent until the company generates some cash flow.

Meanwhile things continue to deteriorate. Rubiales' secretary won't speak to any of us, and refuses to transfer calls. Our people overflow the two small offices, and we begin using Rubiales' luxurious private office to make sensitive company calls. "After all," reasons Flanagan, "he's never there, and it's the biggest office in the place." It's a comfortable office with a big, high-backed leather chair, a wide glass-topped desk, Bauhaus-designed black leather chesterfield and armchairs, and chrome lamps. Soon two or three of us are working in there most of the time. Rubiales' secretary grows more upset by the hour.

However, my first real crisis comes back at the apartment at the Plaza Ruiz de Alda, when Em sends Xan and me out to the local store for groceries. The two of us walk down the wide hallway hand in hand, but when we reach the elevator I realise that I've forgotten my wallet. I tell Xan to wait while I nip back down the corridor to the flat to pick it up. I'm gone for less than a minute, but in that time a big, shiny, empty, silver elevator arrives and the doors open and Xan can't resist the urge to step inside. The automatic doors close and the stainless steel elevator sets off with her inside it all by herself. I arrive back at the elevator where I left her seconds ago, to find her gone. In a panic I sprint down four flights of marble stairs three at a time to the front door. An elderly woman is stepping into the empty elevator. I alert the *portero* to my problem in tragically bad Spanish. "*Mi nina he disparido . . .*" Then I rush back up to the flat to tell Em what's happened,

150

and immediately dash off to search each floor on foot. There are twelve floors in the apartment block. All of them look exactly the same.

After a few minutes I can hear faint wailing sounds, but because the empty marble hallways and stairwells create echoes, it's impossible to tell whether they're coming from upstairs or downstairs. After several minutes of sprinting along empty corridors and running up and down stairs I find Xan on the seventh floor, pounding her little fists on the identical door to ours (which is clever of her), and weeping terribly. I pick her up and she buries her head in my chest. I tell her that everything is fine, and very soon it is. But it's been a long few minutes, full of all the fears that a parent can have.

It's only a ten minute walk from the Plaza Ruiz de Alda to Rubiales' office in the Avenida de la Constitution. The route takes me past the bus station and around a busy traffic circle to the Murillo Gardens and the university. Orange trees line most of the streets in Seville, and by the end of January the trees are thick with fruit. When the oranges ripen they fall to the ground, and then they lie on the sidewalks where they're trod upon, and in the gutters where they're squashed into a slippery mash by the wheels of passing cars. City workers harvest the fruit from the streets and parks early in February and send it off to Dundee in Scotland, to be made into marmalade. After the pickers have gone the fallen fruit slowly turns rotten in the heat and begins to smell of old socks and burned rubber.

But a month after the harvest the air in Seville is heavy with the sweet, exotic scent of orange blossoms. Then the orange blossoms fall in their turn and the jacaranda trees burgeon with electric blue flowers. Hibiscus and bougainvillaea grow like weeds and splash orange, lavender, yellow and red up and down the city's streets and alleyways. Work crews appear with high ladders to pluck dates from the tall palms in the park by the Alcazar.

Seville is humming with activity. Expo '92 will be the biggest World's Fair since Montreal in 1967. It will commemorate the five hundredth anniversary of Columbus's voyage of discovery to the New World. The disintegration of socialist rule in Eastern Europe, and all the political developments related to this, are opening up new horizons for business, technology and cultural exchange. It is important for Spain—particularly the south of Spain, which is still emerging from the social and technical freeze of the Franco era—to show that it can stand alongside its new European Community partners.

For these and other reasons, the 1992 World Fair will become a testing ground for nations trying to gain trading advantages, and for multinational corporations vying for technical superiorities. In the realm of high definition television technology for example, the Japanese, Germans, and Dutch, as well as the British and Americans, will compete with each other for billions of dollars of contract and development work.

This is the reason we're here. The Spanish-Canadian joint venture company that GD has put together is backed by the Banco Bilbao Viscaya, the biggest bank in Spain. The BBV has formed a special service company called Desarollo '92. D'92 is one of only five corporations that have been licensed by Spain's Expo Corporation to work with the participant countries and corporations directly on the Expo site. D'92 expects to do well out of the Exposition.

Conditions at Rubiales' office continue to decline as our colleagues trickle in from North America and other parts of the world. Most of them have experienced working in the pressurised environment of a World's Fair—at Expo '86 in Vancouver, and again at Brisbane in 1988, one or two of them at the Japanese Expo in 1989.

The 1986 World Fair in Vancouver pulled the international expositions business out of the doldrums after several consecutive, high cost disasters. It was well marketed, enthusiastically and efficiently run, and it generated a lot of interest and participation from governments, international corporations, and the public. Brisbane, two years later, was a financial and cultural success as well, and consolidated the importance of these events to the development of international trade.

More than one hundred countries and thirty or more multinational corporations are expected to exhibit at Seville's World Fair on a site covering hundreds of acres at the edge of the city. All of these participants will finance and build free-standing pavilions. In addition, the Expo organisation—the Sociedad Estatal, what in Canada we'd call a Crown Corporation—is building several theatres, five hugely expensive showpiece Theme pavilions, and a multitude of cafés, bars, restaurants, canals, public works and a massive showcase lake in the centre of the site. In addition to this core of activity and development, each one of Spain's sixteen *Autonomias*, or Provinces, has also demanded its own exhibition site, along with extortionate levels of financial support from the Spanish government in Madrid.

It has cost the BBV a lot of money to create D'92 and procure an inside track to all this contract opportunity. The Expo Corporation has extracted outrageously high licensing fees from each of the five service organisations they've licensed to work on the site. But there will be plenty of work; not a building can be designed, and hardly a hammer lifted, except through one or other of these service organisations.

Apart from the work on the Expo site, the Andalusian government has commissioned extensive refurbishment programmes for Seville's ancient buildings and houses. Some of these are magnificent architectural treasures, but most of them have had no proper maintenance for centuries, and the city is full of crumbling stonework and cracked masonry. The main railway station on the river by the Expo site is being torn apart to make a special Seville Expo Pavilion, and a terminus for funiculars which will transport visitors across the river to the Fair itself.

Roads are being mended throughout the city, and new highways built across the countryside to far-away towns. A brand new railway line is being laid to carry a two hundred kilometre per hour, high-speed train between Seville and Madrid. To accommodate the expected increase in passengers, a new rail terminal bigger than a pair of Boeing 747 maintenance hangars is being built out on the Avenida de Kansas City, on the road to the airport. At the same time, the Guadalquivir River which runs through the city is being re-routed to recreate its path on the day that Christopher Columbus left here for the new world in 1492. Ambitious ring roads, by-passes and flyovers, new Customs and Airport buildings, digital telephone systems and much more are under construction; all of it happening in what has hitherto been an agrarian society with a labour force that is almost completely unskilled in technical matters.

This is the background to the maniacal activity that we've encountered since we got here and started work in this city, which is like an ant's nest that has been undisturbed for nearly five hundred years. From what we can see the Andalusians seem to be managing these enormous developments and ambitious transitions with a reasonable degree of sensitivity to the architectural and cultural heritage of this ancient city. At the same time the Fair is a long way behind schedule by North American standards. The Expo authorities have a lot of catching up to do.

Our Spanish partners at the D'92 offices are full of confidence. But right at the start of our first meeting with them it's obvious that we need to engage an interpreter as soon as possible. Unlike people in northern Spain, most Andalusians speak very little English. The second language here is not English but French, and few people speak even that. We realise very quickly that the ability to translate accurately is vital if we're going to work successfully here. To make matters more difficult, Andalusians are every bit as chauvinistic about language as most of the English speaking peoples. In fact only one of our Spanish partners at D'92 speaks any English at all. This is Alvaro, and he is the most junior of them all. We see very quickly that none of his Spanish colleagues pays any attention to him because of his lowly status. In time we also discover that although he is the most junior, he is also the brightest.

As a consequence of our language inadequacies, our first meeting with our Spanish colleagues is stilted, unsatisfactory and frustrating. We quickly arrange Spanish lessons for our non-Spanish staff, which at this point is all of us.

More and more of our people arrive from North America and cram into Francisco Rubiales' tiny office on the Avenida de la Constitucion. It sits in a charming location, close to the Giralda and Seville's old Cathedral, and the gardens of the Alcazar, at the edge of the old city near the Barrio Santa Cruz, a labyrinth of alleys and lanes and ancient residences. Ten of us are now trying to use the telephone and the single fax machine. Between us we have two desks and three chairs, and no privacy. Most of us are looking for apartments or houses to rent. A few of us are trying to arrange Expo-related meetings.

GD breezes into the office and announces that he's managed to secure a large apartment for our offices on the other side of the river. Flanagan and I catch the bus over there to take a look. The owner shows us proudly round her spacious, elegant home. The apartment is on the fourth floor, and it has four big bedrooms, a huge kitchen, and generous living and dining rooms with exquisite parquet floors. The front windows and balconies look down on the Avenida de Republica Argentina, a busy shopping street; the back rooms overlook a quiet lane. "Yeah, we can fix this up," mutters Flanagan. We leave GD alone with the landlady to negotiate terms.

As soon as the ink is dry on the agreement GD dispatches Flanagan back to our new company headquarters. Flanagan will perform the renovation work necessary to transform the landlady's well-appointed apartment into a functioning, high-tech office.

Flanagan's crew sets to work demolishing walls, ripping out ceiling plaster, pulling up the floors. They install heavy-duty wiring circuits to carry the hefty power loads demanded by the extensive computer network we're going to install, the low frequency lighting systems, and the air conditioning machinery we'll need in every room to combat Seville's suffocating summer heat.

Flanagan tells me over coffee one morning that GD neglected to tell the landlady about this radical, corporate re-design when he signed the rental agreement. Furthermore, despite its location on a busy downtown street, the apartment is apparently zoned only for residential use. "We've already had two of the neighbours complaining about the noise and the dust," he continues. "You remember that the building's only got that one little elevator?" I remember. It's painfully slow, and as small as a telephone booth.

"The neighbours have been complaining about that too; about the volume of people coming and going and jamming it up so they have to use the stairs."

I can't believe the change in the place when I turn up after Flanagan's crew has been working on it for a week. One wall of what was a bedroom has been removed in order to transform the narrow entrance hall into a spacious entrance lobby. One of Flanagan's electricians has removed the ceiling tiles from all the rooms, and is busily stuffing in what looks like miles of wiring and black tubing. Another plaster wall has been demolished at the back of the apartment to make two rooms into a large communal office, and a pair of elegant sliding doors, which once partitioned the living room, now lie on their sides out on the balcony. I resolve to leave town if the landlady ever makes a surprise visit.

El Pais, the national newspaper, carries a front-page picture of a big girder bridge which collapsed into a dry watercourse beside the Expo site while work crews were demolishing it. It seems that the foremen misread their instructions, and didn't wait for engineering experts to arrive from Madrid. It's a bad accident and six workmen are killed. Things like this seem to happen quite often here for reasons of impatience or incompetence. I ask Rodolpho if he thinks this terrible accident came about because the contractor was taking short cuts. He astonishes me with his reply.

"Andalusia has the best environmental laws in Europe," he says, as we walk down the Avenida de la Republica Argentina towards the office. "It's possible that the accident happened because the construction company was trying not to break the environmental laws."

Rodolpho is an American. He's married to Isabella who is voluptuously Spanish, and he's been living here for more than twenty years. He prefers to be called Rodolpho instead of Rudolph, his proper name, or the Americanised Rudi. He makes a point of correcting us if we forget.

"How can that be?" I ask.

"I think it's possible that they were taking extra care to make sure that no parts of the bridge fell into the river, and that no fuel or hydraulic fluids went in there from their machines."

Rodolpho's answer confuses me, but I decide to leave the matter alone. I also decide not to mention that the watercourse where the bridge collapsed is dry, apparently even in winter. The company has hired Rodolpho for two reasons. He's let it be known, confidentially of course, that he has 'connections', and we've already discovered that virtually nothing happens here without 'connections'. It is how business is done. Rodolpho claims to have a brother-in-law who is highly placed in the Andalusian government.

The second reason Rodolpho has been hired is that he speaks Spanish with an Andalusian dialect. The Andalusian dialect is important because Andalusians have an instinctive distrust of outsiders, even people from other parts of Spain. In our short time here we've already observed how an outside accent seems to cause a clouding of the eyes, a sense that calculations have suddenly entered into the conversation. Outsiders rarely prosper in Andalusia.

Rodolpho's wife, Isabella, has also been hired as an interpreter. She is a good translator, and warm hearted. GD has now hired Rodolpho's oldest daughter, Marina, to work in our office as a translator. This is a mistake. When we ask her, she comes reluctantly along with us to meetings in order to translate. But most of the time she prefers to sit at her desk staring into space, or chatting with her mother, and cracking sunflower seeds with her teeth.

On the surface of it Rodolpho's comment about Andalusia's environmental progressiveness is difficult to believe and I turn to him in surprise, just as a powerful stream of exhaust smoke from a passing Pegasus bus catches me full in the face. It makes my eyes stream and I voice my disbelief as a 49-cc moped without a muffler goes roaring by, taking my words up the street with it.

Rodolpho hasn't heard me and is still speaking. "Yes, it's quite true . . . in fact, the Council of Europe in Brussels has just issued a proclamation congratulating the Andalusian government for its environmental consciousness."

"I don't believe it! " I shout, raising my voice against high velocity Spanish music pounding out of a nearby bar.

He looks at me in genuine disbelief. "You've got to give this new government a chance," he says patiently. "They've only been in power for five years. It takes time for these things to take effect, but don't make any mistake about it, it's happening. All the laws are on the books."

People drop candy wrappings on the street and flip empty cigarette packets out of car windows. There don't seem to be any bylaws about wandering dogs, or their excretions. Pedestrians walk across the city's bridges oblivious to the shoals of dead fish floating belly up in the river below them. Abandoned cars sit deteriorating without wheels and other essential parts on the Prado San Sebastian near our apartment, right in the centre of the city. The outskirts of the city are a linked, random garbage dump of rusting refrigerators, bedsteads and discarded appliances.

But every night while the citizens are sleeping a miracle occurs, and the city is hosed down by teams of orange-garbed city workers. At first light the streets are spotless, sparkling in the early sunshine.

Lorenzo, the Breeder of Bulls

I received an invitation to the *corrida* today. Seville has one
of the finest bullrings in Spain. The old white-circle stadium
sits steeped in tradition beside the river, shining in the
Andalusian sunlight, beside grey stone buildings. It's as big
as a football stadium, and the first time I walked past it the
main doors were wide open so that I could see right onto
the red-dirt floor of the empty arena. Ranks of seats reach
up in terraces to a series of galleries, which flow around its
upper rim like the cloisters of a monastery and give the place
an air of almost religious importance. *La Real Maestranza* was
built in the late 1700's and restored in the 1970's, and it sym-
bolises the grandeur and passion the Spanish hold for the
bullfight. Seville's bullring is the emotional heart of Span-
ish bullfighting.

The spring season starts after Easter, and runs for a month
with contests every night. The tickets were sold out by Christ-
mas and an invitation is greatly prized.

Lorenzo has invited me. I have met him through our work,
as he is the Chairman of the Andalusian branch of Spain's In-
ternational Red Cross Committee, which is developing plans
to construct a pavilion on the Expo site. Lorenzo is also a bull

breeder, and his family has a private box in the shade. All the best seats are in the shade.

Lorenzo goes to the *corrida* every night when the fights are on. He's a short man with jet-black hair and an inclination to tubbiness. He has the casual air and well-cut clothing—the tailored twill slacks, the monogrammed shirts and sports jackets—which often accompanies wealth. His English is good and his wife went to Roedean, one of the top private schools in England. It is important, explains Lorenzo, to see the competition, the bulls produced by the other breeders. He must know quickly whether they've bred good bulls this year, or whether they are *'malo'*, which means they don't put up a good fight.

I've read somewhere that the finest compliment that can be paid to a bull is for it to be allowed to live. But apparently this happens rarely, and only after it has displayed extraordinary courage and tenacity. It seems to me that the bull must inevitably be so wounded by then that it would have to be put to death outside the ring. This too seems to fall within the etiquette of the ritual.

On the other hand, questions have arisen recently about the calibre of the modern bullfighter. Several matadors have fled the ring in fear in the last two years. This kind of conduct has not been heard of before, and when it's mentioned in Seville voices drop into a lower register.

I ask Lorenzo about a recent event in Madrid. A few weeks ago there was a kind of 'tag team' bullfight; two bullfighters working together against one bull. During the contest one of the bullfighters started criticising the other one's technique. This caused great offence, and an argument quickly developed between the two of them. Then, to the astonishment of the crowd, the matadors lost interest in the bull and started to fight each other.

It was nothing but a gimmick, says Lorenzo disparagingly. He shows me a newspaper photograph of the bull watching nonplussed as the two bullfighters slug it out in the middle of the ring. Fortunately, he says, these disgraces have occurred outside Andalusia. He assures me that they cannot happen here. He tells me that he watched some bulls the other night which had come from the same strain as his more than forty years ago. I ask him how it had been. He shakes his head sadly and says, "*Malo . . . muy, muy malo.*"

Because we're living here, I probably should go to the *corrida*. The spectacle of the bullfight is so central to life here that I consider whether going to see it might help me to understand some of the enormous cultural differences we've encountered—the strange structure of the working day, the slow pace of life, the amazing aptitude here for prevarication.

However, I'm not sure that anything will make a difference any more. I suspect that the differences may already be too great. For example, I watched a bullfight on television the other day. They're broadcast daily with full commentary during the season, much as we watch the ice-hockey playoffs at home. The bullfight last weekend was a bloody affair, with an insufferable sameness to the posturing and strutting of the matadors. None of the encounters were really contests at all, each being one-sided and predictable. I concluded that the whole thing was ritual rather than sport, a socio-cultural event that I couldn't see the point of at all. Em says that she sees the point. She thinks the Spanish men have to show that they're smarter than the bulls. I decide not to pass her opinion on to Lorenzo.

In the end Lorenzo doesn't confirm the invitation, and I decide not to remind him about it. Instead, Lorenzo invites us out to his estate for lunch. Sunday lunch in rural Andalusia is a late afternoon meal and quite formal. We hire a car for the occasion, and arrange to rendezvous with Lorenzo at noon at the Puerta de Jerez roundabout, near Rubiales' office, so that he can show us the way. When we get there, another couple is waiting by the big roundabout, and we meet Xandra and Manito for the first time. Manito is a composer, and a chain smoker of cigarettes, a handsome man with spectacles and long, slender fingers. Xandra is tall and elegant, a fashion designer. Lorenzo turns up late, and leads us out into the countryside at breakneck speed in his jeep.

The journey takes an hour and a half on narrow country roads. I drive the whole way with my foot to the floor in the little underpowered Seat we've rented, hanging onto the trail of dust from Lorenzo's wheels, trying desperately to keep him in sight.

Lorenzo's hacienda sits at the base of a hill, far out on the plains near Moron de la Frontera. Lorenzo's parents-in-law greet us when we arrive, and the proceedings begin immediately with fine sherry. The family has extensive financial interests in sherry. Pascual, the father-in-law, is probably in his early eighties, a well-built, fit-looking man with thinning hair. His face is creased and furrowed; it's an intelligent face, full of seasoning and character. His wife is tall and stately, and speaks beautiful English with an easy grace. Her unhurried movements give her a strong, understated presence.

The main house is an old converted sherry press, a building which has been magnificently renovated. Thick throw rugs are scattered across the stone floors, and the furniture is a casual mixture of wicker and oak. The plaster ceiling is held in the grip of great oak beams that are check-marked with age. Beanbag cushions are strewn about the rooms, and the stone fireplace is big enough to walk into. The restoration is tasteful and discreet, not at all opulent. The back door is open, a cool breeze wafts a scent of flowers into the house, and we can glimpse a patch of green lawn, and the sun-bleached prairie beyond.

The palate-stimulating, pre-lunch sherry is followed by quantities of a surprisingly full-bodied Andalusian wine. Our hosts are exquisitely courteous, and curious about Canada, the World Fair, what we think of southern Spain. The curiosity is genuine and not simply politeness; this is a family with international interests. After the drinks we're ushered through to the dining room and seated around a massive dark-oak table. It is 4:30. A small posse of servants stands discreetly against the walls of the room waiting to bring in the food, and more drink.

The main course is a kind of poached egg dish on a bed of spinach—very lightly cooked. It's a typical Andalusian meal, but I recognise a similarity to the 'Drappit Eggs' that are festooned around the pullet in a traditional Scottish dish called Howtowdie. These culinary coincidences arise all over Europe. Differences in customs, manners and food are often differences of shade rather than colour, passed across borders by the political and social alliances of history.

Bread and more wine accompany each course. The maids—four of them, each impeccably dressed in white—hover around the table. Lorenzo's wife's brothers and sisters arrive from various towns across the south of Spain during the meal, and join us at the table. They're casually dressed, unaffected and charming, each with the easy confidence that comes with a good education and lots of money. They all speak perfect, almost accentless English.

Lorenzo's father-in-law tells Em that he subscribes to more than a dozen English language periodicals. He's been a great traveller all his life, and recounts tales that suggest he's won and lost the family fortune several times. He talks more easily with women than with men, and seems like a man who's never been afraid to choose sides, sometimes wisely and sometimes not.

After lunch we all move out into the garden and a waiter brings more wine. Lorenzo's father-in-law confides that he was a supporter of Generalissimo Franco, although, he adds, this is not something he mentions now in public. Even though the Spanish Civil War was fought nearly fifty years ago, the divisions it created still run very deep through Andalusian society.

Then, fuelled with post-prandial conviviality, Pascual leans back in his lawn chair and takes us off to a time when he had an interest in ocean-going ships.

At the end of the Second World War, he says, he was involved with an escape route called the Rat Line. It was run out of Genoa and several small Mediterranean ports in northern Italy, and it was operated, as far as he could tell, by some officials in the Vatican—although he didn't find that out until later. Its purpose was to spirit Nazi war criminals out of Europe before they could be captured and tried for war crimes. Spain was a neutral non-combatant, but Franco was sympathetic towards Germany and his government secretly supported the effort to set up the line.

Scruffy and incredibly dirty Germans would turn up on the wharf; dishevelled and bent, frail and grey, as if they'd aged mightily from the trauma they'd experienced. Pascual would send members of his crew down to help this human detritus up the gangways onto the ships. But always, just as they were about to come aboard it seemed that each of them had one or two big cabin trunks that had to be retrieved from the shadows, or carried up from a safe house nearby. By this time, Allied security forces were watching most of Europe's seaports, and these trunks had to be brought on board at night, and hidden away deep in the ship's hold.

Pascual lights a small cheroot, and takes a sip of Fundador brandy before continuing.

The Germans stayed out of sight below decks as the ship left harbour and set course for the open sea. They remained hidden as the boat sailed past Sardinia, across the heart of the Mediterranean and out through the Straits of Gibraltar. When they started to encounter the big Atlantic swells the captain announced that they'd reached international waters. Then these beaten men would call for their travelling trunks to be brought up from the hold. They pulled out their dress uniforms and put them on and within minutes they were transformed, strutting around the ship as if they owned it. The trunks were packed with money, jewels, paintings and other wealth, and for the rest of the journey these passengers demanded the finest food and champagne and the most expensive drinks. They would sit up half the night drinking toasts to the Fuhrer and giving the Nazi party salute, and carrying on as if they still stood at the centre of the world they'd known; as if it was all still theirs.

Pascual says he often wondered about the origins of these valuables as the high-ranking Nazis crept off the ship two or three weeks later onto the wharves at Sao Paulo, Montevideo, Buenos Aires or any of the smaller South American ports to which he transported them.

I think Lorenzo's father-in-law made a lot of money out of the Rat Line.

House Hunting

We've been searching unsuccessfully for accommodations of our own since we got to Seville a couple of months ago. The apartment at the Plaza Ruiz de Alda is much too small; there's no space in it for Em to have a study, and Xan is outgrowing her little travelling cot. She needs a proper bed and a room of her own, and most of our belongings are still in boxes and suitcases. Besides, the company has told us that it will no longer keep paying our rent—an exorbitant two thousand dollars a month.

We start our hunt for a new apartment in the Barrio Santa Cruz, the old Jewish quarter of Seville; a labyrinth of narrow alleyways which burst periodically out into gifts of tiny, balanced squares brimming with bright flowers and sunlight. We explore it in the evenings with friends, and examine its tiny *tapas* bars and cafés, and from such aspects as these we contemplate life within its pleasant confines.

Parts of the barrio are very run down, but it is only a short walk from the city's main business district. Its thin, twisting streets insulate it well from the hum and buzz of the city's traffic, the impatient honking of car horns and the incessant wailing of security alarms.

Unfortunately, the barrio has started to become fashionable and the rents are rising astronomically. Several foreign embassies have established offices there, and Rodolpho has mentioned that several government agencies are now eyeing its precincts. We soon discover that we are too late; the centre of Seville is too rich for our wallets and so we direct our search out towards the periphery of the city, even as far afield as the old railway station near the Expo site—the *Stacion de Cordoba*.

The World Fair has changed everything in Seville. Properties are for sale at outrageous prices, often four or five times what they were a year ago. Homeowners are willing to rent, but they want rental fees of thousands of dollars a month for the most basic and rundown places. It's as if everyone has suddenly seen the glint of gold. We hear of landlords who will deliberately keep a house empty in order to score a $4,000 monthly rental for two months during the summer of the Fair, when they could let the place for $2,000 a month on a twelve month lease and come out well ahead. Rationality has gone out the window, as if a high rental price has become a matter of prestige amongst landlords.

Eventually we find an apartment that lies directly across the busy Avenida de la Borbolla from the Plaza Ruiz de Alda, where we are living now. In fact, if we lean out of a back window we can just see the Plaza. We decide to take it at 150,000 pesetas, plus *Communidad* of 13,000 pesetas a month. This comes to approximately $1500, plus $130 a month in strata charges. It's a big apartment, with four bedrooms, a maid's room, and a study. There are three bathrooms, one of them for the maid. Each of the two main bathrooms contains an enormous bathtub, a shower, a bidet and a toilet. The floors are marble, which will keep the apartment cool in summer.

The Presence of Absence

I've been working hard at the office for weeks now, helping to set up the company, making business contacts, finding my way around the bureaucracy of the Expo Corporation, and organising our new premises. It's time for a break before Em and Xan and I move into our new apartment. Besides, the weather is heating up, the temperatures already climbing into the mid thirties. We take advantage of one of Seville's numerous *'puentes'* and head for Lisbon, which we can reach in five hours from Seville.

These *'puentes'* are the only kind of public holiday that Andalusians seem to have. Literally translated, the word means 'bridges'. Public holidays are never taken here on a Monday or a Friday, but always on a Tuesday or a Thursday. At first we thought this was inconsiderate, designed to stop people from taking a long weekend. But soon we discovered it to be an arrangement of Andalusian brilliance, as the Spanish simply take the first (or last) day of the work week off as well, to create the bridge.

We rent a little white car from an agency in a cramped back street off *Calle Florida*. Like the last car we hired, this one is also a Seat—a cheap Spanish car made under licence from Fiat. I check it out carefully before driving it away, because the one we rented when we went to Lorenzo's hacienda ran out of gasoline before it had gone a block from the garage. On the only other occasion we rented a vehicle here, on a day we wanted to go to the beach, the car weaved unsteadily out of the city on a set of badly deflated tires.

It takes us a while to find the road we want to take. Although most cities in the world have maps which show north at the top, Seville's maps have west at the top, with the river running right to left, and thus apparently east to west, when in fact it runs almost directly north to south. All the city's maps are oriented this way and none of them show the international arrow symbol for north anywhere. So simple directional matters like north and south, and east and west present problems, and cause confusion. We never find out why the maps are printed this way, and eventually surmise that it's simply because it makes the city look tidier and more structured on paper.

The road to the border winds up into green hills scattered with cork oaks and healthy-looking sheep. The air is cool up here, a welcome contrast to the dust and heat of Seville. We can choose either of two main routes to Lisbon. Rosal de la Frontera, and Badajoz to the north, are both crossing points into central Portugal. We decide to take the turnoff to Rosal de la Frontera as it carries us quickly away from the busy main roads.

Not far from the Portuguese border we come upon an accident at a place where the road is narrow and grass-edged. Fields rise up on either side to low hills, and the road descends gently towards a stream crossed by a narrow stone bridge. On both sides of the bridge the road is dead straight for at least a mile, with no curves to restrict visibility.

Two cars are locked together on the bridge. Huge pieces of masonry have been knocked from the parapet and one of the cars is teetering dangerously over the gully. The other car is badly crumpled, and steam is rising in clouds from its broken radiator. It looks as if the two cars have raced each other to the bridge from opposite directions and tried to pass in a space only wide enough for one of them, neither driver wanting to give way. The road is now completely blocked and we're miles away from the nearest tow truck. The occupants are standing beside the wreckage looking sheepish and dragging at cigarettes. Neither driver will look at the other.

After half an hour a local farmer turns up and hitches a carthorse to one of the cars. The horse strains at its traces and pulls the battered car a few feet to one side with teeth-grating scrapings of metal. There is just enough room for us to edge past and cross the bridge, and we leave the occupants of the broken cars standing in a small, forlorn cluster, staring at the second car, which remains balanced delicately above the stream.

A few miles further on we cross into Portugal. When we told our Spanish friends that we were coming here they shook their heads and gravely told us that Portugal had gone to rack and ruin. Their comments were almost universally disparaging.

"You'll be on your own if you venture over there," they said. "We won't be able to do anything to help if you get into trouble."

As we drive away from the little whitewashed border post the change is quite palpable, the contrast between the two countries stark and immediate. Portugal is clean, the houses fresh and whitewashed, with roofs of red terracotta tile. Flowers grow profusely in neat gardens. The drivers are polite and give sensible signals, and the cars here are newer than they are in Seville and much better cared for. It feels as if we've arrived back in Europe after a long stay on an impoverished continent.

We drive fast to the Atlantic coast, where the road takes us up a long hill to the huge suspension bridge which spans the River Tagus. When I was last here this bridge was an idea on the drawing board. Now it soars high above the river narrows on massive steel towers, and Lisbon rises up like a painting on the north bank.

This ancient seaport is a greatly under-recognised city. Its vitality alone should place it in the pantheon with Paris and

Rome and London. Red-roofed houses stagger up from the river in an intricate variety of alleyways and terraced lanes. It is a city built on steps, and life here seems to go on in layers, the geography of the place making for interesting dances, full of colour and life-affirming character, and a strange, questing energy. Battered blue and yellow and red trams vie with taxis and cars for space in the narrow, teeming streets below the city's hills, and it seems sometimes as if all the peoples of the Mediterranean and North Africa live here.

We follow the winding coast road through Monsanto Park, and out towards the village of Cascais at the mouth of the estuary. The little train from Cascais passes by, running along between the road and the shore, all the way back up the river to Lisbon. In the years since I lived here Cascais has become part of the city's commuter belt. Today's train looks modern, with contoured silver carriages like American Airstream trailers. It's a far cry from the old wooden carriages with open sides and hard slatted seats that I rode on with my German friend Hado all those years ago when I was fifteen and he took me to meet his friend, the lovely Hohenzollern princess, on the Avenida de Liberdade in Lisbon. As today's train cruises past I can see that it still has a certain charm, but in a functional, suburban sort of way.

Down by the fisherman's beach in Cascais the old Café Tavares was demolished in the early 1960's. Now the Hotel Baia overflows the spot and takes up most of what used to be the village square. We arrange at the front desk for a room, and find that the hotel is still owned by Mr. Soares, who ran the original café and once worked with my father at the airport. Mr. Soares is an old man now, although he looks fit and tanned. He remembers me from those far off days and recalls that I became friends with his son Antonio. I remember Antonio, but I remember even more that Mr. Soares had a beautiful daughter, although I can no longer recall her name.

"How is your father?" he asks. Then, "Why does he never come to visit me?" Without waiting for an answer he carries on. "Tell him there is always a room for him in my hotel. Always. I would like to see him again."

There is something different about Mr. Soares which is more profound than the passing of the years. It is some time before I can sort out what it is. His whole demeanour has changed from subservience to equality in the years since I saw him last. There is a big difference between a café owner and an hotelier, but it is more than that. Mr. Soares personifies somehow a more confident, more mature Portugal that has emerged over the intervening years.

When I lived here I was only just in my teens, and my father worked as the BOAC Station Manager at the airport in Lisbon. Portugal was a fascist dictatorship, and President Salazar lived in Cascais. I used to walk past his house on my way home from the beach. His garden was populated with small grey concrete statues, and once in a while I'd see one of his guards, with a sub machine gun hanging on a strap from his shoulder. There were enough stories about Salazar to suggest that his regime was less than benevolent. But Portugal was overshadowed then by Spain next door, a Spain which was also a dictatorship, with Franco exercising an even more authoritarian grip over his people.

Mr. Soares issues an order to his staff and we are taken upstairs to a small corner suite overlooking the harbour. A bowl of fruit stands on the table—fresh apples and oranges, cantaloupe and grapes and melon. A salty sea breeze plays with the curtains in the open window.

When I first came here the young Portuguese girls completely bowled me over. All the young people did, with their colourful clothes and infectious gaiety. They lived on the beach all day, and only went home when it was dark. They looked out for each other and generously allowed me into their circle. The old coral-coloured beach café is still here, where we danced to the songs of Caterina Valente, and someone crooning 'Volare'.

The jukebox has gone now, and the bar which sold soft

drinks and potato chips has been replaced by vending machines. In the evening I ask Mr. Soares about Stoffel. Stoffel was my closest friend when I lived here. He was tall and spare and ascetic, with sleepy eyes and an early, wispy growth of beard on his lugubrious face. Stoffel came from a poor family and, incongruously for someone so young, always wore a rumpled, threadbare suit. All the other kids wore beach clothes and bright t-shirts. But Stoffel knew many things. He was thoughtful and intelligent and the others used to ask him to mediate their disputes. Stoffel was interested in ideas. I felt strangely honoured by his friendship and I wrote to him for a long time until we eventually lost contact. Over the years I often wondered what had become of him.

"Ah, Stoffel," says Mr. Soares when I ask him. "I remember him. Francisco Stoffel." He gazes at me for a long moment and a faraway look comes into his eyes. "He became a famous *fado* singer. You know *fado*? It is the traditional folk music of the poor people and the gypsies in Portugal; sad music."

I remember *fado*. I can still hear the mournful notes of a guitar in the narrow lanes of Cascais on soft nights, and a woman's voice singing of pain and loss. The songs seemed to seep out of the stones themselves. *'Saudade'* is the word the Portuguese use to describe the sense of *fado*. It is a word that cannot be translated into English. The meaning of it is missing someone, but it speaks more of feelings than meanings. Someone once called it *'the presence of absence'*.

"I thought it was only sung by women."

"It used to be. Traditionally. But men sing it too now."

"Does he make records; tapes?" I ask, thinking I can buy some.

"I think so. I don't know." Mr. Soares pauses, and shakes his head very slightly. He makes an unconscious movement with his hand across his chest. "But Stoffel, he was killed in a car crash about five years ago."

✦

The condominium blight has reached Cascais and the rich, scented pinewoods which overlooked the ocean above the town have given way to glossy new apartment blocks. Our old house still sits along the road to Malveira da Sierra, up the hill past the small rococo estate where President Salazar used to live. The house is shuttered and sad, its plaster cracked and peeling, the garden tangled and overgrown, and I turn away—remembering when it had a gardener and a cook and a handyman and sweet smelling flowers and a small, cropped lawn, and my father sitting on the *stoep* with a newspaper on his lap and a glass of beer at his elbow.

Fishermen still pull their brightly painted open boats up on the sandy beach in front of what remains of the square. They stir early these fisherfolk, and ready their boats for the morning catch well before dawn. By the time most of the hotel guests are awake they've already hauled their boats back out of the flat, metallic sea and are shaking out their nets to dry.

Beyond the village, up the coast road to Guincho, lies the *Boca do Inferno*. This great erosion in the rocky coastline funnels Atlantic swells into towering waterspouts when the tide is high. Local artisans set up booths at the roadside and sell fine lace and woven linens and garish picture works to tourists. We pass an hour browsing among the stalls, and buy some throw rugs to brighten up our new apartment in Seville, to soften the hard marble floors. The prices here are much lower than they are in Spain.

Nearby, Guincho is a place of sand dunes and crashing waves, with the power of the Atlantic pounding in here all the way from the new world. '*Guincho*' is another of these wonderfully descriptive Portuguese words. It means 'the song the swallow makes'. There are always swallows here; dodging along the spray line, swooping among the sand dunes like contour-flying fighter jets.

This beautiful, windswept beach used to be a deserted place, renowned for its chillingly cold seas, virtually ignored by the Portuguese. Now a big hotel stands at the edge of the dunes and it is always full. The wind and cold which used to discourage visitors, now attracts legions of windsurfers from Germany, and Sweden, and all over Europe. Beyond Guincho the brooding weight of Cabo da Roca forces itself out into the ocean, the westernmost point of continental Europe, once the last sight of their homeland for the ancient explorers.

Behind us the wooded hills of Sintra rise up from the plain, turreted with Moorish castles. Up there in the pinewoods the air smells of camphor and there are lakes and places shaded from the heat. The sky is clear and blue-glazed, with the purity and depth of baked enamel. The English poet Southey thought this the original Garden of Eden, and brought his friends Shelley and Byron here. High on the castellated battlements on top of the hills the views are enormous, as if you can see right over the curve of the earth.

I was here too when I was fifteen, and Stoffel came here with me and we raced young and laughing up crumbling stone staircases and gazed down sheer rock walls to the treetops far below. We swam that day at the *Lago Azul* deep in the pinewoods, and thought that this was how life was, how things would always be.

Calle Ciudad de Ronda

Our new apartment is completely empty when we move in. Spanish landlords don't even leave light fixtures—they're the responsibility of the tenant. Bare wires hang dangerously from the ceilings in all the rooms, even in the bathroom. The place is dirty as well, because the air in Seville contains a fine dust which perpetually paints every surface.

We have engaged Antonio the mover to truck our belongings over here from our old flat in the Plaza Ruiz de Alda. Antonio is part of a new breed of Euro-Spaniard. He turns up on time, and works hard. His prices are reasonable and remain true to his original quote. He has a small van and one helper. Antonio is unperturbed to discover that our chesterfield will not fit into the tiny apartment elevator.

"We will have to carry it up the stairs," he says. He looks at me. "You will have to help."

The new apartment is eight floors up a narrow stairway, with tight turns at every landing, four turns to each floor. At each corner the chesterfield has to be lifted and manoeuvred and squeezed between the walls and the railing. By the time we reach the third floor, the sweat is running off me in rivers. At the fifth floor I think I will faint. The chesterfield becomes jammed so tightly at the sixth floor landing it looks as if it will have to be sawed in half.

Antonio ignores the heat and the perspiration and his scraped knuckles on the stair wall. He drops to his knees and squeezes himself between railings, chesterfield and wall, figuring out ways to extricate the couch from the grip of the sixth floor landing. When we finally stagger into the apartment Antonio refuses the offer of a cold drink and disappears downstairs to bring up some boxes. I collapse onto the chesterfield.

We set about filling the rooms with furniture, arranging pictures on the walls. Flanagan lends us a television set from his apartment. It's a temperamental device but it works sporadically—well enough to watch the international rugby matches from Britain, which are broadcast live to Spain with a Spanish commentary. The weekend after we move in to the apartment Scotland wins the Five Nations Championship by defeating England in the final match.

Xan's room is at the front of the apartment, and looks westwards to the rural plateau of the *Aljarafe*. It's the only room with bars on its windows, which is just as well because she's an adventurous soul. At the big *el Corte Ingles* department store in the centre of Seville we buy her a magnificent red bunk bed, with a metal ladder up to the top.

Sound travels through the marble floors from one apartment to another and from time to time we can hear people above us, usually late at night, coughing and laughing and scraping chairs at two o'clock in the morning. This background noise is likely to be a fact of life here, a function of the construction materials that were used. We decide that we'll just have to get used to it—and after a while we find that we don't notice it any more.

Sliding doors open out from the living and dining rooms onto a long balcony with window boxes, and face down a canyon street to the Prado San Sebastian. The Prado is ringed by unkempt plane trees, grey and sick from a relentless infusion of carbon monoxide. It used to be the city's old fairgrounds, but now it's little more than a scruffy dustbowl, used as a great big parking lot on weekdays. About half a dozen wrecked and gutted cars lie out there like props from an abandoned Fellini film set.

Beyond the Prado the rooftops, towers, domes and spires of old Seville stand out against a hot, sun-washed sky. At sunset the city's tiled roofs reflect shimmering, opalescent red and yellow colours. The highest building of all is the old Moorish tower of the Giralda, beside the Cathedral. Every night until eleven o'clock soft lights paint it in ochrous, desert colours which accentuate its elegant lines, and hint at its noble, spiritual purpose. The nearby Plaza de Espana on the other hand is illuminated with heavy-duty quartz iodide floodlights, and jumps out of the night like an extravagant artist's fancy. But the contrast works well, the effect magical, like theatre.

The hills of the Aljarafe rise up in the milky distance beyond the city. Ancient folklore states that the Aljarafe is populated by homosexuals, but the people who live up there today deny this vehemently. From our balcony I can see villages and olive groves and smudge fires through the binoculars. The sun touches these hills each evening, moving along the ridge from village to village, a little further to the northwest each day as we draw towards mid summer.

The Plaza de Espana stands at one end of our *calle*, a semi-circular gem of a building built for the 1929 Spanish-America Exhibition, now military headquarters for the Army in southern Spain. It looks like a building that Walt Disney might have designed, with a sweeping frontage and ornate, pillared and turreted towers at its ends; all of it constructed out of sand-coloured brick and polished ceramic tiles. The front of building is protected by an ornamental moat, crossed by small, curved bridges, which lead up to ornate entrances. The bridges and railings are covered with intricate, expressive tile-work, coloured in soft blues, yellows, and oranges. The great porticos at the rear were used in the filming of Lawrence of Arabia, when the Plaza became for a brief and lucrative time the First World War Headquarters of the British Army in Cairo.

On weekends, the broad sweep of open forum in front of the Plaza is a magnet for tourists and *Sevillanas*, and donkeys draw little rubber-wheeled carts full of excited children across it. Rowing boats ply the waters of its moat, and young couples linger on its Venice-like bridges and gaze dreamily at each other. The Plaza is a place full of life and a soporific kind of energy at the edge of the Parque de Maria Luisa, although once in a while a rock concert or a political speech livens the place up and shakes linen-white pigeons from the nooks and crannies of it's domes and towers. Once we came upon a gypsy wedding inside the park nearby, in a clearing jammed with people, and wild with music and dancing.

Steel-helmeted soldiers carry sub machine guns and patrol the Plaza's precincts day and night. Sentries peer impassively at passers-by through slitted apertures in small, white-painted sentry boxes. They appear to be the model of military decorum, these sentries. Little shakes their solid gaze, their concentration on duty. But Em tells me one day that one of them whistled a low wolf-whistle from the dark interior of his sentry box as she passed, and muttered lewd imprecations to her.

Squadrons of swallows swoop over the rooftops as the sun goes down. They dive acrobatically among the chimney pots and television aerials and washing lines, and soar into the clear sky in bursts of furious energy to catch the last rays of the sun. As the light grows dim hundreds of bats come out and weave unsteadily up the *calle*. They fly out of the belfries of crumbling churches, from the rafters of the old bus station and the tumble of houses and tenement attics in San Bernardo across the railway tracks. Every evening they stagger up the street from right to left, from north to south, on their way to the park to feed on the millions of little flying bugs which live there. The swallows buzz the bats like fighter planes, throwing them off course so that they veer down side streets like partygoers who have celebrated too much.

The *Guardia Civil* patrols the street below us day and night, sitting silently in dark green jeeps or standing about in flak jackets, smoking cigarettes. Sometimes they carry sub-machine guns. We often see a man in a rumpled jogging suit with a blue sports bag. He spends much of his time loitering in the doorway of the apartment building opposite, and for a while we thought him very suspicious. He and the uniformed *Guardia* turn and watch every car that drives down our street—the Calle Ciudad de Ronda. Occasionally we see the man in the jogging suit pull a walkie-talkie from his baggy tracksuit and speak into it. No doubt the sports bag contains armament.

All this, Francisco the *portero* tells us, is because ETA, the Basque separatist organisation, has targeted Seville for terrorist attacks. Francisco is the manager of the apartment complex we live in, a roly-poly man who wears his hair slicked back, *en brosse.* Juan the landlord has warned us that Francisco brooks no nonsense from anyone and runs the block like an SS *Gaulieter.*

High-ranking military officers and their families live on our street, Francisco explains. He assures us that he himself keeps his eyes open for unfamiliar traffic and confers frequently with the *Guardia.* He knows them all he adds confidentially, and they pay attention to his observations, rely on him as part of their team. It is true that the newspapers periodically report some new bombing outrage, but these seem to occur up north, where the struggle for Basque independence is more volatile and immediate. It is difficult at first for us to take seriously the little *Comedia del Arte* that we watch every evening from our balcony; difficult to believe that our neighbours, or the innocent street we look down upon, could be a target for terrorists. But after a few weeks we can see from the grim looks on the faces of the *Guardia* that these things must be taken seriously, and we find ourselves scanning the street for strangers too, and watching the actions of passers-by. We realise then that we have moved from the placid Plaza Ruiz de Alda into the heart of a high-risk, security area. The *calle* is a prime target for ETA.

As the nights become warmer, Francisco moves a large dining table and several chairs out of his little house at the front gate onto the dirt verge beside the road, and sits with his family under the trees each evening until late. The *portero's* family eat their meals there under the gaze of the apartment dwellers. The quantity and variety of food and wine is impressive, the whole procedure animated with conversation and laughter, and neighbours and tenants stop to banter as they pass by, and sometimes take a glass of wine.

Our bedroom is at the back of the apartment, overlooking the Avenida de la Borbolla where the traffic runs all day and all night. We chose this room so that we would have the sunrise in the mornings. However the noise is constant and pervasive and the streetlights are so bright that it's impossible to tell, if we wake up in the night, whether it is midnight, or three a.m., or time to get up.

The Hotel Melia Sol, one of the most exclusive hotels in the city, sits on the other side of Borbolla. Noisy wedding parties dine by candlelight around the blue-lit swimming pool below us on the hotel's roof garden almost every night in May and June.

From our bedroom we can see the Plaza Ruiz de Alda, where we lived when we first came here. Children play everywhere in the plaza, which is surrounded by bars and cafés and shops. It is a convivial place despite the fact that it is surrounded by high apartments and always jammed with parked cars. The newsagent over there always gives Xan a balloon when we go into his shop. Em thinks that this is probably because Xan is fair, while most of the Spanish children have much darker hair.

With the arrival of two technical people to work with Flanagan, three new designers for Knowlton's design department, and a pair of Project Managers to deal with our growing list of contacts and potential clients, there are now ten of us here from Canada, a couple of Americans and three Brits. All of us are taking an hour of Spanish instruction every evening. Our teacher's name is Rosa. She is dark, attractive and street-smart, the best language teacher I've ever had, and she doesn't speak a word of English. Rosa has developed her own teaching techniques. Most of us can understand her now when she speaks to us. Rosa comes from Extremadura—a neighbouring state to the northwest—and she speaks distinctly, unlike the Andalusians, who converse in a rapid-fire, slurred dialect which is very hard to follow.

Flanagan has started to see a lot of Rosa. This will lead to trouble. Rosa is strong-willed, and judging from the way she shuts down any nonsense in her classes, I suspect that she has a Latin temper. Flanagan has a girl friend who is flying out soon from Canada to spend the summer with him. She knows nothing about Rosa.

Flanagan, though, is learning Spanish much quicker than the rest of us.

Semana Santa

Seville's population doubles for *Semana Santa*, the celebrations that are held at Easter. We have been warned about this; that doing business is not a priority here in April. In April, one festival follows another. First comes *Semana Santa*, which lasts for a week. *Sevillanas* use the week after that to recover, and then comes the *Feria*, which lasts for two more weeks. The first weekday after *Feria* is a rest day, but right after that comes May Day, which is a national holiday.

Of all the Easter events held in Spain, Seville's *Semana Santa* is at once the most haunting and powerful. Every church in the city—and there are hundreds of them—holds an elaborate procession at some time during *Semana Santa*. These processions involve the whole congregation and can last for as long as twelve or fourteen hours. The processions wind along set routes through the city's narrow streets to the huge renaissance Cathedral in the centre of Seville, and then slowly wend their way back to base.

The crush of people in the streets during *Semana Santa* is astonishing, and the city's narrow thoroughfares are filled with a strange atmosphere of reverence and excitement, as if a great sporting contest is about to start. Old rivalries simmer just beneath the surface at *Semana Santa*, amid cutthroat ecclesiastical politics. Churches contest fiercely for favourable procession times and routings of preferred significance; parishioners, for prestigious roles and positions.

Two thousand people or more might participate in a single procession, one of which is about to start from a nearby church as we push our way through a heaving crowd to Rosa's little schoolroom in Mateos Gago. We have all brought wine so we can sit out on Rosa's balcony and watch the proceedings in the narrow street below.

"Don't let them see you drinking wine," says Rosa, glancing nervously into the street, "it will offend them and they'll be upset."

The participants file out of the church in two parallel lines. All of them are dressed in black. The first group carries tall staves with unlit candles on top. They use the staves to push back undisciplined onlookers and clear space for the next part of the procession. As dusk steals through the narrow streets, they light the candles one by one.

Several Church Elders walk out with the first group, dressed in white vestments. "The designs on their robes are specific to their rank—to their degree of importance," explains Rosa.

None of the clothing is particularly elaborate, and we can't really tell from the balcony what these designs signify. The Elders are carrying maces and rods of pure silver and gold, engraved with incredible, intricate workmanship. These Elders control the pace and movement of the procession, responding to directions from a Parade Marshal who thumps a heavy staff on the ground to signal everyone to speed up, or slow down or—with three heavy thuds—to stop.

The procession moves at an almost imperceptible pace. A huge *paseo*, or bier, emerges from the front door of the church agonisingly slowly, like a difficult birth. The *paseo* has been built to fit with barely an inch to spare, through the church doorway and into the narrowest of streets along its route, and the bearers who support it have to drop painfully down onto their knees in order to ease it under the lintels. The *paseo* is a construction of great refinement and detail, intricate with gold and silver, decorated with thousands of flowers. The figure of the Virgin Mary sits on top of it, painted with gold leaf and adorned with silver and gold fittings, surrounded by a panorama of flowers. The Virgin's velvet train stretches out behind her, embroidered heavily with gold and silver thread. Rosa tells us that most of the *paseos* in Seville are over a hundred years old, and some of them much older.

The crowd falls silent as the Virgin passes and people loudly shush anyone who dares to cough, or make a noise. All we can hear from Rosa's balcony is the ghostly dragging of hundreds of feet. The night has come down suddenly, and all the candles are alight, the narrow street packed with thousands of onlookers. The slow sound of shuffling feet through the silence is powerful, ethereal. I find that I'm holding my breath.

It requires great stamina and co-ordination to carry these heavy *paseos*. As many as a hundred members of the congregation are bent over underneath each one, and each bearer has vied energetically for the privilege. It is an honour rarely given up once it has been obtained, and the bearers train for the gruelling procession as an athlete does for a contest. Some of the movements they have to make, such as the difficult departure from the church that we witnessed, demand considerable strength and coordination.

Heavy curtains hide the bearers from public view. "It must be pretty hot and stuffy under there," observes Flanagan. "These curtains will hold in all the dust they're kicking up with their feet. It must be impossible for them to breathe."

"*Si*," says Rosa. She insists that we speak in Spanish whenever we're around her, and continues in her own language. "And it's much worse during the daytime processions than it is at night when the temperature is more tepid. Sometimes some of the bearers pass out and have to be helped to the side of the road. In fact the work is so hard that most churches have two full teams of bearers so they can spell each other off."

A murmur goes up from the crowd, and we catch sight of some movement in the darkened doorway of the church as the 'Penitentes' make their entrance onto the street to follow the Virgin. These sinners are all dressed in black, wearing hoods and high pointed hats which reveal only their eyes. Each one carries a heavy wooden cross nine or ten feet high. Some carry two crosses. One staggers out of the little church with seven crosses bound together with electrician's tape. His burden must weigh well over a hundred kilograms, and up on Rosa's balcony Flanagan reaches for the wine and speculates about what the man might have done to require such a measure of penance. He will drag this weight through the city from six o'clock in the evening until two-thirty the next morning. We decide to leave Rosa's balcony to follow the procession behind the huge *paseo* of Christ on the cross, which follows the last of the *Penitentes*. Besides, the wine has run out.

A troop of Roman soldiers in full regalia and a number of the Apostles accompany the Saviour, jostling for space in the narrow street. Christ's *paseo* is less ostentatious than the Virgin's, but is nonetheless filigreed and engraved with precious metals, and decorated with flowers. Candles flutter and sway unsteadily in tall holders on the *paseo* as it moves slowly along. A man in overalls ambles along behind it, carrying a paint-stained stepladder. Whenever the *paseo* stops to give the bearers a rest, the man sets up his ladder and quickly clambers up it to light any candles which have gone out.

Applause breaks out spontaneously from the watching crowd as the Saviour's *paseo* passes them. A Cantor steps through a door onto a balcony and addresses the people in the street. The crowd falls silent and the parade comes to a halt. The Cantor begins to sing in a clear voice. A response comes back from one of the Elders, strong and keen in the night air. The scene, in all its light and shadow, and with its aural accompaniments, sends shivers all the way from the top of my head to my feet, so incredibly touching and powerful is it; so simple and elemental. Then, almost before I'm aware of it, the procession moves slowly on.

Rosa explains that all this activity lies in contrast to the *paseo* of the Virgin, which passes nearly always in silence—except for Mary's procession from the neighbourhood of Triana, the old gypsy neighbourhood of Seville—which is always accompanied by much cheering and merriment.

At the end of the procession comes the band. The bands which follow the processions often contain fine musicians, who have to play while they're being jostled and pushed by crowds trying to get a better view. The band from the church near Rosa's little school contains a rich mixture of clarinets, oboes, brass and drums, and five or six guitars. But we have never seen such enormous crowds behave as well as they do here. *Sevillanas* bring their children out for *Semana Santa*, and many of them stay out all night watching the processions. Despite the crush, the people packed together in the narrow streets and squares seem to treat each other with great courtesy and conviviality.

The authorities block off many of the city's streets during *Semana Santa*. Near the centre of Seville, the whole of the Plaza de San Francisco is given over to temporary stadium seating, which contains a large number of ornate family boxes. All this drives the city's normal traffic chaos into amazing confusions. There seems to be no plan to the revised traffic patterns that are produced by the authorities, and cars and buses become trapped into going round block after block in circuits from which there is no exit. During *Semana Santa* it is always quicker to walk.

Maria Luisa, our maid, tells us that she swore many years ago when she was ill with the birth of her first child, that if she recovered she would go and watch the procession of the *Macarena* every year for the rest of her life. It is the longest procession of all. Now Maria Luisa has eleven children and she always watches all of *La Macarena*, staying up all night, scurrying from place to place to see as much of it as she can.

The Feria

I'm sitting on the balcony outside our living room with a glass of *vino* before dinner when a huge hot air balloon floats silently past. A minute later another one glides by, then another. The three brightly coloured balloons travel sedately through the city haze towards the *Feria* grounds, silent and stately like great galleons in the dying sunlight. One of them drifts dangerously close to the high tower of the Giralda. Another homes in on the big neon *CruzCampo* brewery advertisement on top of a tall office building on the other side of the river at the Plaza de Cuba. But they all manage to avoid disaster, and float slowly over the apartment blocks of Los Remedios before dipping down towards the *Feria*.

Last night was the first night of the *Feria* and searchlights played over the city as if they were dancing to music we couldn't hear: sweeping back and forth, coming together and breaking apart, slowly at first and then faster and faster. It was balletic and haunting, like an old *Pathé* newsreel film of London during the Blitz. *Feria* translates loosely as the 'Fair', but it is much more than that. The whole city throws itself unashamedly into the celebrations and nobody does any work for ten days. The *Feria* is serious business. For weeks now, preparations have been going on across the river at the *Feria* grounds in the suburb of Los Remedios. Workmen have built an elaborate arch ten storeys high out of metal and wood, papier-mâché and plastic. It has been hammered and shaped and painted like the Gateway to Unimaginable Delights—perhaps even to heaven itself. Nearby, the cluttered, rambling fairground has blossomed with noisy rides and booths and colour.

It is unlike anything we have ever seen before. A huge shantytown of *casetas* has sprouted on a piece of dusty waste ground, and been furnished with bars, tables and chairs and carpets, and a whole, instant society of its own. Some of these *casetas* have been finished to a high degree of sophistication, with plaster walls and colourfully decorated wooden fittings. All the *casetas* are party places, some of them large, some small. The biggest ones are like meeting halls, put up by institutions like Sevilla Electricidad, or banks or workers' unions. Law firms have *casetas*; so do clubs, insurance companies and travel agents. Even the city bus company and the post office have *casetas*. Each of the political parties has one (the further to the left, the cheaper the refreshment), as do most of the city's local government precincts. Wealthy individuals in the city erect *casetas* and decorate them with paintings and tapestries and bunting, and then invite friends to visit them while they hold court during the ten days of the *Feria*. Our company lawyer, Juan Goya, has a *caseta*.

Invitations to *casetas* are much prized in Seville, and some people collect as many as they can, as a mark of status. There must be a thousand *casetas* set out in neat rows along the dusty, shanty streets. All the streets are named after famous bullfighters—Belmonte, Ordonez, Manolete, Curro Romero—and every street is solemnly noted on the city map, even though for forty-nine weeks of the year the streets do not exist. Some of the *casetas* are open during the day, and all of them are open through every night of the *Feria*. Each one has an address, and the Post Office will even deliver mail to them during the week of the *Feria*. Most of the *casetas* have doorkeepers to keep out riff-raff. These bouncers check the credentials of everyone who tries to enter. Only the *casetas* which belong to the political parties or the various city districts will let you in without an invitation.

There is food and drink, and music and dancing at every one. In some, the host provides everything and the guests simply help themselves. In others, the refreshment has a price. It's all a matter of great prestige, and long lists are kept at City Hall of people waiting to acquire a *Feria caseta*. The city transit authority lays on hundreds of special buses during the *Feria*. In fact it is difficult to find a bus to take you anywhere else but to the fairgrounds. Taxi fares double overnight. Half the streets in Triana and Los Remedios are blocked off in order to funnel traffic straight to the *Feria*. The congestion is appalling.

The funfair lies just beyond the streets of *casetas*. There are hundreds of rides, and sweet things for sale everywhere to the thousands of children and adults who come here. There are rides which throw people up in the air, others which spin around at fantastic velocity and subject their riders to interplanetary levels of 'G' forces. There are rides which loop the loop, and some which seem to be built purely to try and eject the customers. The dodgems are so powerful that they must have Harley Davidson engines in them, and the Ferris wheel, which towers high over the highest apartments in Los Remedios, has no protective bars to stop its passengers from falling out. It is all very ramshackle, and it's hard not to worry about the fact that it's been erected by workmen who are not noted for their attention to detail.

We take Xan over to the big Ferris wheel and find when we climb in that the shell of the gondola and the seats are made only of thin fibreglass. There is no retaining bar or safety harness, and the sides of the gondola are depressingly low. "It might be a good idea to try something else instead," I suggest.

None of it seems to bother Xan. Em is considering my suggestion, but before we can get out the operator starts the machine and whisks us rapidly up into the blue Seville sky. Half way to the top we notice that the fibreglass body of our gondola is cracked. The contraption continues to spirit us upwards, swinging gently all the time, the wheel gathering speed, going faster and faster even though it is still climbing. Soon it is whirling round at a tremendous rate. Then it suddenly stops, leaving us pitching backwards and forwards high above the city. We start thinking nervously about the thousands of nuts and bolts which are holding the thing together, and the last minute rush with which it was all put together a couple of days ago. Far below us the *Feria* streets are jammed with people, and the most amazing cacophony of noise is blasting up at us from the packed *casetas* and rides. Loudspeakers blare at each other from booths only a few feet apart, and it seems as if every stall and attraction is trying to drown out its neighbours with sound. The Ferris wheel starts up again and brings us slowly back towards solid ground. As we come down we watch riders in black hats and traditional *vaquero* outfits forcing their sleek, immaculately decorated horses through the throng. These men and women enjoy a special status and they know it. We can hear them being hailed from *casetas* as they ride past, and see them stopping to converse and accept glasses of sherry.

It's not surprising that nobody does any work in Seville during *Feria* week, even though only one of the days in the week is actually a public holiday. We find Mr. Ramos, the Managing Director of Siemens, in his office looking very depressed. He comes from Madrid, and cannot cope with the reality of Seville's *Feria*. His staff staggers exhausted into work at noon and departs again at two o'clock, leaving him all alone to deal with telephone calls and demands and deadlines from Madrid and Frankfurt. It's the same all over Seville; people who come from outside the city are overwhelmed by such an overload of festivity.

The morning mail brings me two invitations to *casetas*; one from our corporate partner the Banco Bilbao Viscaya, the other from Juan Goya, the company lawyer. I think I shall wait until

Friday before I go back there. Our international clients will not understand it if we abandon ourselves to the *Feria* as completely as the *Sevillanas*.

The city authorities have built a temporary stadium down in the Prado de San Sebastian, in front of our apartment building. We've been watching with great curiosity as this construction has gone up over the past week, not sure what it might be for. Last night it all became clear. A rock band started playing there soon after the sun went down. The noise was staggering, a deep bass pounding up the street at the apartment, shaking the sliding glass door of the balcony in its frame. The screeching feedback from the amplifiers roused hundreds of bats, upsetting their nocturnal schedules and causing them to rush agitatedly back from the park to their homes in the city's towers and belfries.

The crowd that attended the concert was small. The band had no musical abilities at all, and simply compensated for its artistic deficiencies by increasing the volume. The concert went on until two in the morning. I discovered today that it was an American band called 'Cool and the Gang', and that there are no noise by-laws in Seville.

Today it rained, a hard, tropic rain hammering out of low, black cloud. Thunder ricocheted around the city's buildings and up and down the narrow streets. Lightning flashed horizontally across the sky above the *Aljarafe*. Tonight's concert in our little temporary stadium has mercifully been cancelled, but the *Feria* grounds have hardly slowed at all.

The Andalusian Gourmet

Three more hot air balloons float by the apartment this evening. The *Feria* has been going on for nearly a week and these things are now commonplace. I hardly pay any attention to them any more. However, I watch the balloons for long enough to note that the pilots have badly misjudged the wind. When I last see them they're drifting helplessly off towards the *Aljarafe*, nowhere near the *Feria* grounds.

The streets of Seville are still hopelessly clogged. The authorities change the traffic patterns every day, turning normal thoroughfares unaccountably into one-way streets; reversing one-way systems, closing serviceable roads altogether. The whole city transit system—all the schedules and routings—has been scrambled beyond recognition, all because of the *Feria*. It is very confusing, and the authorities refuse to communicate anything about it to the public.

It must make sense to the *Sevillanas* because the buses are always full and it is impossible to get on board any of them. It is much simpler and quicker to walk everywhere, and probably better for the health. This afternoon I have to attend an Andalusian business lunch, which is designed to impress a delegation from La Rioja, the autonomous wine-producing region in the north of Spain. Our consortium wants to open negotiations about building the La Rioja pavilion for Expo '92. We are keen to win the contract.

A number of dignitaries, led by Senor Perez Soria, an important government official, have flown down to Seville from Logrono, the capital of La Rioja. As far as I can tell, there are three senior civil servants in the group, four politicians from the La Rioja Provincial Assembly, and three *empresas*—businessmen. Our business partner, the Banco Bilbao Viscaya, has sent down their top man from Madrid, *el Director Comercial*, Senor Luis Catalan de Ocon. It is to be a classical, formal Andalusian, politico-business lunch, with the proceedings conducted entirely in Spanish.

After drinks we're all ushered upstairs to a private room in the exclusive restaurant that has been selected for the lunch. Luis and I have become friends, as well as colleagues, and I decide to rely on his judgement and advice in culinary matters. Luis is a quiet, thoughtful man with impeccable manners. He dresses in elegant, well-cut suits and speaks knowledgeably about history and customs, and the arts. I trust him completely. Besides, he is tall and slim, and obviously not given to gastronomical excess.

A cream of gazpacho soup comes out first, served much like a very thick, chilled tomato juice. However it's now four p.m. and I'm starving. The preliminaries have dragged on for hours and my stomach has never really adjusted to the late Spanish lunchtimes. I've been ready to eat since noon.

I knock back two big glasses of gazpacho and a bread roll with butter. Big plates of cut meats and cheeses are brought in. I help myself to several slices of meat and another bread roll. After that there's a lull in the gastronomical parade and the conversation ebbs back and forth across the table. A waiter comes out and pours more wine. So far no one has mentioned the World Fair. All the talk is about the *Feria*. Apparently the delegation from La Rioja was entertained at the BBV *caseta* last night and had a grand time.

Half an hour after the plates of sliced meat a waiter carries in three enormous platters of cold potatoes, shrimp and chopped onions. Another waiter follows him, staggering through the swing door with two huge dishes overflowing with crayfish. I assume that this is the main course and fill up my plate. These dishes of seafood are wonderful, and the Spanish prepare them superbly. I eat heartily and finish my wine, slump back in my chair, stifle a belch and congratulate Luis in my bad Spanish for the outstanding meal. He smiles, pleased.

To my surprise the door swings open again and two waiters come in, bent double under massive platters of lamb and crispy, fried seafood. The lamb is served not in the delicate slices we are used to in North America, but in big chunks that seem to have been hacked from the haunch with a blunt machete. As our host, Luis takes it upon himself to act as server. While my attention is distracted by one of our guests Luis loads my plate generously. Conversation among the Spanish diners barely slackens through all this. However I have ceased to participate. I need all my concentration to do what is culturally, socially and gastronomically correct, and to stay awake. It is considered bad manners in Andalusia to refuse the food placed in front of you. Through a haze of over-indulgence I can see that my helpings are no larger than those of my colleagues, all of whom are busily working their plates, and chatting happily.

By the conclusion of the lamb and seafood course I am completely immobilised, a condition which has nothing to do with the wine which, uncharacteristically for here, has slowed to a trickle. One of the waiters spirits my empty plate away and almost immediately his colleague bursts through the door with even more food, on an even larger plate than the one which has just been taken away. He places a massive leg of lamb in front of me with a flourish; a whole leg, like a hindquarter I might buy from the butcher to last for a summer.

By now I'm speechless, unable to protest. The waiter hands me a wicked, broad-bladed Bowie knife. I eat doggedly on, like a contestant in one of those food-stuffing contests. When the proceedings finally conclude at six-thirty in the evening, I take a taxi home. Luis calls later to tell me that the lunch meeting has been a great success.

Flan-aa-gann

Our Technical Director's name is Flanagan. He's young, brilliant and has a string of successes to his credit. Not yet thirty, he has light and sound credentials for international hits like *Phantom of the Opera*, *Aida,* and the Winter Olympics. He has even worked with the people from La Scala in Milan.

For a while now we've noticed that local people chuckle politely when they're introduced to Flanagan. We've sometimes wondered why, but the mirth has always been subdued and polite.

Flanagan comes with me to Manito's house. Manito, who I first met on the day we went out to Lorenzo's hacienda, is a composer and a technician. He is wildly eccentric and something of a genius. His face lights up when I introduce him to Flanagan and he starts to laugh. His laughter turns into a kind of stuttered hooting and he starts to shake uncontrollably. Tears run down his face. This goes on for several minutes. When he recovers himself he grabs Flanagan with both hands and hugs him. Normally, Manito is completely undemonstrative.

When he's calmed down I ask him to explain the joke.

He looks at me gravely and turns to Flanagan and says, "Aaaah . . . Flan-aa-gann. *Magnifico!*" Then he explains, moving his hands in big circles, shaping his words. Flanagan is the name in Seville for Superman. Flanagan is the wild man who bursts through the saloon doors, shoots the gun out of the bad man's hand, rescues the woman who's tied to the chair and puts all wrongs to right. Flanagan is Robin Hood and the Lone Ranger. There is no problem or difficulty that cannot be overcome by Flanagan, no magic that cannot be performed.

No one in Seville is called Flanagan. It is not a Spanish name. "Flan-aa-gann . . ." concludes Manito admiringly, "*es fantastico!*"

This explains some of the odd things that have happened over the past few weeks. Important people from the Expo Corporation have called and asked, not for the company President or one of our senior Vice Presidents, but for Senor Flan-aa-gann. We have a special relationship with Siemens, the giant German multi-national company. Senor Ramos, the Managing Director of Siemens in Seville will do almost anything for Flanagan. The two of them have become great friends despite a thirty year disparity in their ages. We have inadvertently brought a priceless asset with us to Spain; one that our competitors cannot hope to match. But Flanagan now has an image and a reputation to live up to.

I'm sitting on the balcony, gazing out at the city through a forest of television aerials on the roofs of the apartments in front. It is late and the floodlights are playing lazily over the night sky. The air feels cool although the temperature is still well over thirty degrees centigrade.

At eleven o'clock the floodlights on the Giralda go out, and the searchlights from the Plaza de Espana are extinguished. The darkness is immediately pulverised by a loud electronic shriek from the temporary stadium down on the Prado. The stage lights come up to reveal a small crowd of people wrapped in a purple haze of smoke. Six musicians climb up on the stage and a pianist begins to play. Within seconds he's worked himself into a passion, pounding frantically on the keyboard. The frenzied energy of the performance and the battering-ram style sound vaguely familiar to me. Then it comes, loud and clear, charging up the canyon street right at our balcony. *"Great Balls of Fire."*

Tonight's performer is the legendary Gerry Lee Lewis.

I reach in through the window of Em's study, pick up the telephone and dial a number in Canada. One of my friends is an unabashed admirer of Gerry Lee and when he answers his telephone eight thousand miles away I hold the red Telefonica handpiece out at the night, transmitting the ageing rock legend's music live to the Pacific coast. When the piece finishes my friend tells me he has never heard Gerry Lee sound better. "It must be great," he says, "to have free concerts right outside your house every night."

Heaven.

Robert Bringhurst telephones to say that he is coming to give a lecture at the University of Seville. Can we offer him a bed? Robert is a fine writer, poet and scholar from Canada's west coast, a man with a fascinating, wide-ranging intellect. We've known him for years. He arrives on the day of his lecture and immediately sets off to scout out the university, which is located in the old Tobacco Factory featured in Bizet's opera *Carmen*, across the Prado de San Sebastien from our apartment. He comes back and announces that the arrangements for his talk are virtually non-existent. No one seems to know where he's supposed to speak, and the university's scheduling is so vague and muddled that no one will be able to find out where the lecture is being held. Besides, he doubts that the Andalusian students will be much interested in the Haida of the Queen Charlotte Islands, which is the subject he's going to speak about.

When the appointed time arrives Robert manages to find the correct room, and is astonished to find that the place is packed—and not only with students. Many faculty members have turned up to hear Robert's lecture as well. Apparently they are fascinated with the idea that native people live in Canada.

It had never occurred to them. Considering Spain's genocidal colonial record this is perhaps unsurprising.

The lecture is a rousing success, and immensely scholarly and knowledgeable. Robert speaks fluent Haida, and in his lecture he talks for a minute or two in this ancient language, which sounds both magnificent and incongruous in this setting, in the heart of one of the oldest universities in the world. The Spanish are riveted, their eyes fixed on Bringhurst, rapt with attention as he quotes from the oral mythology of the Haida bard John Skaay and explains that the stories he's telling were catalogued by the anthropologist John Swanton a hundred years ago. At the same time Robert's talk gently conveys the power of the intellectual and spiritual gifts that the new world offered the old, which is something of a revelation to the Spanish—most of whom still believe that their conquests were benevolent.

In the end we realise that we're probably the main beneficiaries of Robert's talk, when a Spanish friend tells us that most of the students only attended it in order to try and improve their understanding of the English language. Robert's foray into Haida must have baffled them. But Robert's visit brings us a breath of home, and his lecture offers something of a bridge between cultures—the west coast Aboriginal, the Spanish and the English-speaking—which have caused each other a lot of pain over the centuries.

I've now heard Robert read on three continents: Australia, North America and Europe. The only other person I have heard reading their work on three continents is my wife. This puts Robert in high company and it pleases him when I remark on it. We repair to a bar under the jacaranda trees beside the Murillo Gardens, and drink beer and try to talk over the din of passing traffic. Robert cannot get used to the noise in Spain. This is not surprising, as he lives on a forested island off British Columbia's coast, a place known for its ethereal silence.

Robert's schedule has been so hectic that when he arrived here on Friday from Barcelona, he hadn't slept for three nights.

On Saturday evening we took him over to the studio of our artist friend Mercedes. Robert fell asleep on her floor studying a picture entitled 'Relaxation'. Mercedes was pleased. On the night before he leaves we sit out on the balcony before dinner with drinks, watching the sun sink down over the *Aljarafe*. Every evening at this time the Spanish flag is lowered at the nearby Plaza de Espana. An honour guard of two soldiers marches out from the administration block. One of them takes down the flag; the other plays Taps on his trumpet. It can be a haunting moment. Tonight the trumpeter doesn't quite reach some of the notes and discordant sounds echo down the street. Pigeons launch themselves off the ledges of the apartment buildings and circle the *calle*. I make an apologetic comment to Robert about the trumpeter's inadequacy.

"Oh, that's just fine," says Robert. "At least you know he's real. When I was in Panama doing service in the U.S. Army I used to play 'Taps' every night. I played it the same way everyone else there played it. Perfectly. I took the 'Taps' cassette out of its case, slid it into the tape deck and pushed the play button. If the machine was working, it played. If it wasn't working, there was silence."

Later on another band turns up at the little performance stadium on the Prado. It starts punctually at eleven p.m. The noise is ferocious. At bedtime we offer Robert a choice of rooms, the band at the front or the traffic at the back. He chooses the traffic and sleeps hardly at all. The band closes down at two; the traffic goes on all night. In the morning he leaves for Edinburgh and the Outer Hebrides. It will be a trip into tranquillity, but there are no orange trees on Barra.

The Doctors

A mysterious virus has hit Seville, and Canadians are dropping like flies. Only four of us have made it into the office in the last week. The rest are in their beds, under the care of Doctor Brioso.

Andalusians swear that garlic has medicinal powers against colds and influenza and our Spanish colleagues are completely unaffected by the ailment. So far I feel fine, but I've been eating garlic furiously and swallowing industrial doses of vitamin C.

The President of the company has now gone down with the virus and his temperature is over a hundred degrees. The office manager is in bed. Em is sick. Even Flanagan's Superman aura has been dented. His temperature has hit a worrying 104. There must be a different species of bug here, one that knows how to circumvent our Canadian immunities.

The virus seems to strike at the beginning of a holiday or a weekend, times when prescriptions are difficult to fill because most of the drug stores are closed. However Seville's pharmacists have developed a clever system to ensure that one or two or them are always open in these circumstances. Every Friday afternoon they post the addresses and telephone numbers of the Duty Pharmacies in the windows of all the others.

Xan is having trouble with the alien bugs she's encountering in southern Spain. We have had to call Doctor Brioso in to see her at least twice a month. Dr. Brioso is a transplanted Rumanian, a large kindly man with pockets full of candies for his child patients. Doctor Brioso's solution to every ailment is to dish out a pocketful of sweets and write a prescription for penicillin. Our daughter loves him.

We are becoming concerned that the flow of penicillin from Doctor Brioso will inhibit the development of Xan's own immune system. Our friend Xandra suggests a visit to Doctor Moreno, a fully qualified physician who specialises in homeopathic medicine. I'm sceptical about these alternative practices, but Em and Xan go off to see Moreno and within two days they're both cured.

Doctor Moreno's attentions to Xan have caused a marked improvement in her general condition as well. Now, instead of coming down with a succession of earaches and flu-like bugs every ten days, she's become her old cheerful self once again.

On a visit one day with Xan to see Doctor Moreno, I notice him staring at me. "How about you?" he asks. "Are you feeling all right? You look pale."

"I'm fine," I tell him, "I just have a headache. It'll go away in a couple of days."

"Tell me about it," he says patiently. "Do you get headaches often? How long have you been getting them? How long do they last?"

"I've been getting them for about five years. They last for two or three days then they go away. But it's all right, I know how they work, and as I say, they go away in the end." I'm still unconvinced about Moreno's unconventional expertise and not very keen to try it myself.

Dr. Moreno shrugs his shoulders. "All right," he says. "But I'll get rid of them for you if you want me to. For good."

I don't believe this for a minute. In Canada they've given me prescription Tylenol blockbusters; they've done a brain scan. They've found nothing, and yet these migraine-like headaches return every six weeks or so.

Moreno probes a little deeper. "Tell me about yourself. What sort of things do you eat? What is the work that you do? What kind of hours do you keep?" He prods me along for several minutes.

"Well," he says again, when I finish answering his questions, "I can get rid of your headaches if you want me to."

There doesn't seem to be anything to lose, and in the rising summer heat of Seville the headaches are a daunting affliction. Dr. Moreno leaves the surgery for a few minutes. When he comes back he hands me two small white packets.

"There are three pills in each package," he explains. "Take one package now. Try not to touch the pills with your fingers, and put the pills under your tongue until they dissolve." He watches me while I do this. The pills are tiny, each one the size of a pinhead.

"Now," he continues, "take the other packet in four months time just the same way. Let me know a month after that which one has done you the most good. In the meantime you shouldn't drink any more coffee. Spanish coffee is far too strong and it's not particularly good for you. The only other thing I want you to do is eat an apple every day."

Whatever Moreno has given me—and he assured me it's a natural substance in tiny portions—it works. I experience no more headaches during my time in Spain, and after a while even allow myself an occasional treat of the deliciously powerful Spanish coffee, with a mid-morning 'jamon york y queso'— cured ham and cheese.

Prague

I'm on my way to Prague for meetings about the Czech pavilion at Expo. The taxi driver taking me out to the airport is fed up because Spain lost the World Cup soccer match against Uruguay last night. The team's performance was terrible. *"Malo,"* he mutters sadly, shaking his head.

I had watched the game on television, and heard the whole *calle* erupt with a roar of applause when Spain scored an early goal. The rest of the match was played in silence except for audible moans from the community outside every time the Uruguayans scored. It was obvious just from the street's sound effects that the Spanish team was playing poorly. When the Spanish game was over I watched Scotland being soundly defeated by Costa Rica, a team that was expected to lose to the Scots by many goals. I was told that the Costa Ricans were such rank outsiders that the Edinburgh betting shops refused to take any wagers on the match. The Scots fans, as they sometimes do, started celebrating victory the night before the match. It looked to me as though the players might have done so as well.

I tell the taxi driver that I come from Scotland. This cheers him up. *"Ah, Escocia,"* he says with a derisive chuckle. *"Muy, muy malo."*

The Czech aeroplane carrying me from Frankfurt to Prague is a decrepit Russian copy of a Boeing 727. But everyone on board is cheerful and friendly; a smiling stewardess serves us free bottles of pilsner beer. Great changes have taken place since I was last in Czechoslovakia at Christmastime, a little more than three years ago. Far below us the line of demolished fortifications which once marked the border between west and east runs like a jagged wound across the countryside. Everything is coming down—old border posts and watchtowers, barbed wire and minefields. The Berlin Wall has fallen and Eastern Europe is opening up for the first time since the Second World War.

An election poster for Vaclav Havel is plastered on the window of the Immigration Officer's little cubicle at Prague Airport. It only takes me a minute or two to arrange an entry visa, and the Immigration Officer hands it over with a smile and a receipt for the $10 it costs me. The lady at the money exchange desk chuckles at my bad German and replies in English. A Havel election poster adorns her window as well. Her six year-old son punches numbers expertly into the calculating machine and works out the correct rate of exchange.

Emanuel, who I first met when I came here before, is waiting now outside the terminal with his son Voitja. Emanuel is a little older, but as irrepressible as ever, quick with a grin and a strong handshake.

It's spring and blackbirds are singing all around the car park. The day is warm and sunny; everything is clean and green with vegetation. The taxi driver cracks jokes as he drives us into the city. A change like this was unimaginable three years ago. Emanuel sees the grin on my face and asks me what I'm smiling about. He knows I can't understand the taxi-driver's jokes.

"All this," I tell him. "It's wonderful. It just makes me feel good."

Prague rises up in front of us, possibly the most beautiful city in Europe. It has plenty of bad Soviet-era architecture, but most of that lies in the suburbs. In the old city centre there has been little development for nearly fifty years; a benefit of communism, which unintentionally preserved the ancient city by leaving it alone, in many places to crumble.

When I was here before, the people were depressed and drab and sullen, and hardly anyone would speak in public to foreigners. Now Prague is flowering again, its people dressed in bright colours and fashionable clothes. Red-tiled roofs spill over the city's hills like a Disney fantasy, and streets open out into squares of little shops and cafés full of people; people everywhere, walking, talking, savouring the springtime air.

Prague flows upwards from the banks of the Vltava River, which saunters languidly through the city, crossed by ornate bridges, and adorned with beautiful white swans. The castle and the great, gothic St. Vitus Cathedral sit up on the crest of the ridge, watching over it all.

I've come here for meetings with a Czech design company called Artexim, whose staff have been helpful to us on a couple of technical and design matters. I telephone them from Emanuel's flat, where I'm staying, and they invite me to have dinner with them at the Prague Arts Club, saying that we can discuss business tomorrow.

The Prague Arts Club inhabits a stone building on the riverbank by an old mill lade. It has only just been opened to non-Party members; in other words to real writers, and artists with genuine ability. We have to cross a small bridge to reach the front door. Inside, the place is infused with a fine Bohemian vitality, people are chatting and table-hopping, and a fiddler plays by the window.

"Once in a while," explains Jaromir, who runs the company, "we were able to find ways around the communist government's bureaucratic regulations and get work on overseas contracts. We had to win these contracts on merit in competitive western markets. No one gave us any help. But when we did win, we were able to bring back foreign exchange, and the government liked that. So we slowly gained a few favours, and after a while I think, a certain indispensability.

"Some of our people worked in Canada when the company was called Art Centrum," he continues. "I worked there too. At the time of Expo '86 I designed the interior of the Roundhouse in Vancouver."

The Roundhouse stands now in the centre of Vancouver near False Creek, the oldest building in the city, originally the old Canadian Pacific Railway turnaround and servicing depot. It's a brilliant example of urban industrial reclamation—a social and artistic centre alive now with creative workshops and classes, music and dance and theatre, markets and exhibitions, conferences and local fairs. I know it well, and remember people telling me how astonished they were that these Czechs could fabricate computer hardware and conjure up advanced software applications apparently from thin air, with only a fraction of the technological resources we had in the west.

I ask Jaromir about the Swiss office address on his company's letterhead.

Jordan, who works with him, scratches the side of his nose and smiles. "That's one of the favours Jaromir was talking about," he says. "It's a very small office and we're still not sure why the government authorities here allowed us to have it. And we got something else very important out of the arrangement. We bought a fax machine for the Swiss office—which was easy enough to do in Basel but impossible here. The authorities here didn't know about the fax machine, but after we'd had it for a while we told them about it. They grudgingly gave us permission then to bring another one into our office in Prague so we could communicate with our Swiss office. This became the only privately owned fax machine in Czechoslovakia.

"When things started to move last year in Prague—what the west calls the Velvet Revolution—we told Vaclav Havel about our fax machine and offered him the use of it whenever he needed it. After that he came over to our office every day to send messages to the media around the world."

Jaromir leans back in his chair and gazes up at the high ceiling. "Once the world knew what was going on inside Czechoslovakia the government realised it had to be careful about any crackdowns," he says. "Then it started backing down on some important issues, like free speech and public gatherings. After that it began losing control, and in the end events just moved forward towards the democratic system we've got now. They couldn't stop it."

The international media faxed messages back to Havel at the Artexim office and the revolution in Czechoslovakia received worldwide press coverage. The little grey fax machine was probably his most useful weapon, vital to his ultimate success. "It's still sitting in the office," adds Jaromir. "I'll show it to you tomorrow."

After our meeting the next morning, Jaromir takes me out to lunch at a small, sparsely furnished restaurant near his office. "This is the first privately owned restaurant in Prague," he says. "It would have been impossible to have anything like this a year ago. The authorities would never have allowed it." We select the dumplings and stew.

The Czechs are happy, although they know they have a long way to go. But they trust their leaders and they're finding their spirit. Every surface in the city needs a coat of paint, but there are no paint manufacturing plants in the country and no paint to be found. The grass in the parks is growing fast and untidy, and there are no lawn mowers. Skodas and Trabants belch out black smoke and the roads are full of potholes. The Czech airline is still flying cramped, inefficient Tupolevs and Yaks—obsolete, gas guzzling copies of old Boeing and Douglas aeroplanes. But things here are starting to change; it's in people's eyes, in the air itself.

Emanuel lives with his wife Blanka in a cramped ground floor apartment on Veverkova Street. Their flat has two tiny bedrooms, one of them little more than a storage closet. Sometimes there is water in the taps, sometimes not. Veverkova means 'squirrel' in Czech, and the park where the squirrels live lies just around the corner.

Across the street from Emanuel's flat stands a pub which serves clear, golden pilsner beer in jugs. He brings me in here to watch the Czech soccer team play a World Cup match on television. The patrons are completely absorbed in the game, animated by the action and their national team, which is playing with great flair. No one pays any attention to me at all until Emanuel introduces me to one of his friends. After that everyone is overwhelmingly friendly, and all of them insist on speaking English. The Czechs refuse to let me buy anything—just as they did when I was here before—refuse to acknowledge that a month's salary for them is probably less than a day's pay for me.

Emanuel took part in the student uprisings during the Prague Spring of 1968. He marched in the streets and carried banners. Some of the people I meet in the pub marched too. It all came to nothing in the end, says Emanuel, and afterwards he was often in trouble with the authorities. Now he has a position in the Buildings and Grounds Department at Charles University. He speaks fluent Czech, Polish, Russian and German, as well as some English and French, and earns about eighty dollars a month at his job. Perhaps he can find the motivation to rebuild his life, but I can see it is difficult for him. He has lost thirty years, and much of the energy and optimism of his youth.

When the World Cup soccer match finishes we jump on a tram and head into the centre of the city. The tram is rickety red and yellow, just as the trams were a few years ago, but the conductress who hands me my ticket speaks perfect English. All the people who come on board punch their tickets scrupulously in the manual ticket machine. The system operates on an honesty basis and no one tries to cheat it any more, Emanuel tells me.

The city centre is busy with people but there are no leather-jacketed, black market moneychangers now, no police cruising up and down the streets in cars, staring suspiciously at strangers; no soldiers standing on corners with sub-machine guns. On this bright spring day it is almost impossible to remember how it was only a short time ago.

For forty-five years the state dealt—more or less—with the requirements of Czech society from the cradle to the grave. As a result it is difficult for people here to encompass the idea of private ownership; private enterprise has been banned here for two generations. These generations have never known about incentives for achievement or excellence, opportunities for entrepreneurs. The state didn't require imagination from its people. It never encouraged it; such a thing was considered threatening.

The Czechs need help with all the changes that are underway, but the shop windows are full of bright summer clothes, toys for children, books in bookstores; there's a freshness and energy in the streets. Private enterprise is starting out with small steps, with handcrafted trinkets on sale at little stands on the Charles Bridge, and beautiful music played on street corners for passing tourists by wonderfully talented musicians. Politeness and kindness show up in people's gestures and smiles; concepts of service and quality will no doubt follow in due course.

The people of Czechoslovakia recently elected the playwright Vaclav Havel President of the country, by an overwhelming majority. Despite the utter discredit of the Communist Party however, it was still supported by large groups of miners, who gave it fourteen per cent of the vote. The Party represented the only security they'd ever known.

Emanuel and Blanka have moved out of their bedroom into the tiny closet-room. There's nothing I can do about it; they insist that I must have their double bed. In the morning they wait patiently in the other room for me to wake up. After breakfast they take me for a walk in the park at the end of Squirrel Street, and show me a great, bare plinth where a statue of Stalin stood until a few short months ago. Now it's a place where children play shinny and football, and ride skateboards. We drink warm soft drinks at the park's cafeteria and gaze down at the big brown river as it works its way through the city. When we're finished, Emanuel picks up the garbage lying around the picnic table and drops it in a bin.

Late in the day I leave Prague laden with gifts from Emanuel and Blanka to take back to Spain; gifts full of forethought—a multi-coloured *Sparta Prague* beach ball for little Xan, three china mugs with the *Sparta* club crest, a bright red, yellow and blue *Sparta* towel.

The Cafés & Streets of Old Seville

The streets in old Seville are tight and crowded, the back lanes only wide enough for one car at a time. They twist and turn to no pattern at all, built as they were for horses and people and not for the internal combustion engine. Colourful tobacconist's kiosks are scattered along the wider main thoroughfares, strategically positioned at intersections, festooned with bawdy magazines; little green lottery booths lie in wait to trap passersby. Café tables sprawl across sidewalks, crowded in by parked cars and *motos*. All of it is a jumble to the eye, a confused riot of noise and colour. Gypsy women with tiny children lie languidly in doorways, their hands stretched out for money. Some of them proffer sprigs of thyme and bright flowers for sale, sometimes aggressively. Our friend, Mercedes the artist, says they can put a curse on you if you refuse to buy from them.

As the summer evenings lengthen, horse-drawn carriages slouch against the kerbs waiting for tourists. Parking is a nightmare. Nobody pays any attention to solid yellow lines or 'No Parking' signs. Cars park two, three and four abreast. Drivers return to find their vehicle trapped by two or three others and lean on their horns until someone comes along to let them out. Some people leave their cars unlocked so that people they've blocked in can push the cars out of the way. Sometimes these cars are pushed and left to roll down the road until they collide with other parked cars, or a big garbage scow or some other obstacle.

Drivers ignore painted lane lines and pack themselves five and six abreast at stop lights. Batteries of police complement the traffic lights at every intersection, half a dozen or more, all of them furiously blowing whistles. No one pays any attention to them. Mopeds and scooters weave in and out of the cars, scraping paintwork with their pedals and handlebars. Buses muscle their way down special bus lanes, shouldering everything else out of their way. All the cars and buses in Seville emit clouds of smoke and the noise level from un-silenced motors and honking horns is tremendous. Nobody here pays any attention to car alarms, which wail and scream all day and night.

However, one car owner in our apartment complex has purchased an alarm that is impossible to ignore. The children who play soccer in the street below us are the first ones to discover it. One of them kicks the ball accidentally into this car and it immediately throws a kind of automotive fit. A wailing alarm goes off like an air raid siren and the headlights, sidelights and directional indicators all begin to flash hysterically. Then the car starts rocking up and down, jumping convulsively around on its chassis. The children stare at this extravagant mechanical display in wonder; then, greatly impressed, they pick up their goalposts and move them in front of the car. Now the car celebrates enthusiastically every time one of them scores a goal. I expect the battery will be flat in a day or two.

Occasionally the police decide to enforce the parking regulations and embark on a ticketing *blitzkreig*. As no one pays parking tickets in Seville, the police usually just turn up with a tow truck.

I'm sitting at a table outside the Café Olympia at the Puerta de Jerez enjoying a morning coffee when a policemen rolls up on a fat BMW motorbike. A battered tow truck pulls in behind him, blocking off a lane of traffic. The tow truck driver hops out with his helper, and the two of them slide a kind of cast-iron trolley under a smart Mercedes parked right in front of the café. The café patrons lower their newspapers, put down their coffee cups and turn in their seats to watch.

Manito explained to me the other day that it's the ambition of every motorist in Seville to own a Mercedes. More than any other symbol, a Mercedes Benz signifies success. Mercedes owners in Seville are the only people who wash their cars.

The two blue-overalled tow-truck men crawl around the Mercedes and attach the trolley and a complicated arrangement of hoisting cables. The helmeted policeman sits sideways on his motorbike scribbling notes in his book. The hoist groans and starts to lift the car jerkily forwards. It rises up and up towards the deck of the tow truck and suddenly the wires twang apart and the Mercedes drops, bouncing off the side of the trailer. One of the fenders catches on the edge of the tow truck's deck and tears nearly all the way off. A huge scrape peels a swathe of paint off the passenger door. The Mercedes falls back onto the road with an expensive crash. The suspension appears to be damaged.

A small crowd has gathered. The café patrons sit up straighter in their chairs. Undeterred, the tow-truck men start the whole process again. They attach a new cable and the big car rises slowly up again from the street towards the deck of the trailer. But the new cable parts as well, and drops the car down onto the road with another huge crash. Two hubcaps roll away into the gutter. One of the wheels is bent under the chassis and a jagged crack spreads across the windshield.

The tow-truck men give up, jump into the truck and drive off. The policeman hops smartly onto his motorbike and disappears. A small boy makes off with the shiny hubcaps. The café patrons pick up their newspapers again.

Less than two minutes later the car owner appears. His pace falters as he walks towards the café and then he stops, staring at his battered car in disbelief. He walks over to his Mercedes, moves around it in a wide circle. He wanders distractedly among the sidewalk tables of the Café Olympia, his face turning red as one of the waiters explains the saga of carelessness and damage. Embarrassed, some of the patrons quickly finish their coffee and leave. The Mercedes owner walks back to his car, touches it gingerly as if it is hot, then spins on his heel and hails a taxi.

Sadly, there will be no recourse for him. Margaretha, the most street-wise of the secretaries in our office, tells me later that it takes years for damage suits to reach the courts, and that in any case it's cheaper just to pay for the repairs than to make the payoffs that are necessary to secure compensation.

The theatre of the streets is best seen from a café table, and much business is conducted in the cafés of Seville. Most of the people in this city spend regular parts of the day sitting in them. The waiters wear clean white aprons like tablecloths, fastened skirt-like across their fronts. They float moodily out to the sidewalk tables where they may, or may not, take an order, turning away if they don't like the look of you, to wave at an acquaintance in the street, or simply busying themselves in conversation with a regular customer.

But behind the café counter matters are conducted with great speed and efficiency. Old coffee grounds are taken out of the gleaming silver espresso machine, and a twist and a sharp bang on the base of the machine looses the grounds into a bucket. A fresh batch goes on with boisterous hissing and steaming noises. In a minute the coffee is ready. This Spanish coffee is strong stuff, black and rich and aromatic. In the mornings it is particularly good with *tostadas*; or at lunchtime with a *jamon y queso tostada*, a toasted ham and cheese sandwich.

One lunchtime a platoon of policemen has gathered at the Plaza de Cuba where the new traffic routing is particularly Machiavellian. Instead of simply going round the traffic circle and crossing the bridge, cars are being channelled down a narrow side street into a series of right angled turns and an even narrower backstreet lane before coming all the way back to the river. Motorists honk their horns in frustration at the interminable delays and the policemen blow their whistles angrily amongst all the noise and exhaust smoke.

One of the policemen stands in the middle of the circle like General Patton, white helmet on his head, a short black stogie clamped in his teeth, hands on hips, daring motorists to ignore this complicated, senseless routing. He advances on errant drivers who try to cross the plaza, waves them over to the side of the road and angrily writes out tickets. A taxi driver looks at him hopefully and gives a small salute when he catches his eye. The fierce policeman waves him through.

A small dirt soccer pitch lies down by the river on the other side of the roundabout, below the bridge. Children play there even on the hottest days, chasing after the ball, kicking up puffs of dust with their feet. Rowing eights and canoeists speed over the grey water beside them, and bougainvillaea grows down there in a rampage of purple and white and coral colours.

One morning on my way to the office, with the air still fresh and cool from the night, I drop into a café on Santo Tomas and find there a group of workmen and businessmen, grey suits and blue overalls, standing shoulder to shoulder at the counter in the long morning shadows, drinking tumblers of Fundador brandy before heading off to work.

Later the same morning, Senor Ramos, the head man at Siemens, takes Flanagan and me to a small stand-up café in the lane behind his office in the Avenida de la Republica Argentina. The floor is thick with sawdust and cigarette ends, the customers jammed tightly inside a blue haze of cigarette smoke. Behind the counter the proprietor parades like a football coach, red-faced and overweight, screaming orders through a hatch to the kitchen, all the while scribbling messages and menus and altered prices furiously on a blackboard. He looks like a walking heart attack, biding its time.

I get my hair cut from time to time at a barber's shop next door. The barber himself is a gentle man and always soaks my hair in warm water and washes it before applying his scissors to it. He uses a cutthroat razor when he shaves around my ears, and speaks lovingly of Andalusia as the California of Europe, an economic success story just waiting to happen. Afterwards I go for lunch at a nearby Chinese restaurant, where the Cantonese waiter speaks perfect Spanish.

The buses in Seville are often packed with far more than their licensed allotment of passengers. People cram in so tightly that it's impossible to lift your arms up to the overhead straps. One morning I just manage to squeeze into a bus which will take me to the office. At the next stop our driver lets on two passengers, then decides that his bus is full and tries to close the doors and drive off. The waiting passengers run along beside the bus hammering on the glass doors with their fists and rolled-up newspapers and walking sticks until the driver stops to let them on board. The bus commuters are easily agitated because the only certain thing about the bus service in Seville is its infrequency.

At the office Flanagan tells me about an appalling incident involving Rosa, our Spanish teacher. The cramped street outside Rosa's little school is called Mateos Gago. It winds its way up from the magnificent Moorish Giralda, past tourist shops, cafés and a pair of old churches, growing progressively narrower as it runs into the Barrio Santa Cruz.

The workmen digging up the street outside Rosa's classroom to lay new pipes and power lines have discovered some Roman artefacts. The contractor quickly covers them up. According to Rosa, Flanagan says, the authorities will stop the work and call in the archaeologists if they find out about the artefacts. If this happens the contractor will not be paid for a long time. The workmen dig trenches in a different part of the street for a few days while the contractor tries to think of a way around his problem.

Yesterday afternoon Rosa was walking past the workmen on the way to her classroom. The men in the trench stopped working and whistled and manoeuvred for a better view of her legs. One of them bared his chest provocatively, and unwisely made an obscene suggestion as Rosa went by.

Rosa is tough, an emancipated Spanish woman. Quick as a flash she pulled a Kleenex tissue from her bag, bent down, picked up a piece of dog *caca* from the sidewalk at her feet and threw it at the chest of the offensive workman, who—hemmed in by the sides of the trench—was unable to dodge.

A terrible silence fell over the whole street, but only for a moment. Suddenly the other workmen started hooting and laughing at their hapless colleague. The joke was now on him, explained Flanagan proudly, and Rosa continued unmolested on her way.

This is cheering news, as Em is often subjected to suggestive remarks from workmen, and calls from passing cars of *"guapa, guapa"*, a crude comment on her striking looks. Perhaps the actions of outraged women like Rosa will start to make some of these louts think twice before imposing themselves in such a coarse manner.

Bandits and Motorbikes

Theft is a terrible problem in Seville, so prevalent and widespread that it's an accepted hazard of city life. Thieves break car windows in order to steal radios and cassette decks. They drive up beside traffic-stalled cars on mopeds and the pillion rider reaches in the window to snatch a handbag, a wallet, anything he can see. Then they weave quickly off through the traffic. Margaretha in our office tells me that the city has a huge drug problem, which lies at the root of it all. The drugs are smuggled in from North Africa to remote fishing villages along the Costa del Luth, on Spain's Atlantic coast. According to Margaretha the problem is so widespread that the police don't seem to be able to do anything to stop it. It makes us a bit nervous, and very aware of what's going on around us when we're walking the city's streets.

Flanagan hears Margaretha talking to me, and stops to say that he was walking down the Avenida de la Republica Argentina the other day with Carlos—one of our colleagues from Mexico. The two of them noticed a man on a balcony four floors above the street, levering at a window screen with a crowbar. It was the middle of the day.

Flanagan stopped and stared up at the man. Carlos, who

is much more attuned to what's going on in Seville's streets than most of us, tugged at Flanagan's arm and told him not to pay any attention and to keep moving. But Flanagan had never seen such blatant burglary before and continued to stare. After a minute the man with the crowbar felt Flanagan's eyes on him and turned round. For a tense few moments their eyes locked, and then the burglar seemed to become infuriated with Flanagan's scrutiny. He clambered down the side of the building in seconds like a human fly and chased Flanagan down the street, waving the crowbar over his head. Flanagan and Carlos ran for it. Margaretha nods sagely and says they were lucky to get away without a beating.

Grahame—one of our designers—comes up the stairs to get himself some coffee and joins in the conversation. Two nights ago he woke up in the middle of the night and heard someone moving about in his apartment, he says. His first instinct was to draw the covers over his head, but he got up and surprised the burglar, who shoved him aside and dashed past and leaped over the balcony rail, realising suddenly that Grahame's apartment is three floors up. As the burglar hung onto the rail by his fingertips, Grahame picked up a wooden footstool and bashed the man's knuckles as hard as he could. The burglar fell all the way to the ground, and lay still for a few moments before picking himself up. Grahame threw the stool and it caught the burglar square between the shoulder blades. Grahame watched in his pyjamas from his balcony as the man limped painfully off down an alley.

A couple of weeks after this discussion, one of our engineers has a sinister experience which illustrates to Em and me just how much we're on our own here when it comes to dealing with crime and assault. Kevin is a geotechnical engineer, a generous, mild-mannered young man who lives with Angelica and her son Byron at the edge of the Barrio Santa Cruz. Byron and Xan have become great friends, and Xan often spends the day over there. Angelica told Em that she found the two of them last week under the kitchen table, eating raw hot dogs they'd taken from the freezer.

Kevin is an aficionado of motorbikes and he imported a sleek new green and blue Kawasaki 750 from Canada. Despite all its locks and alarms it is stolen from the street behind the office late one afternoon. Kevin reports the theft to the police. They listen to his story and make sympathetic noises, and then tell him they can do nothing. Kevin has a black belt in karate; he's not about to give up his motorbike this easily.

At his local karate club Kevin manages to discover from someone with 'connections' that his motorbike has been taken to a distant suburb of Seville called Tres Mil Viviendas. He borrows a car and goes there to check out this information. While he's there he actually sees the bike, and contacts the police to tell them where it is. The police refuse again to do anything. Margaretha nods her head when she hears this. She is not surprised. The police do not enter Tres Mil Viviendas, a poor but heavily armed section of the city; it is a place full of drug dealers and gypsies.

The friend from the karate club offers to act as an intermediary, and a few days later Kevin manages to strike up an agreement with the thieves. They tell him that he can have his motorbike back for five hundred US dollars. Kevin agrees to this arrangement, since the intermediary has told him that he'll never see his motorbike again if he doesn't. The intermediary agrees to accompany Kevin to the meeting place, but before they set off he stuffs a small pistol into his waistband. He hands another gun to Kevin.

The streets in Tres Mil Viviendas are unpaved and potholed, littered with wrecked cars and rusting bicycles. Drug addicts slump on the sidewalks and stick needles in their arms. Everyone watches strangers who enter the place.

Kevin places five hundred dollars in American notes on the counter at the bar that's been designated for the meeting. The head of the thieves looks at it and demands more money. Outside, two of his gang race up and down the street on the stolen

Kawasaki, doing wheelstands and spinning the tires in clouds of dust. Kevin—who speaks excellent Spanish—has no more money and says so, and tells the gang leader that he has no honour, that he's breaking their agreement. The leader of the thieves doesn't like this kind of criticism. He picks up a crowbar and advances on Kevin. Kevin produces the gun and tells the gang leader to tell his friends to bring the motorbike to the door of the bar. When they do, he vaults onto it and he and his intermediary friend speed off as fast as they can.

I find Kevin's story chilling, not least because of the utter inertia of Seville's police. I decide not to tell Em about it, but from that time onwards I begin to feel quite unsafe in this beautiful city, aware suddenly that none of us—and Em and Xan in particular—are nearly as secure here as we are in Canada.

Flanagan has bought a *moto*—a 49cc motor scooter—but the transaction has been full of complications. Without a Spanish driving licence he's not able to get insurance, and for obscure reasons it proves impossible for him to acquire a Spanish licence. His only solution is to register the *moto* in Carlos's name. Carlos can then take out insurance and Flanagan can drive the *moto* anywhere he wants.

Every night Flanagan parks the *moto* in the secure car park beneath his apartment. Every morning he finds another part has gone missing from it. First he loses the headlight. The next night the ignition switch disappears so that he has to hot-wire the *moto* to get it to start. Then his whole braking system goes missing. The throttle handle vanishes next, and when he wants to go faster he has to bend down and pull at a wire beside his foot. He thinks that local youths are hiding in the shadows and darting under the automatic gate at night when resident cars enter his apartment's secure garage. In exasperation he takes a bus out to the Continente hypermarket, and buys an anti-theft alarm and a Maserati air horn.

On Saturday morning I come across him working on his *moto* on the sidewalk in front of the office, installing the alarm and air horn with Robert's help. When he's finished hooking it up he pushes a button to test it. An amazingly loud and piercing noise splits the street and pigeons for blocks around take to the air in panic. Pedestrians stagger visibly in mid-stride and everyone stops to stare at Flanagan and his *moto*.

A few days later I ask Flanagan if the new alarm has worked. He tells me it has been stolen. He still drives his new *moto*, but now it is made almost entirely out of replacement parts.

Escapes

Seville is almost uninhabitable in July and August because of the heat. People hardly work at all, and come to life only at night. There are public holidays every two weeks, almost all of them '*puentes*'. However, most Sevillanas ignore all this in high summer and simply go off to the coast, abandoning the city to people who are too poor to leave, and to the geckos and crickets and white pigeons.

We sleep at night with only a sheet over us, but even that is too much. The river smells in the summer nights, wafting a terrible stench of sewage over the city. The air conditioning cannot compete with the heat. Even our refrigerator is unequal to the task and the ice in the freezer melts and drips down on the floor. We invite some friends over to dinner and find that all our candles have melted into a shapeless mess.

Em makes enquiries about sports clubs, the only establishments in Seville with swimming pools. There is only one public pool in the whole city, and it's dirty and overcrowded, and miles away. She discovers that the private clubs all charge extortionate fees—an initiation fee of thousands of dollars to start with, and then an annual membership charge of thousands more. Some of these clubs are magnificent, with horse riding and polo, golf courses and tennis. All of them have pools, which is the only thing we're interested in. But the cost ensures that they're only open to the very rich.

Mercedes sometimes takes us along to a tennis club near where we live. Her family has had a membership there for generations. The club has a pool and a wicker-chaired bar shaded by jacaranda trees and eucalyptus, and a pleasant colonial, gymkhana air to it. It's relaxing to sit there and drink cool *sangri'a*, listen to the plock of tennis balls and the shuffle of eucalyptus leaves in the hot breeze; but the summer heat in Seville is relentless, and what we need is a refreshing pool that's affordable, one we can escape to every day.

Mercedes takes Em one day deep into the dilapidated enclave of San Bernardo on the other side of the railway line that runs near our apartment. San Bernardo is a part of old Seville which has been by-passed by the developers, although they have recently discovered its valuable central location and are starting to make demolitions. The neighbourhood is a quiet anachronism, with quaint, shaded streets and crumbling apartments and town houses which must once have been quite grand. When it was built many years ago, a delightful little swimming pool was established for the exclusive use of the local residents. Mercedes takes Em to this pool and arranges things so that she can go there to swim any time she wants, for only a few pesetas. Within a few days the locals have accepted her as an honorary resident and no one questions her right to be there. No foreigner has ever swum at the pool before, she discovers; it is solely for the use of the residents of the barrio.

On one staggeringly hot day Em and Xan set off on foot to the pool. It is only a ten-minute walk, but it is so hot that they have to gather themselves and move from shadow to shadow wherever they can. They're crossing the bridge over the railway line when the chain stitching at the back of Em's skirt unaccountably unravels. In seconds the only thing holding her skirt together is the waistband.

Cars whizz by and toot their horns, and workmen building the new apartments across the road put down their tools to watch. Xan who is only three years old has the bright idea to wrap a towel around her mother. They turn back to the apartment to make repairs. The heat is too unbearable to go out again and they spend the rest of the afternoon sitting in the bathroom bathing their feet in the cool waters of the bidet.

Something happens to the human body when the temperature climbs over forty-three degrees centigrade. An outside shade temperature of forty-four degrees seems to be the threshold that drains the energy right out of my body and turns my legs to rubber. Even the effort of ascending in the elevator makes me want to lie down. Climbing stairs is out of the question.

The temperature keeps climbing higher as the summer wears on, until it nudges an unimaginable fifty degrees. The conversion chart in my pocket diary tells me that this is one hundred and twenty degrees Fahrenheit. The very best air conditioning systems—which we do not anyway have in the apartment or the office—can only lower this a few degrees. After suffering two weeks of great lassitude I decide to visit Doctor Moreno for some advice.

Dr. Moreno checks me over and takes my blood pressure. "That's the problem," he says, looking at the reading. "Your blood pressure's too low."

"I thought that was supposed to be a good thing."

"Well, it's not a bad thing. It happens to a lot of people when it gets as hot as this." He smiles. "It's easy enough to fix. You must take a spoonful of honey twice a day and try to get away from the city on weekends—down to the ocean or up into the mountains. It will do you good."

"Is that all?" I ask. I'd expected some of his homeopathic pills.

"That's all. If you do these things you'll be fine."

◆

We decide to buy a fast car so we can follow Dr. Moreno's instructions and escape from the heat. The car we buy is a Toyota Supra with a turbo-powered engine and a sporty *targa* roof. Once the arrangements have been made, the car is shipped down from Denmark to a duty-free dealer in Puerto Banus, near Marbella on the coast.

Early on a bright summer morning we climb on board a bus that carries us slowly through the rolling hills south of Seville and starts to work its way up into the mountains. When we reach Ronda the bus driver lets the passengers out to stretch our legs for a few minutes. Then we climb further into the grey mountains and over a final pass before dropping down to the cool Mediterranean coast at Nueva Andalucia. The Danish car dealer meets us at the bus stop and drives us up the coast to his showroom at Puerto Banus.

We inspect the car greedily. It is sleek, and white to reflect away the heat of the sun. It looks as if it will go very fast. The numbers on the speedometer go up to a breathtaking two hundred and eighty kilometres an hour.

The upholstery is grey and the front seats have special adjustments and little inflation pads to clamp the driver tightly into the seat. It even has seat-heating pads, which won't be necessary here. The steering wheel has a dozen different adjustments to fit the build and style of every driver. The air conditioner is cool and efficient, and the radio has six speakers. We sit for a long time inside the auto-dealer's garage playing with these gadgets while we wait for him to obtain bank confirmation for our cheque.

When the transaction is completed we drive off down the coast feeling like millionaires, soaking up the freedom and luxury of it all. Xan is squeezed into the back seat and starts to complain that she can't see anything. It's too hot to remove the Targa roof, so we stop at a sandy beach near Estepona and dive into the Mediterranean. The sea is warm here, a deep, ruffled blue brushed by a strong hot wind from Africa. Floating in the cool water offshore, I'm fearful suddenly of thieves, and start to cast anxious glances up the beach to confirm that the car is still where we left it.

It doesn't take us long to find out that in the whole of Seville only one pump sells lead-free gasoline, which is all our new car will accept. In the next few days we discover that there are less than a dozen lead-free pumps across the whole of the vast, environmentally enlightened province of Andalusia. It is an unexpected problem.

The lead-free pump in Seville lies out at the edge of the city, near the Real Betis soccer stadium. The gas station doesn't always have lead-free gasoline either. Sometimes two or three days go by after the supply runs out before a new delivery arrives. We have to plan our trips carefully, calculating mileages to make sure we don't run out of gasoline. We make it a rule to refill the tank as soon as it becomes half empty.

Mercedes and her family invite us to visit them at their summer house in the Serrania de Ronda, the deep mountain range southeast of Seville. Mercedes' friend is getting married in the village of Villaluenga del Rosario, at the residence her family acquired during the war.

These mountains are a formidable barrier between the agricultural hinterland and the sea. The road winds higher and higher, and carries us up into a wild, craggy high-country landscape. Not long ago bandits and outlaws lived in caves and remote villages up here, and waited like spiders to prey upon unwary travellers. Reluctant to come to such a lawless place, the Guardia Civil were rarely seen in these parts.

Villaluenga is deserted, its whitewashed houses sprawling in a fine disorder up the side of a narrow valley in a soporific silence broken only by the tinkle of goat bells. The village is crisscrossed with narrow lanes and steep, stepped alleyways. Acacia trees cool its tiny central square, providing shade for neat wooden benches and a spattering fountain. A sandstone church fills one side of the square, its varnished doors and polished brass handles glinting in the sun. The steps of the church are neatly swept and geraniums sprout from its window boxes. It is a sleepy place; Mercedes tells us that the villagers rarely show themselves except when there's a celebration.

On this wedding day the little square is decorated with bunting, and fairy lights have been strung through the trees. Trestle tables have been set up in rows, arranged with white linen cloths and fine silverware. The bridegroom is the village policeman.

Mercedes' aunt shows us proudly through her house—a dark, cool place, full of heavy, oak-wood furniture. Inside the front door a narrow covered alleyway leads down under the house and out to the lane behind. It's a strange little thoroughfare, accessible only through the main entrance. Mercedes' aunt explains that in times past cattle were brought through here from the street behind.

When we go out again the preparations in the square are gathering pace, and busy villagers are setting out chairs and flowers for the festivities. Mercedes takes us into a small *pension* at the edge of the square for a cool drink. We ask the landlady how much it costs to stay here, and she tells us she rents out her rooms for $10 a night. It's a simple establishment where sunlight falls into lino-floored rooms as spare and clean as a monastic retreat. We examine the menu in the dining room. An evening meal here costs only five dollars.

After dark Mercedes takes us to an old restaurant, made up of many small rooms flowing outwards from a central kitchen area. She points out browned bullfighting pictures and grey Civil War photographs, arranged haphazardly around the walls in scratched wooden frames. "That one there," she says, "shows the death of Manolete." The sepia print is faded and old, and shows a bull standing over the prone bullfighter, moments after one of its horns has speared into the man's groin. The bullfighter's face is creased with pain.

The waiter who is taking our order for drinks nods his head sadly. "Manolete was worshipped all across Spain at the time," he explains. "He was only thirty when he died, in 1947. And he didn't die at the big *corrida* in Sevilla, or Madrid, but in the little provincial bullring at Linares. His death was the greatest disaster that has ever befallen Spanish bullfighting."

Xan runs off happily to play outside with a group of village children in a tiny playground with a slide and swings. Despite all the photographs depicting pain and death the restaurant is filled with the gentle liveliness of animated conversation, and we sit for a long time talking quietly on a small patio, drinking a fresh *Vino Verde*, shaded by a vine-covered trellis bursting with green grapes. For me it makes a strange, fascinating contrast—these photographs with their depictions of hardship and death, not long ago so characteristic of southern Spain, and the relaxing warmth of conversation and sunlight, and the cool late afternoon of the mountains—as if time past and present have been brought together in this place.

After dinner Mercedes and her father take us for a walk to an old burned-out church standing battered and sombre on the hillside at the top of the village. The grass verge at the side of the lane leading up to the church is lined with vivid red poppies and small yellow flowers, the still evening air laced with the liquorice scent of wild fennel. The church is badly ruined, its stones feathered with smoke; but the graveyard which surrounds it is well kept and fresh flowers adorn the graves. Mercedes' father explains that the church has not been repaired since Napoleon's troops set fire to it nearly two hundred years ago. I don't ask him why this is. Similar places exist in Scotland, damaged by the English, left today as monuments to other times and tragedies. It seems proper to me that this church too has simply been left as it is.

Sheer cliffs, pocked with caves, tower high above us, dwarfing the little church. Donkeys and horses graze in small stone-walled fields in the well of the mountain valley below us.

Following Dr. Moreno's advice, we speed off every weekend to the beach, the mountains, or Gibraltar. Of all these options the mountains are the best. It's cool up there, clean and uncrowded. In fact the hills and valleys of the Serrania de Ronda are virtually deserted, as if they've been passed by and forgotten by Spain's dashing new society. The white-painted mountain villages stand out stark and sun-bright on the grey-green mountainsides, full of history and legend, the people who live in them reserved and careful with strangers. But Los Pueblos Blancos are gradually being sign-posted and developed for tourism, and I'm afraid that this will slowly destroy their charm, and the tranquillity that comes with their remoteness.

Each of the villages has a distinct character. Benamahoma stands at the western edge of the Serrania, at a conjunction of roads. Grazalema balances in a narrow saddle high above a green valley, and combines old village customs with a summertime influx of city people. Zahara has become an enclave for expatriate British residents, and you can buy Watneys beer in its bars.

We drive into the mountains one Sunday to Grazalema and Villaluenga. On the way there we come across a baby vulture sitting on a low white wall high up the steep Pasa de las Palominos. The bird is moping about moodily, taking sandwiches from anyone who stops to feed it. It seems lost, abandoned, but its mother has probably flown off to find food below the *Pasa*, where the foothills are coated with fir and cypress and populated by small animals.

A thin oak wood beside a stream provides us with a fine, shaded picnic place, and we play soccer, and 'catch' with a frisbee. As the cool mountain evening falls around us we build a little fire out of small sticks and roast hotdogs and drink wine, and lie back to watch a pair of golden eagles floating on thermals above the cliffs. A handsome *vaquero* rides past on horseback and waves to Xan. It is quiet and full of peace up here after the city, the silence broken only by crickets and frogs, and the mysterious twilight sounds of birds calling in the mountains.

✦

Down the mountain pass towards Ronda an old hostelry sits beside a quiet road. A ragged European Community flag with its circle of stars hangs listlessly from a pole in the dusty car park. Xan and I pass through here with Kevin and Angelica and Byron one weekend when Em is away in England.

The old Inn is unkempt and rundown, but inside it has a rustic magic. Crooked wooden tables stand unevenly on a flagstone floor, and its thatched roof is supported by rough timbers lashed together with ropes. The menu is local and wholesome, the prices generously inexpensive. The landlady comes out to talk with us while we eat. She was once English she tells us, but she's lived here now for more than thirty years and has become Spanish. Her husband came from this region but died a few years ago. Her sons are Spanish and speak no English at all.

After a robust meal and several glasses of the landlady's earthy, local wine we decide to stay the night rather than make the long drive back to Seville. The rooms in the small cottages she shows us are dark and a little musty, but they're clean and they have baths.

Very early in the morning at the time of the softest light, Xan and I are awakened by the exquisite song of nightingales. They are singing from the thatch on the roof above our heads and from the trees around our cottage. The sound they make is enthralling, liquid and lyrical like angel music; unlike any bird song I've ever heard. The nightingales sing for half an hour, just as the landlady told us they would, and when they finish we dress and go outside into the cool morning to eat breakfast beside an old swimming pool. While we eat we watch the languorous movements of the Englishwoman's sons as they clean the pool of last autumn's decaying leaves in preparation for the summer trade.

✦

Most of the beaches along Spain's southern coastlines are polluted and when we go there we often find plastic and paper and broken glass littering the sand. The Costa del Sol on Andalusia's Mediterranean coast is known as the 'Concrete Cliff' because of the miles of unrelenting high-rises that Spanish developers have built along the shoreline. These ugly buildings have defiled some of the most striking views in Europe, and we've found that some of the people of the Costa del Sol seem to have been overtaken by an uncomfortable blend of greed and dishonesty which has little semblance to the traditional generosity of the Spanish people.

The grasping capitalism of the Costa del Sol has driven us to explore the hundred-mile stretch of the Costa del Luth, an underdeveloped stretch of coast where people seem to live a more rustically Spanish way of life. The Costa del Luth runs west and north from the southern tip of Europe at Tarifa, all the way up to the old Spanish naval port of Cadiz. The Atlantic Ocean is colder than the Mediterranean, but it's cleaner here and the beaches are less crowded, the light sharp and washed by the prevailing winds. Sometimes the wind howls fiercely up this coast, picking up particles of sand and blowing them about like tiny bullets. At Bologna the wind is so strong that most of the sand has been transported from one end of the beach to the other and lies heaped in dunes to the west. The winds have uncovered spectacular Roman ruins which sit grandly among stunted brush beside little white cottages with windblown hedges, and the sand mingles with coarse seaside grasses, like the *machair* on the west coast of Scotland. But the wind blows here all the time; the flying sand stings our bare legs and faces and it's too wild to sit on the beach without screens.

A few miles along to the west, Zahara de los Atunes is a sad, neglected place; the tuna fish which gave the village its name long fished out. The village sits semi-deserted for much of the year until city folk from Madrid and Stockholm and Frankfurt fly down in summer to take over its shuttered villas. Then children roar up and down the bumpy streets on *motos*, and café proprietors chalk northern menus of wiener schnitzel, herring and steak onto blackboards by their doors.

We try out most of the beaches along this coast—Barbate, Chiclata, Conil de la Frontera, Chipiona—and explore from Cape Trafalgar up to the wide estuary of the Guadalquivir river, and beyond it as far as Mazagon and El Rumpido and Punta Umbria. One hot day we accidentally stumble upon a beach at Cabo Roche that is only accessible through a lavish private housing development. Uniformed security men guard a boom gate like a border Custom's Post at the entrance to this enclave. We drive up to it apprehensively, but one of the guards darts out of a little security hut and whips off a smart salute as he lifts the gate and waves us through, as if we're respected residents in our flashy new car.

The security men provide an intimidating presence which seems to dissuade casual visitors, and there are never more than a few people at the beach when we go there. The water is clean and turquoise-green, the beach long and sandy with secluded rocky coves. But even at this private development we come across empty bottles and plastic bags that people have stuffed behind rocks instead of carrying them off to garbage containers.

The old British Crown Colony of Gibraltar is a three hour journey by car through the mountains. The Spanish have strong feelings about Gibraltar, and the government in Madrid makes regular demands for its return. Spanish tourist maps do not name it at all and only the words *'Punta de Europa'* indicate its presence. Our friend Manito, the composer, is horrified when we tell him we're going down there for a visit. Manito is a broad-minded, modern European man, but he turns us down flat when we ask him if he and his wife Xandra would like to come with us.

"Absolutely not," he says. "And I can't imagine why on earth you would want to go there either." We realise that this is actually a backhanded compliment. Manito has been seeing us as local, Spanish.

The quickest route to Gibraltar from Seville takes us down the Cadiz *autopista* to the Medina Sidonia turnoff, then eastwards through the hills to Alcala de los Gazules. The road winds over the mountains from there to the town of Los Barrios, before dropping down to the coast and the huge factory smokestacks which lie between Algeciras and La Linea.

Gibraltar is popular with tourists, and a line of cars is waiting at the Spanish border post. The Spanish are not particularly upset with the British government at the moment and so we don't have to wait long for Customs and Immigration clearance. We drive slowly through the customs shed until a tall policeman in a high British Bobby hat and hot, black London serge uniform pulls us over. He asks two or three cursory questions and waves us on.

When I came here in 1988 it was to meet with people from Gibraltar's Olympic Committee. I arrived the day after British Special Services agents shot three suspected IRA terrorists near the Shell station at the edge of the airfield. A young SAS man in a windcheater and jeans shot two of the IRA suspects against a low wall in the street in front of the gas station, then pursued the third across waste ground and in amongst apartment blocks until the winded IRA man raised his hands in surrender. The SAS man walked up to him, put the gun to his head and pulled the trigger.

When I got off the flight from England the day after this incident, the airport was full of Special Branch people in London suits. The sidewalk outside the Shell station was still splashed with dark blood when I drove past it in a taxi. The Crown Colony was confused and jumpy for days, and the military guard at Gibraltar's little Parliament building was doubled, the soldiers issued with live ammunition.

Now, hucksters patrol Gibraltar's streets, offering guided tours and duty-free deals. One of them advances aggressively upon pedestrians outside the overgrown Trafalgar cemetery, where many of the sailors who died with Nelson are buried. This tout blocks the sidewalk in an effort to make us engage with him, and we have to step into the street to pass him by.

We take the funicular up to the top of the rock. There's a little café up there where we can have coffee and gaze across the Straits to Africa, and northwards up the Spanish coast. The café sits among old Second World War gun emplacements, balanced on a knife-edged ridge bristling with radio aerials and electronic paraphernalia.

Gibraltar is a schizophrenic place, idyllic and peaceful on the surface. Sun-splashed country lanes cling to its steep western side, spread with English cottages and tiny smallholdings. But under its gentle exterior the Rock is packed with high technology military apparatus. This side of its personality becomes more apparent as we climb up towards the summit, where steel blast doors block off subterranean tunnels. These massive doors are painted camouflage green, and they stand twenty feet high in the rock walls. Gibraltar is honeycombed with command centres and dormitories, and hospitals and stores enough to withstand a lengthy siege. The place has been tunnelled out and fortified by generations of British army men reared on Boy's Own Adventure books. It's like a massive barn where children have hollowed forts and hideaways and priest holes and secret places in the hay; like a place of children's games which have spiralled out of control.

We decide to walk down to the foot of the rock, rather than take the funicular. Half way down we come upon a plaque set in a low wall; it reads:

This marks the spot where Queen Elizabeth II and the Duke of Edinburgh first met the Apes in July 1952.

The mind races; one wonders what they thought of one another. The Barbary Apes lounge about moth-eaten and half asleep, their eyes yellow and cunning. They scratch themselves constantly, lying in the crooks of scrawny, barely-leafed trees above discarded soft drink cans and paper litter.

✦

Our room at the Queen's Hotel overlooks a busy street corner and a noisy outdoor bar which plays English pop songs all day and half the night. We can feel the springs in the bed through the thin mattress and the carpet is threadbare, the furnishings spartan. But it's cheap, and clean.

It's pleasant for a while to speak English again, and drink a pint of British beer, eat fish and chips and stock up on vitamins and a variety of simple things we can't find in Seville. Gibraltar is no longer the duty free haven it was twenty or even ten years ago, but its back lanes are cluttered with people and the character of the place still lies richly upon the Mediterranean faces in its streets. Lebanese shopkeepers and Moroccan leather sellers, Maltese insurance brokers and skull-capped Israelis, and North African Arabs in dishdashas wander the sidewalks.

Visitors

Our friends the Stolles have come to visit us. They own a hotel in Cologne, and restaurants across the Rhineland. Now they're trying to build a hotel in British Columbia. Kathy and her daughter Christie drive down from Germany in a brand new Mercedes station wagon. Ulrich flies in from Canada two days later.

We're also expecting Jeff and Janis to arrive from Victoria at any time. Jeff is godfather to Xan, and an old friend from university. He's a lawyer and he travels in order to find adventures and escape from the formality of his work. Janis is new to us, an unknown quantity, tall and red-haired and fair skinned.

We take the Stolles out to an evening performance of the Paris Opera Ballet Company at the old Roman capital of Italica, a few miles outside Seville. Before the event begins we're served cool drinks and chilled wine among Roman pillars, beside statues to Venus and Diana.

The lighting is subtle, the music simple and clear, the performance in the ancient amphitheatre like the work of a heavenly conjuror. The dancers flow back and forth across the stage to the music of Chopin and Hadyn, with the thin black shapes of cypress trees etched against the starry night sky above the rim of the bowl. One of the performers is a young French girl whose movements unfold like shadows from the music. She swoops and pirouettes across the stage with a sublime, poetic grace and showers of perspiration cascade through the lights from her hair like fairy dust. It is very hot.

Jeff and Janis have turned up at the apartment while we've been out at the performance. They've found it so hot here though, that they've taken an air-conditioned room at the Hotel Pasarell down the road. The only room in our apartment with air conditioning is our bedroom, and the air conditioner in there doesn't do much good anyway. Jeffrey mentions diplomatically that the heat in Seville is one thing, the air pollution another, and quite overwhelming. His remarks make me wonder if we're starting to get used to it.

It's so hot that we decide to take everyone up into the mountains for a day and set off in our car with the Stolles following in their Mercedes Benz. The Cadiz autopista catapults us down the wide Guadalquivir valley to the turnoff at Las Cabezas and funnels us off through rolling fields of bright yellow sunflowers. At Villamartin the road begins to climb into the mountains, past Zahara, up and up the winding switchback route to Grazalema.

Clouds drift in, bringing cool airs and a shower of warm rain. We stop at a little open-sided mountain hut to eat a picnic lunch of bread and cheese and tomatoes, and wine. Horses and cattle graze below us in fields delineated by irregular drystone walls, beside tumbled farmhouses. The mountains rise steep overhead, grey rock and yellow scrub etched across a ragged sky. An eagle floats over a cliff on the air currents.

After lunch the road carries us up to Grazalema; the village full of sunshine and children and summer energy, and red terracotta roofs straggling one atop another up the brush-scattered hillside. On a rocky outcrop at the edge of the village sits a magnificent open-air swimming pool. Sheer cliffs drop away on two sides of it, and the pool overflows with splashing children. Squeezed onto its ledge on the mountainside, the pool hangs over a deep green and quiet valley which recedes into a limitless blue haze. The views across the Serrania de Ronda from here are stupendous. The water is deliciously cool and there's a special paddling pool for infants. Watchful grownups sit in the café-bar upstairs drinking wine or coffee. At night, dances are held out on the deck amid whirling coloured lights: all this for only three dollars a day.

The next day is Sunday and we take everyone off to the beach at El Rumpido on the Costa del Luth—the Coast of Light—on the west side of the world-famous Donana Nature Reserve. It's three quarters of the way to the Portuguese border, an area of great natural beauty which is virtually uninhabited. The nearby Donana Reserve is a way station for exotic migratory birds, and a haven for threatened animals. Spanish politicians point to the Donana when environmentalists accuse them of lax ecological moralities, and lassitude in pursuing polluters.

El Rumpido is a pleasant, uncrowded beach and we spend the afternoon picnicking and building sand castles. Ulrich is so tired from his travels and meetings that he falls dead asleep on a towel on the sand and doesn't wake until it's time for us to leave. Xan and I build a car in the sand, with a steering wheel and a driftwood gearshift, just as my father did with me on the beach at F'jara, in Gambia, when I was a child. The sea is flat like beaten metal, rising and falling lethargically with hidden currents. Offshore the sand is slimy underfoot, and after a while we notice a slight sewage odour to the water and decide to leave.

The next day Xan's little face is swollen up like the Elephant Man and we rush her off to Doctor Brioso. He tells us that El Rumpido is badly polluted with sewage from a nearby town, and that this is the cause of her violent allergy.

"Why on earth don't they close off the beach and stop people from swimming there," I ask, "or at least put up signs to warn people?"

Dr. Brioso shrugs his shoulders. "Everyone knows about it, so they don't bother to put up warning signs," he says.

Later, Jeffrey and I are walking the streets of Seville at one o'clock in the morning, which is not considered to be a late hour here in the summer. The city's streets and cafés are crowded, the air full of music. Even though it's late it is still family time. We pass a gaggle of five and six- year olds walking with four adults. Spanish families include children in every-thing they do.

"You know," says Jeffrey, gazing up at one of the city's big electronic temperature signs, "the sun's been down for five hours and it feels cool and pleasant, but that sign says it's thirty-nine degrees celsius. Even in the middle of the night it's hotter here than the hottest summer day we've ever had in Victoria!"

Every day now the temperature climbs up to forty-nine and fifty degrees. Hardly anything moves in the streets outside, ex-cept for a few wilting people who limp like wraiths from shadow to shadow. The pitch of the crickets has risen to a white-hot scream. Even the 49cc *motos* have disappeared; the slipstream acts like a kind of reverse wind chill on the drivers, making them unbearably hot.

Jeffrey and Janis move into our apartment after the Stolles leave for cooler northern climes. Janis spends much of her time under the cold shower trying to escape from the incessant heat. At night she wraps herself in a sheet and stands under the shower for half an hour at a time before going back to bed with the wet sheet over her, to try and get a little bit of sleep. They decide after two days of this that Seville is just too hot and leave for the Algarve in Portugal. We arrange to go down and join them there on the weekend.

Ayamonte's crooked streets are filled with haphazard lines of cars waiting for the ferry to take them across the slow-flowing Gaudiana River to Portugal. Perhaps it's because of these ferry line-ups, but the town seems to be unusually well endowed with ice cream and bakery shops. Children jump out of the cars and wander through the traffic in an air of carnival, eating toffee apples and candyfloss, while music blares out from car radios.

An old ferry battles up the river from the ancient port of Villa Real and empties a small load of vehicles onto the Spanish shore. Unhurried deckhands refill the boat from the line-up at Ayamonte, working the waiting cars into tight, awkward spaces on the sloping deck. When it's full the ferry sets off again, floating downstream to Portugal.

Tall palm trees line the waterfront at Villa Real, and Portuguese Customs men languidly inspect our passports and wave us through. Everything will change here next year when they open the new bridge a mile or two up river. The bottlenecks and congestion will disappear, and Ayamonte and Villa Real will lapse back into an irrelevant quiet.

Most people speak English in the Algarve and the atmosphere is relaxed and cheerful. Once again we feel as if we've come back into Europe, and the fresh air of Portugal quickly spirits away the tensions of daily life in southern Spain. It's a simple matter here, for example, for us to purchase lead-free gasoline, and to follow road signs that are clear and unambiguous. The longer we live in Seville the more resistant Andalusians seem to the idea of social and cultural integration into the European Union.

The Algarve is the nearest part of Portugal to Seville—although it's just as overrun with package development as the Costa del Sol, just as crowded with German and Swedish and British tourists. The towns here straggle along the highways in untidy strips, and creeping condominium developments are relentlessly replacing traditional homes and villas. But the beaches are clean and well maintained, and the sea breezes help to keep the Algarve clear of air pollution.

Jeffrey and Janis have found a small hotel overlooking the sea in Albufuiera, a busy village of winding lanes. Albufuiera has been transformed into a pedestrian-only village, its humble fishing origins disguised under a charming, pseudo-traditional development plan, its economy now prostituted to the thousands of package tourists who fly in to the big airport at Faro nearby. The authorities here have banished cars to huge parking lots on the outskirts of town, and all of them are full when we arrive. After an hour of searching we manage to find a space for the Supra, and have to pay an exorbitant parking fee.

The moon rises out of the sea as we're sitting on a low wall beside the coast path on top of the cliffs. Strollers pass gaily along the winding pathway in front of us—men with sweaters tossed over their shoulders like capes, hand in hand with young women in summer dresses. Jeffrey has found the only genuine bar left in the village. It's a traditional fisherman's hostelry full of smoke and people and we sit up on the wall above the cliffs, sipping drinks and soaking in the cheerful music flowing from its open door and windows. Below us the light from the moon paints the waves silver.

Xan strolls up clutching an enormous drink crammed with melon, apple, oranges, grapes and other fruits.

"Where on earth did you get that from?"

She points over at the bar, her little mouth full of straws, sucking busily at her drink. "Thirsty," she says.

"I saw her go in," says Jeffrey in a voice full of admiration. "She walked into the bar, pushed through the crowd and stood up on her tiptoes in front of the counter until the barman noticed her. Then she said something to him and right away he turned round and made her that amazing drink."

He shakes his head. "Do you realise what she did? She's only three years old and she walked into a bar and ordered a drink from a Portuguese barman in Spanish. The whole thing took her less than two minutes. It took me more than ten minutes to get served in there."

"How did you pay for it?" I ask her. She shrugs her shoulders and smiles sweetly. She doesn't understand yet that you have to pay for things. So I walk across the path and into the bar and in a bad mixture of Portuguese and Spanish I ask the barman about it. He understands me with difficulty, holding his head quizzically to one side.

"*Cuanto custa? Para la nina,*" I repeat, slowly. "How much do I owe you? For the little girl's drink?"

"*La nina?*" He looks over my shoulder. Xan is standing in the doorway. He points at her. "*Este nina?*" He grins. "*Nada. Absolutamente nada.*" Nothing. Absolutely nothing. It's on the house.

"Besides," he adds with a chuckle, in English which is far better than my fractured Hispano-Portuguese, "she was a lot easier to understand than you are."

We've decided to sack our maid Maria Luisa. She's imperious and uncooperative and she's now accused Em of not allowing her to have any food at lunchtime. This is untrue; Maria Luisa has always known that she can help herself to our food while she's here. It's a standard working condition in Andalusia for maids. Yesterday she accused Em of not supplying her with beer. This is partly true, as we don't often have beer in the fridge. But we didn't know that beer was a requirement of her working conditions.

Sometimes Maria Luisa doesn't bother to turn up for work, or arrives late. If our friends telephone when we're out she harangues them with complaints about us. We've begun to notice that small things have gone missing, like the garlic press. Em noticed Maria Luisa admiring it the day before yesterday.

Now we have a new maid called Kati. Kati is tiny and conscientious and unbelievably hard working. She comes from a village in the mountains near Jaen and is divorced, which is still unusual in Spain. Her husband used to beat her, she tells Em one day. Kati has a birthmark on her face and is very self-conscious about it. We don't notice it. Xan likes her a lot, whereas she was frightened of Maria Luisa.

It is necessary to employ a maid in Seville because of the debilitating effects of the heat. As well, the city is so dirty that the apartment turns into a dustbowl without a good mopping and cleaning every day. It's impossible for us to keep up with it when we're both working.

Kati is poor and we pay her more money than we paid Maria Luisa. We'd give her even more if we had it, but the company is now behind with paying my wages and expenses and it doesn't look as if it's going to catch up. So instead we give Kati little gifts whenever we can, and things we no longer need from the refrigerator.

One day Kati asks Em if she can have our stale bread. We hadn't known that things were quite so desperate for her, but they are. Kati's husband refuses to pay her any financial support despite an order from the court. It appears that these court orders are often ignored in Andalusia, and women treated as little more than chattels in the eyes of the law. We think the husband is paying Kati's lawyer to do nothing, which is also not uncommon. Kati has a twelve-year-old son called Rafi who goes to school. She also has an older son who is unemployed and has recently failed his bus driver's examinations. Kati brought Rafi round to visit us the other day, a tall, quiet boy, very polite and thoughtful. It is all very sad and unfair. We worry about what will happen to them.

Trouble has broken out at Flanagan's house. His Canadian girlfriend Megan has turned up and discovered Flanagan's involvement with Rosa, our Spanish teacher. Flanagan should have told Megan about this before she flew over here, but he has avoided the issue. Now it has come to his door and will likely cause no end of difficulty.

Megan is devastated about the affair, and Em tries to help her out as best she can. But I have a feeling that Flanagan could be facing a problem of nuclear proportions down the road, once Megan sorts herself out. In the meantime Flanagan buries himself in his work and avoids all women as his world starts to totter. Rosa retreats into the labyrinths of the Barrio Santa Cruz. After a couple of weeks Megan leaves Seville and travels to Portugal, and then takes her broken heart off to northern Europe. Eventually she goes back to Canada, where she has been living in Flanagan's house in Vancouver.

Not long after she's gone Flanagan receives an urgent message from the tenants who were living in the basement of his Vancouver house. Megan has evicted them. Not satisfied with that, she's sold every stick of Flanagan's furniture to a second hand furniture warehouse and moved out. Now the bank wants to know why the mortgage hasn't been paid, why the telephone and hydro have been cut off.

Flanagan tries to sort out this disaster while tending to important duties in Seville. It's a formidable and time-consuming task and he sets about it reluctantly. In the end he has to fly to Vancouver at considerable expense, and it takes him two weeks to sort things out over there. He returns to Seville greatly subdued.

Expo 92

When autumn comes, Mateos Gago—the street in front of Rosa's school—is still a maze of trenches and a jumble of piled cobblestones, pipes and mounds of dirt. Over the course of the summer this short, narrow street has been dug up and re-surfaced three times, once for the water pipes, once for the power cables and once for the telephone lines. When each job was finished the holes were filled in and the road readied again for public use. But none of the service companies spoke to any of the others before establishing its own plans and schedules, and no sooner was the road re-surfaced than another utility company appeared and dug it up again. The whole operation has probably cost the Seville taxpayers three times as much as it needed to. Rosa has watched all this unfold from her classroom, and tells us that the contractors have managed to ensure that the Roman ruins have remained buried, and the archaeologists blissfully ignorant of the treasures beneath their feet.

It's hard to define the difficulties that we encounter living and working in Andalusia. Most of them are caused by differences of culture and ethics, accompanied by diverse concepts of honesty and honour, and incompatible assessments of priority and reliability. Some of these matters manage to translate themselves across the cultural divide with time, and as they do so some of the problems are smoothed out, although they generally leave a kind of lingering dissatisfaction.

Tensions are rising as the Expo time clock ticks down. Our Spanish colleagues at the Banco Bilbao Viscaya are keen to help us win some big contracts, particularly with the Spanish provinces—the *Autonomias*—who will all build pavilions on the Expo site. It's probably as much a matter of honour with our BBV partners as a matter of money. Luis Catalan de Ocon, my main contact at the Bank's head office in Madrid, has been seconded to our Spanish-Canadian joint venture company, Desarollo '92, to help us win some contracts. He telephones me to say that I should fly over for meetings in the *Canarias*, the Canary Islands. He knows a Minister in the provincial government there, he says, and they'll listen favourably to a pitch for business from us. The next day Luis calls again, to say this time that an opportunity might be about to break with *Asturias*, one of the provinces in the north, where he tells me the Bank has considerable influence. Perhaps, he adds, I should fly up there instead. I try to explain to Luis—an immensely conscientious and cultured man—that it takes several people many days of research and design to work up a properly professional presentation in our business, and that we need to have a very firm opportunity before we commit the time and expense that this involves.

Meanwhile the French have been digging a huge hole for their pavilion out at the Expo site on the Isla de Cartuja. They've designed an underground building that only protrudes a few feet above the surface, reasoning that this will keep their pavilion cool in Andalusia's extreme summer temperatures. The French architects have pushed forward with great flair, but our geotechnical engineer Kevin tells me that they didn't order a proper geotechnical study of the building site before they started construction. A geotech survey would have given them vital information about the quality and consistency of the subsoil, says Kevin; an important matter, as the Isla de Cartuja lies beside the Guadalquivir River and the whole Expo site stands on alluvial soil.

Over the last few days the huge French hole has slowly filled up with water, drowning millions of dollars worth of expensive excavating equipment. Planeloads of French engineers and technicians have flown down from the north to try and sort out this expensive disaster and avoid an embarrassing black eye. French engineers have set up massive suction machines in an effort to pump the water out of their hole. This morning the sides collapsed into the hole and buried everything, including their big pumps, under tons of mud and rubble.

The Spanish, annoyed with the French for what they perceive as the Gallic arrogance and high-handedness with which they've gone about their business, have been slow to offer assistance and sympathy.

On another part of the Expo site the Latin and South American countries are now proclaiming publicly that Columbus's explorations led to the widespread destruction of their ancient civilisations by the Spanish conquerors. One of the Latin countries has brought up the subject of pillaging, pointing to the hundreds of churches and cathedrals across Spain which are adorned with precious stones and metals stolen from the Americas. The Discoveries are not something to be celebrated, they say; they might even be a proper subject for a United Nations enquiry into unresolved genocide, and a cause for financial compensations.

The Spanish appear unperturbed by these harsh accusations, having long ago effected a mental disengagement between the visible opulence of the churches, and Spain's colonial conquests. Authorities in Madrid quietly put it about that the fuss is a fabrication, a front in order to blackmail the Spanish government into paying the Expo participation costs of the South Americans.

It's true that riches from the Indies are paraded widely across the country and glorified in Spain's churches. Every one of the sixteen Provincial pavilions at the World Fair is planning to have a display of plundered artefacts. There is no shame in Spain about this at all, no concession to any sensitivities from South America or anywhere else. In fact we've noted that there doesn't seem to be any embarrassment about the excesses of the Inquisition either. On the contrary, these brutal oppressions are commemorated each year across the country at *Semana Santa* and other Easter celebrations.

However, somewhere in the deep recesses of Spanish government these criticisms about the *conquistadores* have struck a delicate nerve. Not wishing anything to mar the Expo event, the Spanish government announces a few days later that it has agreed to pay considerable sums of money towards the construction of each of the Latin pavilions at the World Fair, towards the design and manufacture of their displays, and to meet the costs of transporting the artefacts to Seville from all the South and Central American countries.

These Hispano-American governments are masters of the art of brinkmanship, having learned it well from the Spanish colonisers. Despite the concessions they've won from Madrid they continue to roll out threats to withdraw from the Fair, and the cost of their participation continues to climb. It has not taken them long to realise that a World Fair celebrating the discovery and settlement of the New World will be a disaster if the New World refuses to turn up.

The Commissioner of the Belgian Pavilion announces that one of the five Expo-approved service companies has tried to bribe him in order to win a contract to build their pavilion. A brief scandal erupts in the British and Belgian newspapers, but little is heard about any of this in Spain and the affair is quickly swept under the carpet. Our company, D'92, is one of the five Expo-approved service organisations, and there is much speculation in our office about which company is involved in the bribery scandal. The Belgian Commissioner has presumably been told to shut up by his government, and refuses to divulge names. All we know is that we are not the culprits.

The Italian Pavilion catches fire during construction. The Expo fire crews are disgracefully slow to get underway and by the time they reach the Italian site the fire has taken a strong hold. When the firemen attach their hoses to the new Expo fire hydrants they find that there is hardly enough water pressure to put out a candle. They stand back disconsolately and watch the Italian Pavilion burn to the ground.

Construction crews have finished dredging out the enormous Expo Lake in the centre of the Isla de Cartuja. All of the Spanish pavilions will stand around this magnificent man-made lake; the host pavilion itself, and the pavilions of all sixteen of Spain's *Autonomias*. At great expense the Expo Corporation has excavated canals to link the lake back to the Guadalquivir River, and constructed a complicated series of lock gates so that pleasure boats can climb up water-borne steps into the heart of the fair grounds. The Expo engineers filled the lake with water from the river and moved on to the next stage of their preparations. But, due to the permeable soil, the huge lake drained itself completely in three days. The Spanish held a series of emergency meetings but have decided it is too expensive to seal the whole lake. They're now installing giant pumps to replenish it constantly from the river and maintain its surface level.

The Spanish engineers are refusing to examine the question of where the water is going when it drains out of the lake. Our geotechnical engineer Kevin says that a loss rate of this magnitude must be causing serious subterranean erosion. Now one of the French engineers has told *El Pais*, the biggest newspaper in Spain, that it was water leaking from the lake which flooded the French pavilion; that the Expo Corporation is really to blame and the French will be launching a legal claim for compensation. The Frenchman then throws everyone into a panic by going on to say that all the pavilions around the lake will probably collapse into the water soon after the Fair opens. Meanwhile weeds and other long grasses are growing extravagantly out of the lakebed, multiplying daily and fouling the neat, canalled waterways which thread through the Expo site. Soon the weeds will interfere with the technologies which are being installed to produce the nightly sound and light spectaculars during the Fair itself.

I'm now dealing with provincial government representatives in several of the Spanish Provinces—La Rioja, Navarra, Pays Vasco, Aragon, Valencia and Galicia. My meetings with most of them are dragging on and on without much visible progress. Sometimes I travel north for these meetings, or if the Ministers or senior bureaucrats come down to visit the Expo site we hold the meetings in Seville. But such contract negotiations move imperceptibly slowly in Spain and I can't tell if I'm wasting my time or not. Luis, at the Banco Bilbao Viscaya in Madrid, is working his magic on Cantabria, the Asturias and Extremadura. He telephones to tell me that he has a lead into the Baleares.

"*Si Miguel,*" he sighs when I ask him about it, "it is a tenuous lead, but I have spoken to them and if you fly up to Palma de Majorca at your own expense they will receive you."

It's more than ten years since I've been to Palma. It will be much more temperate up there at this time of year than it is in Seville, but I decline. There has already been far too much flying about Spain with too little to show for it.

Rodolpho spends much of his time in meetings with the commissioners of the Andalusian Pavilion. These meetings have been going on for months, and Rodolpho's communications about them are always vague.

"They want more designs from us," he says. Then a few days later, "They want to meet Flanagan. They've heard that he can solve the lighting problems they're having in the tower of their pavilion."

Rodolpho's exasperating vagueness goes on for weeks, but it mirrors what is going on with the clients I'm meeting. It's almost impossible to pin anyone down. Meanwhile time ticks on and everyone's schedules are tightening up.

Of all the Spanish *Autonomias*, the commissioners of the pavilions from Valencia and the Pays Vasco seem to offer us the strongest possibilities. But nothing has come yet to a definite conclusion, and no signatures have been inked onto contracts. Finally the people at the Banco Bilbao Viscaya come to the conclusion that it cannot take a chance that its home province—the Pays Vasco—will sign a contract with a rival service company.

Luis telephones from Madrid to tell me that we have the contract to build and fit out the Pays Vasco pavilion; that the deal is secure. I'm very excited to hear this, and ask him how he's managed to pin them down. In my dealings with them I've found the people up in Bilbao to be quite evasive and non-committal.

"Ah Miguel, you mustn't ask too many questions about these things. It is the Bank's home *Autonomia* after all, and we have some influence up there."

I ask him about our next step.

"Now," he says, "we must embark on meetings with the *'jefes'*—the decision makers of the *Pabellon de* Pays Vasco."

The Basques produce their head architect at the first meeting, in the manner of a pre-emptive strike. Luis Angolotti is a gaunt French Basque with wild hair and a manic cast in his eye. He looks like one of those ageing endurance athletes who are too obsessed with their sport to hang up their Addidas. He immediately launches into an impassioned exposition about the virtues of his design, and I wonder at first if he's quite stable. He proudly unrolls his architectural drawings and sits back and asks us what we think of them. We converse in a mixture of French and Spanish; he speaks hardly any English.

"It's wonderful," we tell him, "a very adventurous design, and we particularly like the way you allow so much natural light to enter the building."

Luis Angolotti is pleased. "Now we have to decide what to put inside it," he says.

This is a perennial problem for almost every one of the Expo participants. Most of them have designed buildings without first developing any idea of what they will be used for. This is because the project development process in each country invariably starts at the political level and politicians tend to see buildings as monuments, the functions of their interiors more as ideas with unreliable provenance and doubtful staying power.

"How flexible are you to design changes?" asks Knowlton, our chief designer.

"What do you mean!" exclaims Luis Angolotti.

"Well, your colleagues in the government have asked us to design the interior of the building; the flow of traffic from one exhibit to another, displays about the early Basque explorers, food services and so on. The Commissioner has already said that he wants us to include a three hundred and sixty degree theatre-in-the-round." Knowlton points at the plans. "If all these things have to go inside it there will have to be some changes."

Luis Angolotti takes a felt pen out from his pocket and quickly sketches thick blue lines across his blueprint. In seconds he changes the design completely.

Knowlton is aghast at this instant, radical re-design. "We should talk about it first," he suggests.

I ask the Commissioner about the fundamental message of his pavilion, what he wants to accomplish through the Basque presence at Expo.

"The Future," he says, then almost immediately, "the Past."

Our discussions carry on intermittently for most of the day. After a long lunch with wine we feel as if we're homing in on the commissioner's basic philosophies. But it's very difficult to get him to say anything we can latch onto.

"It's our image," he confesses at last. "People see us Basques as a bunch of bomb throwing anarchists. We've simply got to change this view into something more positive if we want to encourage European investment here."

By the time our next meeting comes along we've given the Pays Vasco Commissioner's comments a great deal of thought. I confirm our basic understanding with the Commissioner first.

"You want to look to the future, but show strong roots in the past through the history and tradition and the unique culture of the Basque people?"

The Commissioner nods.

"You want to show this through a series of displays, artefacts, regional food in the restaurant, and a 360 degree film theatre."

The Commissioner nods again.

I explain that it will be expensive to make such a film. We know of only two companies with the technology to make it and both of them are American.

The Commissioner brushes off this concern. He's used to this sort of thing; every company in Spain tries to get more money out of him. "Our budget is four hundred and seventy million pesetas," he affirms stubbornly.

This is about four point seven million Canadian dollars—a little over three million U.S.—for the whole interior. The budget must cover design, fabrication, film scripting and production, projectors, lighting, sound, kitchen and restaurant equipment, tables and chairs, fittings, signage, toilet paper, everything—and any additional costs necessary to change the building design to accommodate all the extra things they've now decided they want to have inside it. However we believe that our thinking has uncovered a brilliant solution for his problem of re-positioning the image of the Basques; one that will meet all the requirements the Commissioner has set out; one that will fill him with enthusiasm and the desire to find extra money. I decide to ignore his comment for the moment and tell him about the concept we've developed.

"The best way to get your message across is this. We will make a film of wonderful colour and sweeping imagery. It will contain all the elements of life in the Pays Vasco, your wonderful art and culture, commerce and industry, expansive scenery with spectacular vistas of the mountains and coast. We'll include sports and culture, and city life and fishing and farming. But we'll script the film as if the Pays Vasco and all its rich history and traditions and culture are being seen through the eyes of a child—simple and straightforward, with stunning visual and audio effects. The film will be full of innocence, and because of the child it will carry a powerful message of hope and expectation for the future." I pause for effect, then carry on.

"This approach will have two benefits. First it will explain the Basque region and your people quickly and simply to visitors who know nothing about it. Secondly, if these visitors do know anything at all about the Pays Vasco, it will probably be what they read in the newspapers: terrorists and bombs and assassinations. However, the child narrator and the whole atmosphere of the film will make it impossible for anyone who comes to the pavilion to relate what they see and hear with terrorism. The people who come to your pavilion will see the Pays Vasco of the future through the eyes of the child."

We think this is a brilliant solution, but the Commissioner is greatly unsettled. His head is shaking before I've finished.

"No, no, no," he says gravely. "Children do not run our province. People will laugh at us if we present ourselves as children. Besides, you can't expect me to believe that the people who come to our pavilion don't know about the Basque country."

"Well they don't," I tell him bluntly, and my colleague Luis shifts uncomfortably in his chair. "You've already said that people have got the wrong impression about the Pays Vasco and you want to change it. Besides, how much do you know about Oman? Or Papua New Guinea? People always think other people know more about their country than they actually do."

The Commissioner doesn't buy this at all and continues shaking his head. I'm obviously miles off target. "No, no, no," he says. "We've got to have something much more sophisticated than that."

Even the Swiss are having problems with the concept and purpose of their pavilion. The prime contractor for the Swiss Pavilion has sent a small advance team into Seville. Ulli turns up at our office. He speaks six languages fluently, and moves effortlessly from one into another. One moment he's speaking English to our support people, the next he's conversing in flawless Spanish with our accountant, quizzing him expertly about banking arrangements. A Munich restaurateur we're working with joins us for a few minutes, and Ulli tells a joke in German and doubles the Bavarian over. Ulli also speaks Dutch, Italian and French.

It turns out that the main problem the Swiss have concerns the ice tower on top of their pavilion. I'm convinced Ulli is pulling my leg when he first tells me about it.

"It's an important symbol of our country," he explains, "snow and ice—the glaciers. Besides we've spent a lot of money developing the technology for this."

It transpires that the Swiss have spent millions of francs developing and testing a new type of refrigeration plant in a bid to show their technical prowess. But we think they've miscalculated badly. The technology does not yet exist to maintain a tower of ice in the baking fifty-degree heat of the Andalusian summer. Even if it did, the hydro bills would be unimaginable.

But months have rolled by with no effective technical solution in sight, and in the end the Swiss reluctantly decide to drop the idea. Recriminations follow. Much time has been wasted on this ambitious design feature and Expo building deadlines are approaching fast. Shouting matches erupt over the long distance telephone line between Zurich and Seville. The Swiss Ambassador to Spain flies down from Madrid to solve the crisis. Switzerland's Expo project team invites me to dine with the Ambassador at an exclusive restaurant near the Plaza Nueva. Ulli confides that my presence will help ensure that the Ambassador remains calm. "He's unlikely to stage a scene with a foreigner present," he says. Ulli selects a restaurant which specialises in seafood. The Ambassador likes seafood.

The dinner conversation is glum and subdued at first, but it slowly brightens under the steady flow of fine Spanish wine. Around the table we discuss the problem of the ice tower and the Ambassador agrees that it should be dismissed once and for all. The conversation moves on to themes of technology and mechanics, and then touches upon the matter of culture. This excites the Ambassador, who is an enormously cultured gentleman. The Ambassador has been trying all through dinner to grapple with the essential purpose of Switzerland's presence at the World Fair.

"The problem," he says with a sigh, "is that we Swiss have no native culture."

This simple statement sparks off a furious argument between the German-Swiss, the Italian-Swiss and the French-Swiss around the table. All three languages are going at once.

I like the Ambassador and lean over to reassure him. "I think I've heard this before. It's the sort of thing we talk about in Canada all the time."

He helps himself to more wine and pours me a healthy belt as well. The two of us drift into a small oasis of tranquillity as the cross-cultural argument rages around us.

"You know," he confides, "I think the most appropriate thing for us to do would be to build a great big washing machine in the middle of the pavilion and fill it up with bank notes from every country in the world, and then watch it going round and round and round during the whole length of the Fair."

The Gulf War

For months now I've been dealing with the Government of Oman, trying to win a contract to design and build the interior of their pavilion. We've floated concepts and designs, and even entered into an alliance with the English company which is managing the construction of their building. It's a frustrating process though, partly because communications between Spain and Oman are difficult. Despite massive investments in technology the Spanish telephone system is still an unreliable analogue service. To compound things, the Omani system only seems to work intermittently and is even more temperamental.

The situation is complicated further because the Omanis have almost as many holidays as the Spanish. But theirs are Muslim holidays as opposed to Christian ones, and the two calendars rarely coincide. Nor do the weekly days of rest. Sunday in Spain is a holiday, and Sundays in Seville are often followed by *'puentes'*. The Omani weekend covers Friday and Saturday. Sometimes this leaves only one or two days in the week when both countries are open for business at the same time. The time change adds to these difficulties, and the start of the Gulf War with Iraq adds even more uncertainties.

Spanish airspace closes down completely when the Americans bomb Baghdad. Long-range US Air Force B-52 bombers roar out of bases at Torrejon near Madrid, and Rota on the south coast. The B-52's unload their bombs over Iraq and fly on to re-fuel and re-arm at Diego Garcia in the Indian Ocean, the exquisitely beautiful island airbase the Americans lease from Britain. Then they make a shuttle-run right back to Spain again, dropping more bombs on the way. Out of prudence or nervousness the Spanish authorities cancel all domestic air traffic whenever the US Air Force takes to the air. The result is chaos at every airport in the country, and thousands of passengers stranded all over Spain.

Our negotiations with the Omanis have slowly come to a head and I'm supposed to fly out to Muscat to sign a contract at the beginning of February. It's a big contract and the signing date was established before Christmas in order to fit in with the Omani Trade Minister's schedule.

When the Gulf War broke out in mid-January I was ready to believe the propaganda. The United Nations forces would have the situation cleaned up in less than a week. "It'll be over in four days max," said Chilton, one of the Americans in our office. "We'll clean 'em out. No problem."

By February 1st, the Americans have been pounding Iraq for nearly two weeks and the whole Middle East is a definite no-go area for infidels. It's time to telephone Muscat. The war in the Gulf is showing no sign of coming to an end.

Hassan Muhammed Ali is my Omani contact and he's unimpressed when I suggest that we ought to postpone my visit.

"What are you talking about?" he asks.

"Well, there's a war on," I respond dryly, "in case you haven't noticed."

"There's no war here," he replies with some heat down the creaking telephone line. "Whatever is going on up north doesn't have anything to do with us. It's hundreds of miles away."

I try to explain. "It's not the idea of *being* in Oman that worries me. The problem is *getting* to your country. The US government, and the British, Canadian, and Spanish govern-ments are all telling their nationals to stay away from the Mid-dle East right now."

"I can't help that. If they're saying that, it's your problem not mine. British Airways and Gulf Air are still flying out here every day from London." He waits for this to sink in. "What-ever is going on in Iraq doesn't seem to bother the airlines. If you want a contract with us you'd better be here for the meet-ing with the Minister on the 9th." He hangs up the telephone.

I send a fax to Muscat the next day. I'll fly out on Gulf Air on the 5th.

I don't feel comfortable about British Airways. The Royal Air Force is bombing Baghdad along with the Americans and I can't see either the Iraqis or the unpredictable Iranians shed-ding tears if anything with the name 'British' attached to it has an accident. At least the name 'Gulf Air' might give them the idea that it's locally owned, and besides, the Iraqis still own shares in it. In fact it was my father and a Colonel someone-or- other who originally started up Gulf Air as a regional sub-sidiary to BOAC (now British Airways) in Basra in 1951, with an old Dragon Rapide biplane.

When I discuss all this with my father on the telephone he tells me he is appalled at this war. "The Iraqis are among the most civilised, decent, educated societies on earth," he says. "The Americans have demonised Saddam Hussein, and in do-ing that they've made the Iraqi people out to be little more than a bunch of illiterate savages. I'm sorry to say that our people have just followed along behind." By 'our people' he means the British government. "None of them have got any idea what they're doing out there, and it'll cause them a great deal of trouble in the end, you mark my words."

Gord Donald, our company President, promises to buy me life insurance and spends three days lining it up. It's impor-tant to make sure that Em and Xan will be covered financially if I don't make it back. Before I leave Seville GD assures me that they've found a good policy; in the unhappy event that I don't return, my family will at least get some money. This is reassuring. The company is rarely more than an inch or two from the financial abyss, and I know my heirs won't see any money from them if I collide with a Scud missile in the next few days. I know that Em is nervous about this trip, but it seems to me that—as Hassan told me—the airlines wouldn't be flying out there at all if things were not pretty safe. Besides, the purpose of my trip is to sign a contract for several million dollars, and I'm expecting that this will help the company to catch up on the back pay it owes me.

Early on the morning of February 5th, I set out for Seville's airport only to find that the US Air Force is flying again. Nothing else is moving in the sunny Spanish skies except for birds. Miraculously the authorities open the airport at noon and Iberia sends off a direct flight to London. It's the only passenger flight out of Spain this whole day.

London is coated with grey-white slush. The terminal at Heathrow is surrounded by tanks and armoured personnel carriers, and patrolled by burly paratroopers in camouflage jackets and red berets. Metropolitan policemen dressed in bulky flak jackets pad up and down the halls in rubber-soled boots, with stubby sub machine guns cradled in their arms. This overbearing military presence seems right over the top to me; I've never seen anything like it in England before. Inwardly I congratulate myself on my decision not to fly with British Airways.

The women at the check-in desk turn down my request for information about Gulf Air's flight routing. "Why do you want to know?" they ask suspiciously.

"I'm just interested. I want to make sure the Captain is making the right choices."

"Well, I'm sure he is sir," they intone smoothly. "Besides that information is completely classified. We don't even know what route you'll be flying, and even if we did we wouldn't be able to tell you."

"They sure seem to be nervous about things around here," I observe, motioning towards the army and the armed policemen.

"Oh that; that's got nothing to do with the Gulf. Haven't you heard?" She takes a deep breath. "The IRA fired two mortar bombs at 10 Downing Street this morning. I don't think they killed anyone but they broke a lot of windows and made a dreadful mess."

I hadn't heard about this. It must have happened while I was waiting at the airport in Seville, or during my flight up here. It's a bit unnerving, as if the world is beginning to fall apart.

I spend the day sitting in the terminal watching the police and the army walking back and forth and, through the windows, a wet snow falling. My flight is called just before midnight, and I file onto a Gulf Air Airbus with the other passengers. I'm surprised to see that the aeroplane is full. Once we're all on board we sit and wait for an hour while the ground crew sprays the fuselage and wings with a de-icing compound.

I'm nervous about the flight routing because I don't trust in the innate common sense of big companies like airlines. I'm also cynical enough to believe that governments sometimes like to make grand gestures on the big stage in order to influence international opinion. I believe that they're sometimes tempted to do this by sacrificing small items, like airliners full of people.

If we take the shortest route out to the Gulf we'll cross directly over Iraq, as I did a long time ago when I flew out to Bahrain on my way to India. This seems improbable under the present circumstances. On the other hand, airlines don't like to make radical changes in the way they do things, and our routing may be only slightly to the south, perhaps over part of Syria and the bulk of Saudi Arabia. It seems to me that this would be almost as dangerous.

A third option would be to route the aircraft well up to the north. But this would mean skirting Iraq by flying over Russia and coming close to dangerous areas like the Eastern Caucasus and Afghanistan. This route would bring us down on a southerly track over Iran, which seems inconceivable given Iran's violent anti-western reputation.

The fourth and most likely option would be to fly eastwards up the Mediterranean until we're past Libya, then move down over northern Egypt, touch perhaps the southern tail of Israel and Jordan, and then cross Saudi Arabia. But it's clear that any route out to the Middle East presents problems of one sort or another; each one like threading a needle.

We take off into the night and I find it impossible to get any sense of direction from the stars I can see after we've climbed up through the cloud. Eventually I drift off to sleep.

When I wake up, bright sunshine is flooding through the window. Below us lies a barren landscape of grey-brown hills and scattered mountains with snow on their tops: scarred, semi-desert country without any roads or settlements. Here and there dirty snow lies in gullies.

Our cruising altitude is about 35,000 feet. I look up the Airbus's cruising speed in the flight magazine, and then adjust my watch for the change in time zones. I point the hour hand at the sun and bisect the angle between that and twelve. It's an old Boy Scout trick to find direction, and it tells me we're flying almost due south.

These examinations indicate that we're north of the Persian Gulf, and probably east of the Caspian Sea, somewhere near the Russian border, over northern Iran with the main part of the country still to cross before we reach our destination. The mountains below us are vestiges of the Caucasus in the west and the far off Hindu Kush to the east. It's an empty and little travelled part of the world.

An hour and a half later the aeroplane descends over soft blue water and lands at Abu Dhabi, in the southern Gulf. On the ground it quickly becomes hot inside the aircraft and the cabin crew open the rear doors to let in the breeze. It's early in the morning and the air smells clean, like freshly ironed sheets. The heat of the desert day is still a couple of hours away.

A long line of US Air Force DC-10 tanker aircraft sits nose to tail on an auxiliary runway nearby, stretching off into the distance as far as I can see, their wings and fuselages painted matt green and grey. There must be more than a hundred of them.

New passengers file aboard our aeroplane, the doors close and we take off for Muscat, in the south.

Hassan Muhammed Ali is waiting for me in the bright, marbled Arrival's Hall at Muscat Airport. He nods to the uniformed Customs Officers and they wave me past their counter.

"I'm impressed with your influence," I tell him.

"Oh that? It's nothing," he says. "You're a guest of the Omani Government, and because of that we've eased the passport and immigration proceedings a little bit. They're not particularly stringent in any case."

As we sweep out of the Customs Hall a well-groomed businessman in a pinstriped suit is pulled out of the line behind me and led off to a room for questioning.

Hassan's driver is waiting outside, a tall tribesman in leggings and a loose white shirt. His clothing is less formal than Hassan's starched dish-dasha, and looks more suited to the hills, and to riding horses or camels. He takes us to my hotel in a white government four-wheel-drive Toyota.

The hotel is a box-like Hilton with doormen and bellboys in quasi-military, maroon-coloured uniforms with epaulettes and high collars. The bellboys look uncomfortable in the heat. Plush lounges lie at either side of the big marble-floored lobby. Upstairs in my room a wicker basket overflowing with peaches, apples, oranges and bananas sits on a table. Two big king-sized beds take up most of the space. I shower away the travel grime, and go out for a walk.

Muscat lies like a scattering of villages among rocky grey wadis. Ribbons of road join up sections of the city, linking the city's different districts with pieces of strip development. The Hilton is situated on the edge of a newly developing downtown area.

The sun is fierce and there's little greenery to relieve the rock-dark, moon-like landscape. About twenty soccer games are underway on a big, bare expanse of waste ground opposite the hotel. Some of the games are quite formal, with referees, and teams wearing matching strip; others are obviously pickup games, with people running around in street clothes. There's not a blade of grass to be seen and the players are kicking up clouds of dust as they dash around after the ball. The whole area is a confused mass of joyful noise and movement.

Hassan tells me at dinner that he wants to give me an intensive course in the culture of Oman over the next few days. He explains everything he's going to show me in detail; the schedule he's planned is crammed to the minute.

The next morning we drive up the coast to a Bedouin village near the town of Sohar. An irritating bell tinkles constantly inside the car as we drive along.

"The speedometers of all the government vehicles in Oman are fitted with governors," explains Hassan when I ask him about it. "The bell rings whenever the driver goes more than sixty kilometres an hour."

"But there are no other cars on the road," I point out. We're driving across a flat, empty, semi-desert landscape. "Why do you have to drive at sixty?"

"It's the law," he says impassively.

"Yes, I see. But the bell's been ringing ever since we left Muscat. Why can't you just disconnect it?" I ask.

"We can disconnect the governor so we can go faster," he explains, "but we can't disconnect the bell."

It's impossible to drive as slow as sixty on these long straight desert roads. Hassan's driver presses on with a fixed smile on his face, oblivious to the chimes. At first they drive me nearly crazy, but after a while I don't notice them either.

The women at the Bedouin village are expecting us, their faces covered with the *yashmak* so that only their eyes are showing. Some of their eyes are arrestingly beautiful. The Bedouins are a nomadic people, noted for their fierceness and loyalty. They live in elaborate tents, which they pack up and take with them whenever they move. But Hassan explains that the Omani government is now trying to get them to settle in one place, and learn trades and develop indigenous crafts.

The women show us their workshops and weavings with a shy pride and I purchase a small, exquisite rug from one of them, and a weaving to hang on a wall at home. It's a strange thing, as we negotiate the price, to communicate with someone without being able to see their face or witness their expression: to have only a suggestion in their eyes as a guide. None of the men show themselves while we are in the village.

On the way back to Muscat Hassan tells me that his Minister has finally chosen a design for the Omani Pavilion at the World Fair.

I pretend that I'm surprised, and I give him a hard time about it. We've become friends.

"You mean you've already decided to build a particular kind of building, without any reference to the purpose of your exhibit; before you know what will go on inside the building?"

"Yes."

"I'm amazed," I tell him. "Would you build a supermarket if you wanted a building where you could teach children? Would you build a school with classrooms and then decide to use it as a hospital?"

"The Minister has decided on a dome," he says.

I've been dealing with the government of Oman for many months now. Delays no longer surprise me, but I've also become used to sudden resolutions. I think I'm slowly learning the desert art of immense, timeless patience.

On the one hand, the Omani government seems to have decided that they want our company to build their country's World Fair exhibit. It has been a long and complex negotiation and during the process our designers have come up with a variety of different concepts for the Omani pavilion. On the other hand, none of these concept designs has yet been approved at a level high enough to ensure that we have a contract. The over-riding purpose of this visit to Oman is to finalise design concepts, and to sign a binding Memorandum of Understanding with the people who will pay the bills. This will give us official direction and approval, and the security we need in order to allocate expensive resources to the Omani project.

At the end of the day I walk out in the soft evening light to a village not far from the hotel. At a small restaurant there a waiter takes me up some stairs to a table on a first floor balcony above the street. The other diners examine me curiously; all of them are men, and all of them look quite rough and unshaven. The place is untidy, the plastic tablecloth coated with fine sandy dust. The waiter brings me wafers and a paste-like dip. The wafers are brittle and crumble into crumbs and the paste tastes dry and spicy like couscous, and instantly removes the moisture from my mouth. I'd like a drink but this is a Muslim country and no alcohol is served outside a couple of western hotels. I settle for water. The waiter brings me a light, curried lamb and some heavy speckled bread which I use to mop up the gravy. The other diners look away as soon as I start to eat and pay me no more attention. I'm hungry, and the food goes down quickly.

In the morning my stomach is in turmoil. Hassan comes to the hotel early with his driver to take me off to Nizwa in the interior of the country. My condition dictates frequent halts on the drive through the Jebel Akhdar, the rugged mountain range which rims the coastal plain. Because of this the journey takes much longer than it should, but we eventually reach the ancient town of Nizwa in the afternoon.

Nizwa is an oasis, a gathering place for wandering desert people, standing at the conjunction of un-mapped desert tracks. My legs feel like rubber as we climb a flight of dusty stone stairs to the top of Nizwa's old fort. From its great flat roof we gaze out over palm trees and mud-brown buildings to a limitless grey plain. The town is scrambling with activity today; teeming with people calling and shouting to one another, buying and selling and bartering supplies in a maze of narrow streets.

"Nizwa is an old military post as you can see," explains Hassan. "It's a centre for this whole central area of Oman, and people journey here from many miles away to buy and sell things. Today is market day, and it will give you an idea of the culture and the commerce in this part of our country."

I tell him gently that it looks fascinating, but I don't think my stomach is up to any extended exercise, such as pushing my way through the crowded streets. We make our way back to the government Toyota and drive away from Nizwa across a flat desert landscape. At an isolated gasoline stop miles to the south we come across a camel sitting in the back of a Toyota pickup truck, chewing insouciantly as if its mouth is packed with gum. I'd always thought that the Toyota advertisement depicting this scene was a set-up, but Toyota trucks are ubiquitous here and camels are valuable. They're like trail bikes; the desert people don't ride them everywhere, just in the places where they're needed, where they're the only thing that will work.

We drive on across the desert on a flat, straight road to the coast at Sofar, where boats ride gently at anchor on a china blue sea. Children are splashing in the shallows beside big Arabian dhows and brightly painted fishing boats, and the little port is busy with a relaxed air of purpose. Hassan takes me into a boat yard where workmen are building an elegant, wood-planked dhow. They're building it to an ancient design but they're doing it, he explains, from memory and experience, without written plans or blueprints, using skills and crafts that have been passed down through many generations.

As we drive back through sun-flayed desert hills towards Muscat, Hassan realises he's left some documents behind in Sofar. It will take an hour for him to go back and retrieve them. I'm starting to feel better, and tell him that I'd like to get out and wait here in the desert silence for him to return. It will give me an opportunity to contemplate the desert by myself, to absorb some small piece of its atmosphere.

It's mid afternoon. The sun is high overhead, and it's very hot. An Imperial eagle climbs majestically up the air currents searching for prey. It's the only living thing I can see. The landscape is dusty-dry and barren except for a small patch of grey-green scrub in a rocky wadi. It's an empty, beautiful place, peaceful with the silence of ages.

The next morning Hassan tells me that he has made arrangements for us to fly down to Salalah and Dhofar in the south of his country. The aeroplane leaves right after lunch. It's a bumpy flight and takes about an hour before we drop down onto a lush green plain beside the Indian Ocean, and taxi past a grove of date palms to a little terminal. Salalah is a fertile, well-farmed enclave with plenty of water, says Hassan, and many varieties of tropical fruits and vegetables are grown down here and exported to other countries.

Twenty years ago the British SAS had an important base at Salalah during the unspoken war against Communist Yemeni insurgents from the south. My friend W., from the south of Scotland, ran a MASH unit here for nearly two years while the war was going on.

The local government agent drives us out into the desert to find frankincense trees. We come across them in an arid wadi south of town, scrubby and skeletal, holding their bare branches up like crooked supplicating fingers to the blue sky in a landscape utterly without greenery: just dust and rock and these strange trees. But the air here has been painted with a magical aroma and it hangs in the windless atmosphere, thick and sensuous like music, or fire. Hassan shows me how to scrape the valuable gum off the bark, its scent at once seductive and cleansing, as sharp as pine resin but incomparably more exotic. Local people harvest the gum from the branches and tree trunks and dry it into hard crystalline blocks, and send it off to markets all over the Middle East.

Not far away lie the ruins of a very old fort, once the scene of a great battle and terrible massacre. A sandy-gold beach brushed by soft white surf curves away from a small salt-water lagoon, and all around us the landscape is pockmarked with holes and diggings and crumbled stone.

"Two thousand years ago this was the site of a small city called Khor Rori," explains the government agent. "Italian and American archaeologists have examined it, and they have discovered coins and inscriptions that show that the city was originally established as a seaport, probably to ensure control over the frankincense trade. The archaeologists say that the ancient Greeks had two different names for the city. They called it Sumharam, or Mosca."

Far off across the plain a rocky hillside shows the dry scar of a once massive waterfall the size of Niagara, which must have tumbled down the mountainside in ancient days; like the silted up lagoon perhaps, a sign of more temperate times.

The aeroplane taking us away from Salalah climbs over fields of fruit and vegetables and black, fertile soil, and soars over the rocky Jebel, where tough tribespeople live in high, isolated villages.

This is the rugged mountain country where the Sultan and his British allies fought the rebels from southern Oman and Yemen. Oman's present ruler, Sultan Qaboos bin Said, took charge of the fighting when he was a young man. His father had mismanaged the country's affairs for years, and his older brother was corrupt. Qaboos had only just returned from England, and three years of training at Sandhurst Military College. He used his new contacts well after he received his Commission, and spoke to a sympathetic Foreign Office, exerting his influence on British friends who understood the strategic importance of his poor country. This ensured him British military support.

It was politic for the British to help build up Qaboos's growing reputation as a leader and fighter, but their assistance had to be discreet. They therefore employed the clandestine SAS, and highly specialised elements of the Royal Air Force. The hard and merciless British Special Services are arguably the toughest and best-trained fighters in the world. They managed to subdue the guerrilla campaigns emanating from the Yemen in one of those secret, dirty little wars that are still not admitted by the British government. W. could never speak of it because of the threat of serious penalties under the British Official Secrets Act.

Back in Muscat, Hassan leaves me to my own devices and so I head for the centre of town, walking past mosques and the calls of the *muezzin* summoning the faithful to evening prayers. Most of these calls now are taped and come out of loudspeakers placed high up in minarets; the ancient customs are changing as technology moves through this part of the world.

The Soukh sprawls through the centre of old Muscat. This huge market is an exotic rabbit warren of alleyways and shops and awnings and hucksters. Mysterious smells, wrought by chemists and perfume sellers, leather makers and potters, assail my senses as I pass. Watchmakers and metalworkers hammer away in the shadows. Colour flows from the brushes of painters, is woven into fabrics by tailors, and string-based eastern music pours out of hole-in-the-wall cafés. Baskets, cushions, chairs, rugs, and a thousand trinkets and pieces of merchandise overflow tiny shops and litter the narrow passageways. Children play up and down the laneways and the whole place is shaded and cool and bursting with a kind of somnolent energy.

Oman has been renowned for centuries for the excellence of its perfume makers. Hassan explained to me that these alchemists can analyse and reproduce the finest Parisian perfumes with an exactness which confuses experts. Exotic whiffs of sandalwood and myrrh float through the shadows of the Soukh in the company of reproductions of Cologne

4711, and the whole of it mingles with the smell of raw leather and rich Arab coffee and a host of other things.

Sultan Qaboos bin Said lives in a magnificent waterfront palace not far from the Soukh. He's a strange and secretive man and little is known about his personal life. There is no opposition in Oman to his rule, which seems to be firm but fair. His people remember his reputation as an uncompromising guerrilla fighter and this commands something greater than respect. Omanis seem almost to deify him.

The next morning, well before the Soukh comes alive, Hassan takes me to a high place by the sea and we watch the sun rise out of the Indian Ocean and sparkle majestically on the towers and minarets of the Sultan's palace, turning it into a glittering artist's fantasy. The facade is decorated in splendid gold and aquamarine, set off and surrounded by lush green lawns and the clear blue sea. The sight of it, in this desert landscape, is surreal; like a dream.

The Omanis have still not decided what they want inside their pavilion at the World Fair. "What sort of message do you want to convey to the world about Oman?" I ask Hassan at breakfast, not for the first time. We're going to meet his Minister today.

"Our government will decide that," intones Hassan.

"Yes, I understand that, but it's very hard for us to design something if you won't settle on a central theme. You want us to present you with ideas, but we've got to have something to hang them on—some concept you approve of."

"We must have designs," he says emphatically. "My Minister will not sign the Memorandum unless you show him some new designs for the interior."

I've brought a big folder of designs with me, but I want to try and make sure I show the Minister the right ones. I'm fishing; I know very well I won't have a lot of time in the meeting. "Right!" I agree. "I know it's important for your Minister to see design ideas. We also want him to get an idea of the range of work we can do. But we must have some direction from him, otherwise we're all wandering around in the dark."

The conversation continues round in a circle as it has done for months. Hassan's problem is that he can't risk going out on a limb for fear of losing face—perhaps even of losing his job. It's taken me a long time to realise this.

I take a deep breath. "Tell me, what objective does Oman have in coming to the World Fair in Spain? Do you want, for example, to attract international investment; or perhaps build up Oman's tourist industry; or deliver a cultural message; or inform western countries about potential trade opportunities?" This, too, is a subject we've discussed before.

Hassan ignores my questions. "We told you we wanted to see new designs. That is what we asked you to bring. The Minister didn't like the last ones he saw. There was too much hocus pocus in them. We don't like that kind of thing in Oman."

He's referring to the design devices we recommended to give each new audience an introduction to Oman's history and culture. Like the Basques, the Omanis refuse to recognise that most of the people who visit their pavilion at Expo will be ignorant of all but the most basic facts about their country. We think it's necessary to counter this with a brief, entertaining crash course about Oman before engaging the audience in the serious business of the exhibit. The design concept Hassan is referring to takes visitors into a small amphitheatre made to look like a traditional courtyard with a pool in its centre. Through mediums of water and light, smoke and projection, an Omani narrator appears on the surface of the water in the pool. He tells a story, which is projected in still and moving pictures on the courtyard walls.

"But you liked it when we explained it to you in Seville, Hassan." Because of Hassan's earlier enthusiasm we put a lot of work into the concept. The full colour drawings we did for his Minister were expensive to reproduce.

"I liked it but I am not important," he says blandly. "My Minister has to make the decisions, and he didn't like it."

I persevere. "You said that water was important to the culture of Oman."

"Yes. Omanis were the first people to develop scientific irrigation systems. The *falaj* has been the basis of Oman's agriculture for millennia." He goes on. "For centuries Oman has stood at the conjunction of important trade routes. Our navigators explored the world; they invented the first sextant so they could cross the oceans." He gazes patiently at me. "You know all this."

The Minister is a tall, imposing gentleman. He spends several minutes giving us his thoughts, speaking in articulate and educated English with barely a trace of an accent. "The Omani government," he explains patiently, "is not particularly interested in portraying this country and culture through technical gimmicks, even if the main themes of the World Fair are largely concerned with technological advancements."

The Minister's chair is placed in front of a window, and bright sunlight flows around him, making it impossible for me to gauge his expression while we're speaking. This enhances his formidable intellectual presence, which already fills the room. "We are a very ancient people," continues the Minister. "We are proud of our inventions; of the pivotal role that Omanis have played for thousands of years in the advancement of knowledge and science in so many practical fields, like farming and irrigation, the development of metallurgy, navigation and trade and world exploration. We are also very proud of our traditions of art, and the relationship that these have in so many practical ways to the sciences I have just referred to." He glances at Hassan. "I think Hassan has shown you some of these things, taken you to one of our smelters, shown you the origins of the frankincense trade, conducted you around one of our modern perfume factories, and introduced you to some aspects of Omani culture."

I'm impressed; the Minister is clearly up to date with what's going on with this project, and he's done a fine job of explaining to me the challenge of the World Fair as he sees it—from his government's point of view. He seems to be the sort of man to shape destiny rather than wait for it, and it isn't difficult for me to imagine him riding the desert beside Lawrence. He's certainly not someone whose judgement and vision I can question: not the sort of man to accept something as trivial as the Gulf War as a reason for delay. It's rude to write in the presence of the Minister, so I make mental notes while he's speaking, notes which revolve around words like traditional, static, artefact. I add the word dignity, because the Minister seems to personify this virtue above all. Hassan says nothing at all during the meeting, although he bows his head slightly whenever the Minister makes a reference to him. I'm resigned to flying back to Seville to start our design team off on a completely different tack, still without a contract. But just as the Minister stands up to leave, his aide pulls out a sheaf of papers and we sign a preliminary agreement.

The Omanis have been wary of me, I realise as I climb up the steps to the aeroplane that will take me back to London. Ever since oil was first discovered under the desert sands a procession of westerners has journeyed out to this part of the world with creative and devious schemes for getting their hands on Arab riches. It occurs to me that the Omanis probably view the World Fair along similar lines. It's a western event they're not completely sure about, but one they don't think they can afford to ignore. They're right to be suspicious. Europe's business practices in the lead-up to the World Fair must sometimes seem as brutal and cutthroat as the fighting that Sultan Qaboos encountered in the Jebel behind Salalah.

Madness and Disaster

The central features of the World Fair will be four huge, cantilevered Theme Pavilions. These are to be known as the Pavilions of the Future, Navigation, Discovery and the XVth Century. The construction manager for the Discovery Pavilion calls up and asks us to a meeting; he says he wants our company to work on the interior. If this is true, it will be a huge contract. The meeting goes well and the construction manager assures us as we shake hands at the end of it, that we'll be contracted to do the necessary work when the time comes.

However I'm concerned about schedules. The opening date for the Fair is approaching rapidly. "When will the Pavilion be ready for us to start installing the interior?" I ask before we leave him.

He gazes around the horizon as if he's looking for an answer. "December 31st," he says at length.

"But that's only three and a half months before the Fair opens," I point out. "The fit-out will take at least six months for such a highly technical exhibition."

He shrugs his shoulders and stares at me. "It's what the construction contract specifies."

"Okay, but if that's the case, we need to be sure we'll have a clean, dust-free environment to work in on January 1st."

"Oh no," he replies. "On that day we'll have to start installing the electrical and plumbing systems, and the air conditioning."

Even though we're now used to such things, this is still hard to believe. Nobody can start putting delicate exhibitry—a good deal of it priceless and irreplaceable historical material—inside the pavilion until everything else has been done, and certainly not without functioning temperature controls and lighting.

"When will you finish all that?"

"April the first," he says.

The Fair opens on April 20th.

An even more serious matter has arisen in the case of the Spanish Pavilion, the centrepiece of the World Fair. The host pavilion is to be a symbol of Spanish achievement and the focus of the country's pride. King Juan Carlos himself has selected its design, and Spain's international prestige is wrapped tightly into the concept and design of this building.

The managers of the Spanish Pavilion are beginning to realise that there are problems with it, and they've asked for our help. It only takes us a few minutes to examine the plans and come to the heart of the matter.

The Pavilion's basic concept calls for a one hundred and fifty-seat theatre at its centre. Scenes of Spain's glorious past, present and future will be projected in here, and the theatre will host some of the country's finest performance artistes during the fair. We can see right away from the plans that the rest of the Pavilion is a maze of tiny rooms. The next biggest room in the Pavilion will barely accommodate twenty people. The more we look at the design, the more apparent it becomes that the place is a traffic-control nightmare. The way the building is designed, it will barely handle a flow of even four hundred people an hour—never mind the tens of thousands of Spaniards who will want to visit their national pavilion. We ask to speak with the architect and discover to our astonishment that he has not collaborated at all with any of the interior designers who have conceived the exhibit. We explain these basic flaws to the Pavilion's Commissioner and his management team, and tell them that the building will have to be modified.

"Out of the question," says the Commissioner. "Don't you understand? The design has been selected by the King. It cannot possibly be changed." He waves his hands in the air and tells us not to worry about it. "All these things are under control. They will all be fixed."

We ask him how, but he refuses to talk any more about it.

Before we leave we point out that his management team should make some provisions to shade the huge queues of people that will form outside the pavilion. The people who want to see the exhibits and performances will have a long wait, we tell him. They will collapse like flies in the blinding Andalusian heat.

The Commissioner smiles indulgently at our comments. "The people here are used to heat in the summer," he says. "This is not a problem for us at all."

We point out that Expo's own publicity anticipates hundreds of thousands of visitors from all over the world. "People from the United States and Sweden and Germany won't be used to the heat in Seville in summer," we tell him. "It will look bad if your foreign guests start to faint."

A few days after this meeting one of the national newspapers announces that a fifth of all the money advanced for the Spanish Pavilion has been siphoned off into the coffers of the Socialist Party, the governing party in Spain. The Spanish Pavilion is the most expensive project on the Expo site by far, with a budget of hundreds of millions of pesetas. This scandal briefly rocks the Fair, but like the other difficulties Expo has encountered, the problem of the Spanish Pavilion is swept quickly under the rug. Work on the pavilion stops for a few days, and then resumes again.

Dave Moon, the construction manager for the New Zealand Pavilion, has been in trouble with the Expo authorities several times. Soon after they agreed to participate in the World Fair the New Zealand government signed a contract, under duress, with one of the approved Expo service companies. This service company missed its first deadline for construction and supply, and has now poured the concrete slab for the building to the wrong dimensions, using a cheap cement mix. Dave shows me this by kicking big chunks out of the slab with his boots.

A few days later he orders all the Spanish workmen off the New Zealand site. "They won't work, they can't read plans and they won't pay attention to anything we tell them to do," he tells me.

He arranges for forty skilled construction workers to fly to Seville from New Zealand. The Spanish government refuses to issue them work permits. The New Zealand government threatens to withdraw from Expo '92. After a week of brinkmanship, the Expo authorities and Spanish Immigration relent. The Kiwi workers are allowed to stay.

Dave has been obstructed by the Expo authorities all through the construction process, and harassed with a wide variety of petty regulations. His New Zealand crew has also had to dig up the faulty foundation slab and pour a new one. But unlike any of the other pavilions, each of which had to be built by one of the five Expo service companies, Dave's pavilion is now almost finished.

Dave tells me that a big shipping container was delivered to his site yesterday. It was lowered onto the sidewalk at his gate on top of thick boards Dave's men had put down to spread its weight. After the container was emptied and taken away, a senior Expo man turned up. "You've damaged the sidewalk," said the Expo man, pointing to wide, jagged cracks across the concrete. "You'll have to pay to have it repaired."

Dave looked down and spat, just missing the Expo man's

shoes. Then he danced up and down on the sidewalk in his boots, kicking chunks out of the pavement just as he'd done with the original slab. "Nah," he said. "That wasn't us. That's bad workmanship. You guys used the same cheap concrete mix on the sidewalk as you did on the foundation slab for my building."

No doubt Dave would be considered a diplomat's nightmare in many embassies, but we have a sneaking feeling that the Kiwis like to have people like him around. As it is, the New Zealand Pavilion will be finished well before the British Pavilion, which is slowly rising next door. But Dave tells me that he's instructed his men to slow down.

"Why on earth are you letting the Brits catch you up when you can beat them by at least a month?" I ask. Usually the Kiwis are just as ready as the Australians to beat up on the Poms whenever they can. We're standing up on the flat roof of the New Zealand Pavilion, gazing over at a group of workmen who are busy installing the pipes for a waterfall which will cascade down the glass façade of the British Pavilion.

"Nah, that's uncharted waters," says Dave, grinning, "being the first one to finish I mean. No one knows what roadblocks the Spanish will throw up at completion. But you can bet they'll think of something. We'll just watch what happens over there. I'm happy to let the Brits have it."

Three weeks later the British fly out two hundred businessmen and politicians for their topping-out ceremony. They are to receive official congratulations and some sort of prize from the Expo Corporation for completing their Pavilion first. I'm up on the roof again with Dave, watching the rehearsal. The British have brought an outsize Union Jack with them, and they're having trouble snapping it open at the top of the flagpole on the roof; the lanyards keep getting twisted.

"Look," says Dave. A small green van draws up outside the British pavilion. Three men in white hard hats get out and march inside, each one carrying a clipboard.

The next day Dave telephones to tell me that the British topping-out ceremony has been postponed.

"Good God, and they've flown all these people out. It must have cost them a fortune. How long's the hold up?"

"Dunno," he says laconically. "I expect someone from the Expo head office will have a chat with the building inspectors. But there'll be some to-ing and fro-ing and it's bound to cost the Brits a packet."

We've just found out that our company President's real name is Gordon Donald McTavish, although he always calls himself Gord Donald and signs contracts and other things with that name. Margaretha accidentally came across a fax the other day from GD's Vancouver lawyer, referring to proceedings for legally changing his name to Gordon Donald.

This sort of thing makes me nervous. Why would anyone change a perfectly good name unless they want to get away from it because of something that's happened in the past?

Before Gord Donald came along the company was wholly owned by Lon Knowlton, who started it more than ten years ago. Knowlton is the Chief Designer; he's quick-minded, but wilful and stubborn. He now holds half the shares in the company. Apart from a small distribution to one or two other people, Gord Donald owns the rest.

Soon after Knowlton brought him on board, GD went out and hired the best people he could find: Flanagan for technical, Robert Thomas for fabrication, myself for marketing, Dick Lott for project management, and several top-flight designers. In fact the company's design section has grown and grown; GD always seems to give in to Knowlton's requests for more designers.

GD is a nice fellow, but he's not a very good manager and I think he has little concept of budgeting, and almost none of cash flow. He's never been able to understand the vagaries of the Spanish system of doing business, where nobody considers paying bills for at least ninety days. Although he quickly managed to grasp the system of "irregular compensation" which sometimes turns up here, he seems to use it inappropriately, either at the wrong time or with the wrong people.

While he's hired some pretty competent people, GD's judgement is occasionally flawed in the matter of personnel. He hired Doris last year, a highly efficient head of Pavilion Operations for an American company at the 1988 Brisbane Expo. But it was a poor decision to hire her when he did because we didn't need her skills for another eight months.

Soon after Doris joined the company, GD began to take her out. Within a month they moved into an apartment together and held a party to announce that they were going to get married at some undefined date. With Doris's cooking GD is starting to put on weight. The two of them often kiss and snuggle in the office, go out for lunch together and hold hands in the elevator. This doesn't enhance GD's status as company President, particularly with the Spanish staff, who frown on this sort of behaviour in public. Some of them have started calling him 'Don Gordo'—which basically means 'the fat boss'.

Our friend Mercedes was crossing the Plaza Nueva a few days ago when a taxi skidded to a halt in front of her. Both rear passenger doors flew open. GD shot out of one door and began shouting at Doris, who was climbing out of the other. People around the square stopped and stared. Doris screamed something at GD, then jumped back in the taxi and ordered the driver to drive off. GD was left standing at the side of the road staring after the departing taxi.

In the end he strode off by himself. He has thick white hair and he's over six feet tall, taller than the average Spaniard. Mercedes has no doubt about her identification. There have been other arguments just as furious, in the office and in the street, one of them right outside the offices of our main corporate competitor, Sevilla Service, according to Flanagan. It is not a good situation.

The company has now spent more than a quarter of a million dollars on computer hardware, software programmes and a hugely expensive and unnecessary office network. We have the third largest computer network in Andalusia, and a far greater intranet capability than our small company requires. No one but Knowlton can grasp how it all works or what it can do. Our internal communications software is so complicated that a technician has to be flown out from Canada whenever anything goes wrong with it. One thing or another has gone wrong with it every week since it was installed, usually just after the technician has disappeared back to Vancouver. It also seems clear to me now that the company is under-financed. It owes money and expenses to everyone on staff. It hasn't even paid my original travel costs to come to Spain, as well as about thirty thousand dollars in back wages.

Nervous about the company's finances, our joint venture partners at the Banco Bilbao Viscaya insisted several months ago that we hire a Spanish Director of Finance. So we acquired José Serrano. Unfortunately it has been very hard at management meetings to get any kind of financial statements from him, or any proper project accounting. However José talks a good line, although he speaks no English at all.

Last week Manito told me that it's possible in Spain to become a doctor or a lawyer or almost any other kind of professional by simply purchasing a qualification. Some of us are not sure now if José has any serious accounting qualifications at all, although the finer points of this situation are lost on GD, who doesn't speak very good Spanish.

Senor Torquato of Valencia is refusing to pay his bill. Throughout our difficulties with other Spanish clients Senor Torquato has been a paragon of honesty and efficiency. He has personally signed off every stage of his project, after receiving the correct approvals from his supervisory government committees in Valencia. Armed with these signed approvals we've moved on through concept to design, and now into the manufacturing phase of his project. Our joint venture colleagues at the Banco Bilbao Viscaya have been quick to reassure us about

Valencia's reliability every time we've raised the matter of the unpaid bills.

Chilton, our Project Manager for the Valencia Pavilion, is devastated. He sits in his office in a glass-enclosed balcony among a jungle of potted palms and ferns and stares gloomily into his computer. Chilton thinks he and Torquato have become friends and cannot understand what has happened. Flurries of telephone calls and faxes bounce back and forth between our BBV partners and Valencia and our offices, but still no bills are paid.

Each morning when I reach the office Chilton is already there, perched in his glass eyrie above the street. He always looks busy, hammering away at the keys of his Siemens computer. Chilton is an American from Washington, DC. He has been living in Seville for four or five years, and now he's fallen in love with a girl from a traditional Spanish family.

Macarena is tall and dark with smouldering *Carmen* looks. Chilton thinks he is in charge of the relationship, but it's clear to the rest of us that he is not. Macarena speaks no English. Although Chilton has a good command of Spanish, we now know that North Americans can never speak Spanish well enough to satisfy the contorted etiquette and customs of Andalusia. He tells us one day that Macarena's family has pulled powerful strings so that he can take part in one of the *Semana Santa* parades. This is a much sought-after honour; normally it is only granted to those who have supported the church for years.

I ask him what his role will be. One of the Marshals with a heavy staff perhaps, resplendent in a long cloak? Perhaps he will be a *'penitente'* to cleanse himself before his marriage to Macarena? There is a certain glamour even to them.

Chilton admits that he will be none of these. He will be one of the anonymous labourers under the heavy *paseo*, invisible behind the thick velvet covers that fall down the sides. Chilton will toil away in the suffocating heat for fourteen hours. His particular procession is one of the longest of all the celebrations. He has been told that he must start serious training immediately, like a representative rugby player, months before the event.

Meanwhile he sits pecking away at his computer, his glass office heating up unbearably as the sun climbs overhead and the morning wears on. After several more days without any resolution to the Valencia affair I pay him a visit, pushing through his steamy forest of tropical plants. Chilton is playing computer golf.

"You should try this," he says excitedly. "I'm playing Pebble Beach today." He picks at the keys, and something like the hour hand of a clock whirls downwards and the computer makes an electronic clunking noise as an imaginary golf club connects with an imaginary golf ball.

"Look at that! Two hundred and eighty yards . . . right down the middle!"

"Is this what you've been doing all day?" I'd thought that he'd been worrying away at the Valencia business, trying to sort it out.

"No. Sometimes I play Muirfield, or Augusta. But there's nothing happening with Torquato. The Bank can't get any money out of him and there's no point in getting bent out of shape about it. Things will sort themselves out eventually." Chilton has learned more than he cares to admit from his Spanish family. He continues to punch away at the computer keyboard. He points at the little clock-like symbol at the top of the screen.

"This is how I know how hard to hit it," he explains. "Watch this. This is a delicate one. I've got to chip it over a bunker and stop it dead on that sloping green."

The temperature in his office is over a hundred degrees but Chilton is oblivious to the heat. "I played St. Andrews yesterday and beat the course record. Damn!" The computerised golf ball disappears into a yellow sand trap.

Chilton is becoming acclimatised to the customs of the region. He gazes up at me like a child. "There's nothing we can do about Valencia," he says patiently. "It's all in our partners' hands now. If the Bank people can't get him to pay his bills then we certainly can't."

He turns back to his golf. I go back to my office.

I'm working hard on the Oman project; writing up the basic contract, re-developing the concept outline for the exhibit. Part of what I have to do involves writing a script for a multimedia presentation in the Pavilion: however, irritating changes have somehow been appearing every day on the script that I've been typing into the computer.

The deadline is fast approaching for sending the script off to Hassan in Muscat. On Saturday morning I make my way to the office to finish it up, and when I turn on my computer and bring up the file I find the script is radically changed, almost unrecognisable. I call Em and tell her we won't be able to take a promised trip into the mountains. It takes me all day to rewrite the script.

On Sunday morning I go back to the office to apply the finishing touches in peace and discover that the script has been completely re-written again. The English is ungrammatical, and the context changed so that most of the facts in it are now badly mis-stated. The Omanis would have a fit about the inaccurate references that are in it. Once again it takes me all day to correct the grammar and inept phraseology, and rewrite the misleading descriptions.

The next morning Anna, the translator, complains to me that the script is still not ready for her, and the deadline (already extended twice because of the strange changes) is tomorrow. "The time is already much too short for a good translation," she says. "But if I don't get the script right away I won't be able to do anything at all."

"What do you mean it's not ready, Anna?" I ask her. "I printed it out and put it in your tray last night."

"Lon Knowlton took it away," she says.

I run down the stairs to see Knowlton. I also know that he's the only person in the organisation who can get inside anyone else's computer. He's sitting at his desk, typing away at his keyboard.

"Who's changing my Oman script, Lon?" I ask, trying to stay calm in spite of the fact that days of hard work have been altered and erased; despite the fact that I flew out there in the middle of a war to get the contract.

Knowlton turns round slowly and stares at me. He doesn't like being interrupted when he's working at his computer. "I got Walter to change it," he says coolly. "I didn't like the way it was written."

"Walter? Who the hell is Walter?"

Knowlton stares at me, obviously offended by the tone I'm using. "Walter used to teach design at the University of Winnipeg," he says primly. "I've hired him to oversee the scripting on all our projects."

I find it difficult to speak. For a second I think I'm going to faint. "Three times? You got Walter to re-write my script three times and you never said a word to me about it?" The fainting sensation lasts only a second or two before I completely lose my temper.

"And who the fucking hell do you think *you* are then?" I shout, sweeping all his books and papers off his desk onto the floor in a fit of fury. Knowlton dives under his desk. I storm out of his office.

Walter is the scruffy-looking, elderly man we've seen hanging about in the reception area. It turns out that he comes into the office every night after we've all gone home. Without telling anyone else, he and Knowlton have been changing all the contracted projects.

Walter speaks no Spanish. Knowlton has hired him to advise the designers about the Oman and Andorra contracts; contracts I've won for the company; contracts made with clients who are my responsibility. Walter speaks no Arabic either, nor has he ever been out to the Middle East. I find out he has no idea where Andorra is.

Marty has been given the job of General Manager in an effort to keep costs down and make sure things run efficiently. I plunge into his office. "Marty, you've got to tell that Walter guy he can't come in here."

"Can't do that Mike. He's a friend of Knowlton's."

"You don't understand Marty. If I see Walter in here again he's going out the window."

"Um, I'm afraid GD and I agreed to his appointment," Marty says.

I lower my voice to a whisper, very angry. "If you don't stop him from coming in here and fucking about with my work, Marty, I'll throw you out the window with him."

I steam out of Marty's office and blast through the door into GD's office and lose my temper with him as well.

Half an hour later Marty saunters into my office and tells me that Walter will be gone by the weekend. This calms me down.

The company's staff complement is expanding rapidly to meet the pressure of contracts. The design department alone contains at least a dozen designers—Czechs, Poles, Brits, Canadians, Spanish. Flanagan has hired several technicians. Robert has hired technical designers and factory workers from London. We've now taken over the apartment downstairs and Flanagan wants to drill a spiral staircase down through the living room of our main office. I'm not at all sure that this expansion has been properly costed out, or even well planned. I doubt very much that it has been cleared with the landlady.

One morning I walk past a dented white van parked in the street outside our offices. I notice it because the van has its steering wheel on the right-hand side and raw metal patches riveted over a number of rusted-out panels. It's an old British Bedford.

Marty has hired a shifty-looking Floor Manager to run the fabrication factory the company is building on the outskirts of Seville, but won't be able to pay for. The new Floor Manager's name is Bradley and he comes from London.

"Is that your van in the street?" I ask him when I get upstairs.

Bradley's gaze fixes on my third shirt button. "What ov it?" he says belligerently.

I make a mental note to keep my hand on my wallet. "It's got UK plates. It'll get towed."

"Company's buying it," he says in a round, Millwall accent. "Marty says he can get it licensed 'ere. He needs it for the factry, and Flanagan needs somefing to carry 'is gear about in." He leans towards me and whispers, "'ave you been paid lately? Marty hasn't given me my expenses yet."

I shake my head and walk away.

Walter has turned up in our offices again, languishing in the reception area. The sight of him drives me into a fury. I march straight into Marty's office and slam the door.

"Marty, I've changed my mind. I think you should go out the window first. I can deal with Walter later. "

Marty glances nervously out of his window. A narrow interior well plunges five floors down through the centre of the building. A tiny, litter-strewn courtyard lies at the bottom of it, ankle deep in cigarette ends. Depending on the speed of Marty's exit he could bounce off the walls three or four times on his way down.

"Relax Mike," he says, reaching for a cigarette. "Walter's duties have been changed. He's only been hired to walk Riley now." Riley is Lon Knowlton's dog.

I can't believe this.

"Riley doesn't get enough exercise," continues Marty. "Knowlton worries about him. It interferes with his work."

I'm almost speechless, but not quite. "Are we paying wages to Walter?"

"Well . . . yes, we are."

"Do you know how much back pay the company owes me Marty?" I lean over his desk and he slides his chair away from me, until the wall stops him from retreating any further. "Do

292

you? This company owes me thousands and thousands of dollars and that idiot downstairs has hired his old university art teacher to take his bloody dog out for walks?"

"We're all in the same boat," Marty mutters, picking up his telephone.

Last Christmas GD made a decision to purchase land at La Rinconada, just outside Seville, and start constructing a factory—a fabrication plant so that the company could build all the interior exhibitry for our contracts. This decision flew in the face of the advice GD was given by the company's senior management and most of its Directors. It was pointed out that there would be a glut of useless factories in Andalucia when the World's Fair was over, that the company would lose a lot of money when it came time to sell it. Our partners at the BBV told GD they would not back the factory financially.

GD simply waited until the office was closed and the staff and Directors away for the Christmas break to confirm his decision. Now we find that the factory has been financed, not out of capital loans from the bank, but with operating funds which are desperately needed for day-to-day wages, office expenses, marketing initiatives and so on. Since Christmas it has been José Serrano's job to make sure that we have enough operating money to stay afloat. He's been doing this for some time, but in a kind of decreasing pyramid, through a succession of lenders and contacts. It turns out that José has been dashing from one bank to another borrowing money, often pledging the same, non-existent collateral. He's kept no records of these complicated, desperate transactions and now he's run out of bank friends and contacts. Things are all coming to a head.

The cash-flow situation is now beyond critical. Most of the designers have left to work for other companies. Grahame tells me that two of them are working at home so they can protect their work and retain ownership of it if they're not paid.

Flanagan buries himself in his work and refuses to talk about finances. This is understandable. Flanagan has invested a lot of money in the company over the last year and recently signed for and guaranteed some expensive electronic equipment through his own bank account in Canada. Some of the others think Flanagan is silent because he's confident and sure of things, but I know it's because he doesn't know what to do. Conditions are very tense.

Knowlton tries to steal Grahame's design drawings. Grahame threatens to kill him.

Marty is throwing up every night, and sits in his office shuffling papers all day. Creditors are calling daily, hourly, by the minute. None of the staff have been paid for weeks, and many of them are experiencing real hardship. The remaining designers have been on strike for two days and are threatening to leave with all their drawings.

Lon Knowlton rarely leaves the sanctity of his computers. Robert hides downstairs with the engineers. Chilton is playing golf at some electronic Spyglass Hill. Over the last few months our two clever secretaries, Margaretha and Jennifer, have perfected tested Spanish techniques for fending off creditors. But every day now they're finding it more and more difficult to plug the dykes.

On the way to speak to Robert about one of our projects I find the downstairs hallway jammed to the ceiling with boxes of new computers. I turn round and steam right back up to Marty's office.

"What the hell's going on Marty?" I'm trying hard to keep my voice calm. "We're all owed money. The banks are owed money. Our creditors are jamming the switchboard and I've just tripped over another hundred thousand dollars worth of computers which someone has bought for people we can't afford to hire. Are you guys all mad?"

"Relax Mike," says Marty smoothly. "We don't have to pay for them for ninety days."

The power goes off while we're talking, and a commotion

starts out in the stairwell. We can smell smoke, and run out to see what's going on. A jangle of fire bells comes from the crowded street. Flanagan dashes past and dives down the stairs, taking them three at a time. Marty and I follow.

Our building's electrical system was never designed to carry the massive loads that we've placed on it. The block where our office lies is zoned only for residential use, and for a few small shops. We find Flanagan standing down at the front door staring at the main electrical control box. The metal box is glowing red, and an ugly, grey-black gluey liquid is dripping slowly out of it onto the sidewalk. The smell is terrible.

"What's the problem?" asks Marty.

"Cooked," mutters Flanagan. "Completely fried."

It turns out that our air-conditioning system and our high-powered computer network have completely done in the building's ancient wiring circuits. The damaged circuitry services fourteen residential apartments, and two small shops on the ground floor. Repairs will be expensive. Flanagan thinks we might even have destroyed the wiring for the whole block.

Meanwhile Knowlton's car provides a small diversion. Knowlton's personal effects have started to arrive from Canada just as his company is collapsing. For some reason this puts me in mind of what it must have been like in the Berlin bunker when the Allied armies were closing in on Hitler; the sense of unreality as the Nazi Commander-in-Chief moved his non-existent armies around a map of Europe.

Knowlton was told months ago that the container with all his goods in it had been jettisoned from a freighter during a wild Atlantic storm. He initiated complex negotiations with insurance representatives in Spain, which dragged on and on without resolution. He was surprised two weeks ago to receive a call telling him to go and collect a big container from the docks at Cadiz.

Among his effects is an ugly brown Fiat sports car. Knowlton is pleased to have his car and drives it daily to the office, even though he lives in a house less than five minutes walk away.

He parks the car in the street behind the office. We've told him not to do this, particularly as the car is a convertible. Auto theft is rife in Seville.

When he goes to collect the car after work, his British Columbia licence plates are missing. Later in the evening a policeman stops him for having no licence plates on his car. Knowlton tells him angrily that if the police did their job properly and protected personal property he'd still have his licence plates, and drives away leaving the astonished policeman standing on the pavement.

Knowlton seems unaffected by the situation he's in. The authorities will catch up with him eventually; without licence plates he will have to import his car officially into Spain, and pay a thirty-three percent duty on the value the customs authorities choose to assess it with. Without licence plates he has no motor insurance, as the Spanish policy he's bought is rendered invalid. It is not legal to drive a car in Spain without insurance.

The next day the Fiat's headrests disappear, along with the ashtray.

The company's crises grind inexorably onwards. Each one has now flowed seamlessly into all the others with the inevitability of a tide of black lava at the foot of a volcano. The telephone company has disconnected the telephones. Now we have to walk up the street to the luxurious D'92 offices to make essential telephone calls to clients. Creditors have stopped telephoning the office, but they now come personally to the office instead. They crowd into the reception area and shout and gesticulate at our Spanish secretaries while the company principals hide in their offices, and we attempt to shelter important international clients from these distasteful events.

José Serrano resigns and goes back to live in Madrid. He refuses to admit the incompetence of his dealings with the banks, and it is true that GD's manoeuvrings probably left him little choice. Meanwhile GD continues valiantly to try and mount a rescue package with a mysterious group of Spanish investors. We often see him deep in conversation with a grey man called Julio Lopez. Julio is supposedly connected with powerful Expo figures and rich businessmen.

Knowlton comes into the office in a state of agitation. Margaretha asks him if he's all right.

"Someone has stolen the steering wheel from my car," he says. Without the steering wheel of course, the car cannot be moved, and it's parked in an area where it will soon be towed away by the authorities.

Flanagan rather heartlessly points this out. "Getting your car towed in Seville is about the same thing as having it stolen," he adds helpfully. It could take hundreds of dollars of encouragement, and endless negotiations to release it from the city's towing compound.

While Flanagan is speaking a thought seems to pass through Knowlton's mind. His face brightens and he disappears downstairs into the office of our engineers. Late in the afternoon I see him driving down the busy Avenida de la Republica Argentina, steering his car with two metal vise grips locked onto the stub of his steering column, his elbows jutting out as he manoeuvres in and out of the traffic. As I'm watching, a car darts suddenly out of a side street, causing Knowlton to swerve violently. One of the vise grips comes off in his hand and he's left waving it around in the air, trying frantically to steer with the one in his other hand. He narrowly misses running into a line of parked cars, and just manages to bring his car to a stop with only the one tenuous vise grip to steer with. I turn away, leaving Knowlton sitting in his stalled car, pointing the disengaged vise-grip angrily at the errant motorist.

Work has stopped at the factory at La Rinconada. The builders have not been paid and the workers have sealed the doors shut with big, industrial padlocks. Thousands of dollars worth of expensive equipment is trapped inside, including the pricey electronic gear that Flanagan is on the hook for in Canada. He grows more silent than ever.

Bradley, the factory foreman from London, now spends his time sitting in the reception area grumbling aggressively and threatening to go on strike unless he is paid. This will make no difference to anything.

The carpenters and electricians that Bradley has hired, and flown out from London at the company's expense to work at the factory, have turned up at the office as well. They cannot get into the factory and they haven't been paid either. All of them are skilled people, and most of them resigned jobs in England to come and work here in Seville. They're a beefy, tough-looking bunch and they all seem to know Bradley well. They're angry and want to meet with GD.

The electricity company has cut off the electrical supply to our offices, and our expensive computer system is now useless. People are openly looking for new jobs. GD's efforts to put together a rescue attempt have come to naught. This is ironic as the company actually has well over US $30 million in verifiable, signed contracts. However, with a fragmented and diminishing work force, and without BBV's backing to ensure a healthy cash flow, time has finally run out. There is nothing to do but make preparations to leave.

The lease on our apartment is a problem. The Spanish won't hesitate to arrest foreigners who run out on their leases. Besides, our landlord, Juan, is a decent man and we don't want to leave him without a tenant. But the company owes me several months of back pay and expenses, and we can't afford to keep the apartment for the remaining six months of the lease. Fortunately the Swiss Pavilion people are interested in taking it over, and Ulli comes round to inspect it. He finds it suitable for their purposes, and we inform him carefully about the lease terms, the frequency and size of payment. He agrees to everything.

Juan journeys up from his home in Malaga to meet Ulli. All that needs to be done is for them both to sign the lease agreement, which we've had legally re-drafted and notarised at our own expense. To our horror Ulli starts to dicker with Juan about the rent. An argument begins, and flows back and forth before it is finally resolved. I am upset at Ulli's vacillations but Juan accepts them without complaint. It is how things are done here.

The company offices on the Avenida de la Republica Argentina are a different matter altogether. It is impossible to return them to the residential splendour they were in before the company took them over. There is no money left to do the necessary work, and the structural alterations that have been made are virtually irreversible in any case. GD signed the lease and approved the alterations, but now he doesn't want to meet with the landlady. He arranges to leave the keys with Juan Goya, the lawyer. The lawyer will plead ignorance.

Em and Xan fly off to Canada. They'll come back to Europe in three weeks and meet me in Scotland.

Andorra

It's nice and cool when I wake up in the Los Olivas Motel outside Madrid. It has been a difficult night; a squadron of mosquitoes turned up just as sleep was taking me away, and buzzed about my ears, jerking me back to wakefulness. I killed six of them during the night and laid them out on the bedside table. They're lying there in an untidy row when I open my eyes.

The shower is cold, but without the vagaries of Spanish showers, which usually throw water all over the place. This water-jet flies true and the shower curtain even stops it from flooding the tiny bathroom.

It took me all day yesterday to drive up here from Seville. I got up early and took a shower, keen to get on the road. Our empty apartment echoed like a vault, the furniture all carted away by the shipper, already on its way to Canada. On the way out I stopped at the portero's little house by the gate to leave the keys and say goodbye, but Francisco was away on an errand and so I left my greetings with his son.

The insurance on the car we bought in Andalusia expires in two days, and because it's a duty free car the insurance has to be renewed in a country that is not a member of the European Community. The rules concerning this matter are very complex and not entirely clear to me, but I've been assured by people who know about these things that motor insurance in Andorra is reliable and inexpensive, and effective throughout Europe. Andorra does not belong to the EC, although its neighbours—France to the north and Spain to the south—both do.

It's a Sunday morning and there's hardly any traffic on the roads. Wide freeways spirit me around Madrid, past acres of waste ground and building sites, and onto the Guadalajara – Zaragossa road. I open the car out and soon it's clicking along at a steady 180 kilometres an hour. There are not as many Guardia on the roads up here as there are in Andalusia.

The road climbs up onto the Navarra plateau, and the land stretches as flat as rolled pastry to washed out blue horizons on every side. By early afternoon the temperature has warmed up, although the heat is not as taxing and oppressive as it is in the south.

After Zaragossa the wide Barcelona road takes me eastwards as far as Llerida and the muddy Rio Segre. There's more traffic down here than there was up on the plateau. I turn onto the narrow C-1313 and head for Seu de Urgell, and wind slowly up towards the Pyrenees, past tattered ochre and red villages clinging to the steep hillsides.

Andorra lies deep in the mountains like a secret, sandwiched between Spain and France. At the border a Spanish Customs Officer asks me how much money I've got with me. I tell him I've got two hundred thousand pesetas and he immediately tells me to pull over. A worm of anxiety, awakened by this official in uniform, gnaws at my stomach. Has he told me to pull over because I don't have enough money? Because I have too much? Because he wants a bribe?

But a long line of cars has already formed behind me and there's no space to back up or park. The official looks disgusted, curls his lip and mutters, "*Continuar*", and I drive off, relieved.

Just beyond the Customs post a sign points to Andorra La Vella and the road squeezes through a narrow defile. But a workmen's barrier closes it off at the first corner, jamming up the traffic until two men in blue overalls saunter out of a hut and move the barrier a few feet over to one side. The Eurohotel lies on the north side of Andorra La Vella, the cramped urban centre of this tiny country. The girl at the counter offers me a room for three thousand one hundred pesetas, and tells me the price includes breakfast. The room she takes me to sits on the edge of a sharp slope, over a tumbling stream which falls straight down the mountainside.

Tomorrow I have an appointment to renew the Supra's insurance at the offices of Gestoria La Vella in the Carrer Dr. Villanova. After a cool shower I wander off to explore the town, and ask six different people for directions to Dr. Villanova Street. No one knows where it is, and there are no street maps here. But eventually I look up and find the offices of Gestoria La Vella standing in front of me, nondescript and grey. The street where they sit has no name.

I sit at a table in a sidewalk café, sip a glass of wine and order steak and chips, and contemplate the life of this place. Andorra is a tax haven and a hideaway, for the moment at least outside the prying eyes of Brussels and the European tax authorities. It can only be approached through a couple of narrow defiles, or three high mountain passes that are often blocked in winter. Three narrow valleys make up the country, with a few farmable benches on the mountainsides. Nearly all the level bottom land has been built upon. Above me, construction cranes reach over the town centre like broken fingers. New buildings are going up, old ones coming down.

Three young girls stop and order ice cream, and sit down at the next table, casting sideways glances at four older boys drinking beer. The wind comes up and the boys pick up their glasses and move inside. The girls shrug and content themselves with making comments about the people walking past.

The sun leaves early in this high-sided valley, and arrives late each morning. Sheer, scree-sloped mountains rise high above the town, locking it in on all sides. In winter when the sun is low there will be little sunlight here at all, and these steep faces will be prone to avalanches when the snow comes. Lightning flashes off to the south and a few drops of rain start to fall. The sun touches the mountaintops above the north end of town.

In the morning it takes me more than two hours to complete my business at Gestoria La Vella. It's a complicated procedure, conducted almost entirely in Spanish. By the end of it I've spent about a thousand dollars to acquire new licence plates for the car, and new insurance of a sort. The agent assures me the insurance will protect me from all claims, as well as Customs and other authorities on all the roads of Europe.

By noon I'm on a narrow road which is carrying me up a wide valley towards the French border. As the car climbs higher and higher the countryside opens out into grassland and patches of scrub heather moor. At the side of the road a sandwich board by a tumbledown barn advertises food. The air up here is cool and clean, the sky patterned with mountaintops. The barn is rustic inside, smoky and low-beamed with alcove windows and rough walls that have been slapped with whitewash. Red checkerboard tablecloths cover the wooden tables.

A girl no more than about twelve years old seems to be in charge. She barks orders in a husky voice to her parents and sisters, who flit in and out of a dark kitchen like shadows. In a minute she brings me a bowl of hot soup; as soon as I've finished it she turns up with a thick beef stew, and chunks of bread torn from a loaf.

After lunch I drive off and a series of steep hairpin turns quickly takes the road up into the clouds and a clammy darkness. I turn on the headlights. Then I'm over the top of the pass and descending, picking my way around more sharp bends. France can't be far away now. The road descends to a misty skiing village where a long line of cars is stopped at a border post. French gendarmes and Customs officers are checking the cars, one by one.

Two Customs officers walk up and start to examine the Supra, moving carefully round it from front to back. One of them points at the new licence plates. The other one waves me over to a parking space at the side of the road, and hails a colleague who's wearing plain clothes. The plain-clothes man walks over and immediately asks me for my passport. He circles the car once, and comes back to my window.

"Turn off the engine please," he says in English, "and come with me to my office. Bring your papers; the papers for the car too."

Inside the Customs office he sits down and directs me to sit in a chair on the other side of his desk. His questions are fast and professional, leaving me little time for answers; little time for thought.

"How long have you owned this car? Where did you buy it? How much did you pay for it? When did you buy the insurance for it? The licence plates?"

His English is good. I answer all his questions. He calls through the open door to a passing, uniformed superior. The two of them hold a short conversation in French. He turns and asks me a question in French.

"I beg your pardon?" I reply in English.

Satisfied, he continues conversing with his superior. Things don't sound good. They're saying I can't bring the car into France.

He turns back to me. "You cannot drive this car in France."

"Why not?"

"Because you have owned it for more than a year. If you bring it into France you must pay Import Duties. European Community Import Duties amount to thirty-three per cent of what you paid for the car."

I stare at him and digest this information, and suddenly I feel very tired. He waits for me to answer.

"I'm only passing through France on my way to Scotland. *Ecosse.*" I let the word slide off my tongue in the hope that it might evoke past associations. "I won't be spending more than three days in France and I don't have any intention of selling the car in Europe. I want to ship it home to Canada, where I live."

"You don't understand," he says. "You cannot drive this car anywhere in the European Community, not without paying Duty."

"You mean I've got to leave it in Andorra?"

"Yes."

"Well, you might as well take the car then," I reply, filled suddenly with a mysterious lassitude. "I'll just catch a bus from here. I've got no intention of paying Duty when I don't want to import the car into Europe . . . even if I could afford it." I toss the car keys onto his desk and stand up.

This takes him completely by surprise, and he calls out to his superior who is once again walking past the office door. They have a rapid conversation in French.

"Where are you going?" he asks, glancing again at my Canadian passport.

"Scotland."

He laughs, and his mood has changed. "Even if we let you through you'll never get past the English Customs at Dover."

But I can tell that his attitude is different. For the first time in an hour I'm starting to think that things might work out. "I can worry about that when I get to England," I tell him.

He shrugs his shoulders. "Okay, you can go." He hands me the passport, and I pick up my keys and walk out of his office and down the front steps of the little *Douane*.

The road down to Aix is steep with switchbacks and curves. I drive fast, wanting to put as much space as possible between myself and the French Customs Post in case they change their minds. The sun comes out for the first time in hours.

Das Reich

The foothills on this northern flank of the Pyrenees are riven with steep-sided canyons, and the road curls and constricts itself around rocky walls and outcrops, and drops down towards a silver river far below.

The traffic around Toulouse is slow and heavy. It is hot down here, August hot, and the French truck drivers are impatient, quick to use their horns. But I find the road out to the Corréze and head north at a good pace. This route was laid out by Roman armies and it reaches compass-straight for its horizons, rising and falling across a pale, olive-green landscape, breaking up and floating in the haze. The air is thick with damp, high summer heat; soporific and enervating, even with the Supra's air conditioner at full blast.

I don't stop until I've driven for more than an hour. A small roadside stand offers peaches for sale in baskets, and bottles of wine. The peaches are plump and full of juice, and refreshing in the heat. The wine will taste good later. The purchases cost hardly anything.

This is the route that the SS Das Reich Division took to Normandy in the days after the D-Day landings in the summer of

1944. The allied armies had assaulted the beaches and gained a toehold on the European mainland. The 2nd SS Division—the Das Reich, stationed in southwest France—was ordered north immediately. The success of the German defence depended on them making the journey quickly, in a few short days.

The French Resistance attacked them all along the way and it took the Division more than two weeks to reach the Allied beachheads. By the time they got there it was too late for them to make an impact on the battle for Normandy.

It was a journey which should not have taken them more than two or three days. One young and enterprising British Special Operations officer named Tony Brooks managed to distribute a special abrasive oil, which the Germans unknowingly applied to railway rolling stock and even to some of their tanks and half-tracks. This oil completely wrecked the ball bearings and joints, and seized up the moving parts. It caused huge delays and great frustration.

On their way north that summer the Das Reich Division passed through the villages of Tulle and Oradour-sur-Glane. Here they exacted fearful reprisals upon the civilian populations for the delays they'd suffered. At Tulle they hanged a man from every lamp-post along the length of the town's main street—any Frenchman they could find wearing blue workman's overalls. Some of the deaths were particularly barbaric and slow, where they bound the men and then hoisted them up by meat hooks thrust under their chins, to dangle from balconies above the river. The SS held no trials, made no effort to establish that any of the men they hanged had anything to do with the Maquis.

At Oradour the SS herded all the women and children into the village church, and barred all the exits before setting it on fire. The men of the Das Reich Division waited outside and watched it burn, shooting anyone who tried to climb out of the windows, firing off their machine guns from time to time to drown out the screams of the people inside. Nearly six hundred villagers died in the church at Oradour, none of them combatants.

Oradour has been left as it was on that summer day in 1944, a burned out skeleton of a town, complete with rusting metal tram tracks and broken telephone wires. It stands as a monument to what men can do.

A fierce thunderstorm erupts at seven o'clock, just as darkness is falling. I turn off the main road towards the village of Couzance. There is an inn here. It is almost empty and I take a room. Outside the rain pounds down, rattling the roof of the conservatory, bouncing high off the tarmac in the empty car park while I eat my supper. The bed in my room is like many French beds: soft and springy, and bowed in the centre. It folds over me and I sleep, deep and dreamless and long.

The Customs man at Dover takes only a cursory look at my passport and waves me through, reminding me to keep to the left side of the road. It takes a bit of getting used to in the left-hand-drive Supra, but the car takes me quickly round London and then northwards up the M1. By the end of the day I'm standing up on the hill at Carter Bar on the Scottish border, gazing over fading green fields as neat as patchwork, as ordered as a painting. In the distance stand the gentle Eildons, strong and familiar, the hills of home.

Acknowledgements

There are many people to thank.

First of all, my wife Marilyn Bowering for all her help in going over the book many times, and guiding me in the writing of it. Marilyn shared many of the experiences in it, collected blisters on her feet, got wet, froze and baked and slept on lumpy beds in rundown hostelries. During it all she made quiet observations, offered perspectives and interpretations that were unfailingly insightful and intelligent, sensitive and provocative.

The poem 'Native Land' is from Marilyn Bowering, *Love As It Is*, (Victoria, BC: Beach Holme Publishers Ltd., 1993).

Thank you to Doug Beardsley for offering me helpful strategic advice at an early stage in the writing of the book.

Thanks are also due for the content of the book, for all their help to me and for the teachings and experiences without which life would be dull, to:

My late father, for sharing firesides and beer and wonderful stories with me, and linking things—past to the present.

Carm Borg in Valetta, for being such a generous host, and for opening little windows into the ways of his people.

David Black, for asking me to take on the challenge of the Europeans and sending me off on some fascinating travels, and to Sandy Peden.

Pierre Leduc for his invaluable help when he was Canadian Cultural Attaché in Paris. And to Tommy and Françoise and the butcher, who live near Place Gambetta, just around the corner from Jim Morrison, Edith Piaf and Oscar Wilde.

Rick and Cathy Stolle for the use of their attic apartment in Cologne, for memorable meals, for their advice and company in Germany, Spain and Canada, and for introducing me to Marc de Champagne.

Helene Detry-Gustin for inviting us into her cottage in Grune, and for telling us about things that happened a long time ago; particularly the small important things, the things that still keep her awake at night.

Jacqueline Pietri in Nice, and Alice Maria. And to John Rebman at the Beach Regency for his hospitality.

Emanuel Borovian and his wife Blanka in Prague, for wreaking miracles when things were bleak, and later for so generously handing over their comfortable bed in Squirrel Street. To George (Jiri) for giving us all but the shirt off his back, and to Gerry (also Jiri) and Vera Simek.

Jaromir Hnik and Jordan Stoyanov for their help when I went back to Czechoslovakia three years later, and for showing me the little grey machine that helped their country to finally break free.

Some of the names in the "Seville Diaries" section of the book have been changed in order to protect what I might call innocent bystanders. But special thanks are due to José Ignacio Narvaez and Xandra in Seville for their friendship and generosity, and for glasses of fine wine and whisky. To Mercedes and her family, to Enrique Moreno de Cova and his, and to the wonderful Luis Catalan de Ocon in Madrid for his trust and friendship. To Paul Flanagan for propelling me into the whole unforgettable experience, and also to Kevin Johnston, Rosa, Angelica & Byron, Chilton, Marty, Graham, and Robert, for sharing in it. And of course to Marilyn and Xan for coming to Spain with me, and making it home.

Thanks are due as well to Jeff Green, who came to see us in Spain, endured the heat and made trenchant observations, which invariably enlivened matters. Jeffrey also looked over parts of this manuscript, and offered me invaluable advice.

Lastly, whatever you think of it, this book is a lot better than it would have been without the very professional care that Ron Smith and Hiro Boga of Oolichan Books have applied to the challenges of editing it. I am most grateful. Any errors of fact, or omissions, of course remain entirely my own responsibility.

Much local and general knowledge, and a considerable amount of research went into the historical references and anecdotes sprinkled through the book. Chief among the sources for this information were:

John Swettenham, *To Seize The Victory: The Canadian Corps in World War I* (Toronto: Ryerson Press, 1965)

Charles B. MacDonald, *A Time Of Trumpets* (New York: Bantam Books, 1985)

Douglas Botting, *In The Ruins Of The Reich* (London: Grafton Books, 1986)

Russell Braddon, *Cheshire V.C.* (Watford, UK: Odhams Press, 1956)

John Erickson, *The Road To Berlin* (London: Weidenfeld & Nicolson, 1983)

Marie Vassiltchikov, *Berlin Diaries 1940-1945* (Toronto: Random House, 1988)

The Royal Air Force Pilot's Flying Log Book (Form 414), of my late father, Stan Elcock.

The epigraph at the beginning of the book is taken from:

Martha Gellhorn, *The Face of War* (New York: Atlantic Monthly Press, 1988), pp. 115-116. ISBN: 0-87113-211-7.

Michael Elcock was born in Forres, Scotland and grew up in Edinburgh and West Africa. He emigrated to Canada when he was twenty-one and worked in pulp mills, in the woods, on west coast fishing boats and as a ski instructor—earning along the way a B.A. and M.Ed at the University of Victoria, having undertaken post-graduate studies in Quebec, Sweden, Germany, Belgium and Scotland. He was Athletic Director at UVic for ten years, and then CEO of Tourism Victoria for five. In 1990 he moved with his wife and daughter to Andalusia to work on developing Spain's Expo 92. He has lived in a number of different countries, and has travelled extensively in Europe, North America and the Middle East. He has published many articles in periodicals, newspapers and magazines in Canada and overseas. He now lives with his family outside Victoria, BC.